Professor Lesley Regan runs the [...] miscarriage clinic at St Mary's Hospital, London [...] gest referral unit of its kind in Europe. In addition to caring for women who are trying to find out why they have miscarried repeatedly, she has built a team of dedicated doctors and midwives who help her to look after these women throughout their future pregnancies. Lesley Regan is Professor of Obstetrics and Gynaecology at the Imperial College School of Medicine at St Mary's – the first woman in the country to hold this position. She is a renowned teacher in the field of reproductive medicine, and having previously been director of medical studies at Girton College, Cambridge, continues to enjoy teaching general obstetrics and gynaecology to medical students.

Lesley Regan's contribution to research into the causes of miscarriage is recognised internationally. She is an adviser to several national and international organisations and currently holds the prestigious post of Visiting Professor to the Harvard Centre of Excellence in Women's Health. Her high profile, expert knowledge and common-sense approach have resulted in her being in demand for both television and radio; *Good Housekeeping* magazine and the *Evening Standard* list Lesley Regan as one of the most influential women in Britain. The mother of twin schoolgirls, she has also helped to raise four stepchildren. Lesley Regan lives with her husband John Summerfield and family in central London.

This book is dedicated to the memory
of my brother Martin: and the celebration of
the two little girls he loved so dearly –
my twin daughters, Clare and Jenny.

MISCARRIAGE

WHAT EVERY WOMAN NEEDS TO KNOW

A POSITIVE NEW APPROACH

Professor Lesley Regan

ORION

An Orion Paperback
First published in Great Britain by Bloomsbury in 1997
This revised paperback edition published in 2001 by
Orion Books Ltd,
Orion House, 5 Upper St Martin's Lane,
London WC2H 9EA

A CIP catalogue record for this book
is available from the British Library.

ISBN 0 75283 757 5

Typeset at The Spartan Press Ltd,
Lymington, Hants
Printed and bound in Great Britain by
Clays Ltd, St Ives plc

Contents

PART THREE: PRACTICAL ISSUES AND ANSWERS TO QUESTIONS

INTRODUCTION

Miscarriage is extremely common, indeed it is probably the commonest cause for young women to be admitted to hospital apart from the happy birth of a baby at term. Losing an early pregnancy is often a shattering experience as it represents the loss of life just at the time when anticipation is highest, but because it occurs so frequently and because the baby is not fully formed, it is not regarded seriously by doctors and staff, which makes the situation even more distressing.

Several other factors contribute to the emotional injury caused by miscarriage. Firstly, the reason for miscarriage is often obscure and the medical team may not make vigorous attempts to establish the cause – few things are worse than having an unexplained medical problem. Secondly, women who have miscarried naturally tend to blame themselves for 'causing' the problem, even though it is certain that very few miscarriages are caused because a woman has not taken proper care of herself in early pregnancy. Another problem is that some women who miscarry tend to be infertile – it is extremely depressing to have great difficulty in getting pregnant only to lose the baby when victory is in sight.

This book is therefore extremely timely and I am very pleased to recommend it highly. Professor Lesley Regan is an acknowledged expert in the field, with an international reputation, who has been responsible for some of the most innovative and valuable advances in the management of miscarriage. Perhaps even more to the point, with this excellent book she has produced the definitive account of the causes, prevention and treatment of miscarriage. It will be useful to many professionals as well as those who sadly have had personal experience of the disheartening event. This sympathetically written book is clear, comprehensive and elegant, and many couples will draw great comfort from it as it will help them understand this condition and learn what so frequently can be done to help.

PROFESSOR ROBERT WINSTON

FOREWORD

Why did it happen?
Was it something I did?
How can I make sure it doesn't happen again?
When should I try again?

These are some of the most common questions asked by women who have suffered pregnancy loss through miscarriage or ectopic pregnancy. Their feelings of grief and emptiness are often compounded by a lack of information, by the fact that no one took the time to explain what was happening or that explanations were in terms which they could not understand.

Here at last is an excellent book which not only addresses such questions seriously and thoughtfully, but is written with real sensitivity to the emotional aspects of pregnancy loss.

Professor Lesley Regan has drawn on her extensive experience at St Mary's Hospital, together with research from across the world, to remove much of the mystery, fear and confusion surrounding pregnancy loss. She explains the often unexplained with clarity and compassion. She invites the reader to learn more about the processes of conception and pregnancy as a tool to understanding what happens when things go wrong, yet does not shrink from acknowledging how much yet remains unknown. She examines both popular myths and diverse medical opinion, explaining her own conclusions and practice. Types of loss, causes and treatments are set out clearly and medical terminology interpreted.

One important observation is the powerful positive effect which an open pregnancy unit can have on the outcome of pregnancy, even after several losses. Where women have open access to a medical team for consultation, monitoring and reassurance at all stages of their pregnancy, their pregnancy is significantly more likely to succeed. Let us hope that all clinicians will adopt the 'tender loving care' approach which Professor Regan advocates.

Grief, loss, fear and anxiety are often at a high level amongst couples who experience pregnancy loss. With this very welcome publication, Professor Regan brings clarity, comfort and hope. It will be on the top of our recommended book list.

RUTH BENDER ATIK
NATIONAL DIRECTOR, MISCARRIAGE ASSOCIATION

PREFACE TO THE SECOND EDITION

Why do we need a second edition of this book?

The answer is simple and also very exciting. Over the last three years there have been some important advances made into our understanding of the causes of miscarriage. Armed with this knowledge we have been able to develop new investigative tests that are helping us to identify a further group of women with previously unexplained miscarriages. It will only be a short time before these women can also be offered treatments that will help them achieve their goal – a live take home baby

Perhaps the best examples of the progress that has been made are the newly discovered pro-thrombotic disorders (see Chapter 12). We now recognise that a significant number of miscarriages are due to an abnormal or an exaggerated haemostatic (blood clotting) response to pregnancy. In short the normal balance that is needed in our blood stream, between developing damaging blood clots and bleeding uncontrollably becomes disturbed and shifts towards forming clots – hence pro-thrombotic. When the first edition of *Miscarriage* was written, only a few prothrombotic abnormalities were recognised. Now we know that there are lots more and that many of them are genetically inherited.

The other reason for the second edition is that my patients keep asking me for further information and updates on the medical advances that they read about and the research projects that they have contributed to. They quiz me (and so they should!) about the details and want to ensure that they have the most up-to-date information. In fact over the last few years the type of questions that my patients ask have changed. I think this probably reflects that so much more medical information is now so easily available via the Internet and other sources. Paradoxically, this volume of information can cause confusion, leaving women desperate to know what is fact and what is not.

So in this edition I have tried to provide answers to these newer questions. There are further sections on exercise and air travel in pregnancy, vitamin supplements, new types of ultrasound scans and treatments for fibroids, medical methods of dealing with a proven miscarriage, minimal access or keyhole surgery techniques, auto-immune problems, new prenatal diagnostic tests, the power of the new molecular genetic techniques, and of course lots more details about the phospholipid syndrome, other pro-thrombotic disorders and the safety of aspirin and heparin treatment in pregnancy.

Sometimes the questions cannot be answered with facts alone because they are dependent on the individual situation and the woman's personal views and circumstances. Here I have tried to offer advice based on my previous experience or my personal opinion without being too directive. I hope that you enjoy the new edition and that it provides you with the information, reassurance and determination you need to embark on another pregnancy.

THE NEED FOR THIS BOOK

A quarter of all women who become pregnant will experience at least one miscarriage – it is the most common complication of pregnancy. The aim of this book is to take the mystery out of the subject. I want to make this difficult and confusing topic understandable to the millions of people it affects by providing clear, comprehensive, up-to-date information about the known causes and treatments of miscarriage. I hope that, by reading my book, you will be able to approach the subject without fear or confusion.

Women frequently arrive at my clinic having been shunted from one doctor to another, not fully aware of what has happened to them and what is likely to happen in the future. Some have miscarried on several occasions, yet have never been able to find out why. Others have been given different advice, diagnoses and treatments from every doctor they have consulted. Often patients who have plucked up the courage to ask questions about their miscarriages have been ignored by doctors too busy and overworked, or sometimes, regrettably, too superior to spend time explaining to them the nature of their problem. Every day I meet women who have come to believe that they will never experience the joy of a successful pregnancy, women who blame themselves for the loss of their babies.

The clinic where I work, St Mary's Hospital in London, is the largest referral unit in Europe. We see 700 new patients every year and continue to look after several thousand more. Few of their cases are straightforward. By their nature they have come to the clinic because of a recurring problem for which no answer or solution has been provided. I am constantly amazed and inspired by their fortitude, courage and tenacity. Some of the stories they tell are heartbreaking. As a mother, I am regularly filled with admiration and humility for their ability to put bitter disappointments behind them and their determination to carry on and reach their goal.

This book is, in part, a tribute to those patients and their partners, whose desire to bring life into this world has been unswayed by loss, and undaunted by the often perplexing advice and treatments of modern medicine.

I have set out to describe the causes and treatments of miscarriage which, from experience, I have found most easily understood by the women who attend our clinic. The emphasis is on understanding what doctors know already and what they are trying to find out. As a practising consultant gynaecologist and obstetrician who is also engaged in research, I have seen the distress and confusion that may be caused by differing medical viewpoints. Often this is simply a reflection of the clinician's particular expertise – or even bias – and I hope that, with accurate information at your fingertips, you will be able to identify and get round this problem.

I also stress the importance of entering clinical trials. This is a positive way in which you can help yourself to understand and receive the dedicated care needed to solve your particular problem. I have found that women who join clinical trials are more likely to succeed next time – even if they are in the control group!

This book is for everyone who has a question to ask about miscarriage. I do not pretend that I know all the answers but I hope that you will feel encouraged by the knowledge that doctors and scientists all over the world are trying to find out more about this problem. Above all, this book reinforces the fact that, given time, luck and a little medical help, you are more than likely to enjoy a successful pregnancy.

ACKNOWLEDGEMENTS

The writing of this book was a challenge, and I want to thank the people who have helped me. Without doubt, the most important contributors have been my patients, and my thanks go out to every one of them. The problems, fears, courage and honesty they have shared with me are a continuing source of inspiration. I hope that I have done justice to their repeated requests for more information. Their baby photographs are now displayed in our 'Rogues' Gallery', which brightens up many of the walls of the clinic office.

I am indebted to Maggie Pearlstine for her friendship and encouragement. Her certainty that I could and would 'write it all down on paper' has been a driving force. I have been very fortunate to have the benefit of the practical help and skills provided by Matthew Baylis. I am enormously grateful to him both for his advice and his enthusiastic interest in my subject.

The readers of this book will quickly recognise how much I rate the importance of research. I consider myself lucky to have had such excellent research fellows and want to thank them for their dedicated contribution to the clinic and its patients.

My family have made an enormous contribution to this book. Although they know how much I value their love and support, I welcome the opportunity of paying them a special tribute. My husband John has maintained his role of chief supporter and critic, and tolerated my preoccupation with good humour. Ollie and James have helped by generously entertaining the twins. The last chapters were written on holiday watching Jenny and Clare (and my papers) flying around the garden and reflecting on the fact that being a mother is a very special joy and privilege.

PART ONE
THE BASIC FACTS

ONE

WHAT IS A MISCARRIAGE?

The readers of this book may wonder why I have chosen to devote the first chapter of a book about miscarriage to the definition of medical terms. At first glance, it must seem a very cold and clinical way to start writing about one of the most emotional topics in medicine – losing a baby. There is no doubt in my mind that miscarriage is one of the most devastating blows that nature can deliver. However, experience has taught me that clear explanations of the terminology used by doctors and nurses are very important. Many of the couples I meet in the miscarriage clinic are both distressed and confused by the words they have heard to describe their problem. I believe that once you understand the medical terminology, your miscarriage problems will become much less frightening and, most importantly, more understandable.

A miscarriage is a pregnancy which ends naturally before the baby (fetus) can possibly survive outside the mother's womb. The medical term used to describe a baby's potential ability to survive outside the womb is 'viability'. Viability may be defined in terms of the gestational age of the pregnancy (the length of time since the last missed period) or the size and weight of the baby.

The reason for including two definitions of viability within the definition of miscarriage is an important one. Most babies will have reached an average size or weight which corresponds to the gestational age (measured in weeks) of pregnancy. Some babies will be smaller (weigh less) and a few babies will be larger (weigh more) than is expected by the dates from the woman's last menstrual period. However, the weight of the baby at the time of delivery is a crucial factor in determining whether it can survive outside the womb, irrespective of how long it has been in the womb. The bigger the baby, the better the chances of survival.

Many of the women who come to my clinic are uncertain about the difference between a miscarriage and a stillbirth. Essentially, it is a difference of timing, but the terms used can make a lot of difference for the women who have had to go through the experience. Miscarriage may occur at any stage in a pregnancy from the time of the positive pregnancy test until 24 weeks of gestation. After this date, the delivery of a baby which then dies is called a stillbirth. A baby which dies in the womb after 24 weeks is called an intrauterine death. These definitions are described in more detail later in this chapter.

Early deliveries

The survival of a baby delivered very early depends upon whether the baby is healthy and upon the medical expertise (neonatal services) available to nurture the baby after it leaves the womb. Neonatal services have improved dramatically over the last twenty years in the United Kingdom. As a result we are now able to offer the hope of survival to much younger and smaller babies, as long as they do not suffer from severe abnormalities at the time of their birth.

When I started my training in obstetrics and gynaecology, babies born before 28 weeks of gestation (or weighing less than 1000g) were rarely capable of surviving, despite the efforts of the neonatal doctors (paediatricians specialising in newborn babies). Nowadays, babies born between 24 and 28 weeks of gestation have a much better chance of survival, as long as they are delivered in hospitals that have special care facilities for tiny babies. This fact is so well recognised that obstetric units now operate a policy of 'in-utero transfer' for women in established premature labour. This means that pregnant women who are considered to be at risk of premature delivery are transferred to hospitals with the appropriate neonatal facilities before they deliver. This policy ensures that every baby born very early has the best chance of survival because the neonatal doctors are on hand at the time of delivery. The treatment that the baby receives during the first 24 hours of his or her life is crucial.

Miscarriage versus abortion

I am very conscious of the fact that many of the patients I see in the miscarriage clinic have felt distressed and angry with doctors and nurses who have referred to their miscarriage as an 'abortion'. Medical terms used by doctors are designed to be a precise way of describing the medical problem to other doctors and nurses. Unfortunately, for a patient who has suffered a miscarriage, this medical description may seem an insensitive way of describing the facts.

The words are not meant to be deliberately hurtful or insensitive. I think that most of the misunderstandings and distress stem from the fact that many people in our society use the word 'abortion' to describe a pregnancy that is deliberately ended. For a woman who is miscarrying a much wanted pregnancy, hearing the word 'abortion' will always be distressing if she is unaware of the correct meaning of the words used.

'Abortion' is the correct medical word for any pregnancy that ends before its time. A spontaneous abortion is a pregnancy that ends before the baby is viable – in other words, a miscarriage. A termination of pregnancy is a pregnancy that is deliberately halted. The term 'induced abortion' may also be used to describe termination of pregnancy. The termination may be performed for social reasons (an unwanted pregnancy) or it may be performed for medical reasons. There are many medical reasons for performing a termination of pregnancy – to protect the life of the mother, because the baby has an abnormality which is incompatible with a healthy life, or because the baby has died in the womb – another type of miscarriage – which we refer to as an 'intrauterine death' or IUD.

There has been a definite move by doctors and nurses over the last ten years to manage miscarriage problems with greater sensitivity and understanding. When I first started seeing patients with a history of recurrent miscarriage, the referral letter from the general practitioner or hospital doctor almost always started with, 'Thank you for seeing this unfortunate woman who has suffered recurrent abortions . . .' I am glad to report that 'recurrent abortion' is rarely used now. Most referral letters now refer to 'recurrent miscarriage'. Similarly, when I am invited to give a lecture, I no longer have to change the wording of the title from abortion to miscarriage. Several eminent gynaecologists have written newspaper articles about the importance of using more sensitive words when talking to a woman who has miscarried. And if you meet a doctor or nurse who refers to your lost baby as an abortion, I suggest you explain to them, calmly and firmly, that you find the word distressing – I suspect that they will respond positively to your feelings.

Miscarriage and stillbirth: legal definitions

The legal definition of a miscarriage in the United Kingdom at the present time is the spontaneous loss of a baby with a gestational age of 24 weeks or less. This definition (made by an amendment to an Act of Parliament in 1991) takes into account that the neonatal services currently available offer a baby born at 24 weeks the chance of survival. Before 1991, the legal definition of miscarriage (which had been in force since 1929) was the spontaneous loss of a baby with a gestational age of 28 weeks or less and corresponding to a birth-weight of 1000g.

The World Health Organisation (WHO) uses a different definition of miscarriage – the loss of a baby weighing 500g or less, which corresponds to a gestational age of 20 to 22 weeks of gestation. The problem with the WHO definition is that it leaves any baby who is miscarried between 20 and 24 weeks in a sort of no-man's land. Fortunately, the legal definition in the UK has prevented the WHO recommendations from causing confusion.

After 24 weeks of gestation, the spontaneous loss of a baby is called a stillbirth. If the baby dies in the womb but is not miscarried spontaneously, it is called an intrauterine death. The physical process of miscarriage has to be induced artificially, but the baby, when delivered, is a stillbirth and not a termination. A baby of any gestational age or birth weight who demonstrates signs of life at the delivery is defined as a liveborn infant. The death of a liveborn baby during the first seven days of life is called an early neonatal death.

Having explained some of the terminology that you are likely to come across when talking to doctors about your lost baby, the following chapters of this book are aimed at helping you to understand why the miscarriage happened and what you can do to minimise your chances of it happening again. Above all, what I want to draw the reader's attention to is that miscarriage is very common, that doctors do not understand all the reasons why miscarriages occur and that the only way to improve this situation is to support and contribute to future research in this important field of medicine.

TWO

THE SIZE OF THE PROBLEM

Miscarriage – the loss of a pregnancy before the baby can possibly survive – is extremely common. It has been estimated that one in four of all women suffer a miscarriage at some stage in their reproductive life. This means that miscarriage is the commonest complication of pregnancy. As you walk down the street, visit the supermarket, catch a bus or go about your work today, every fourth woman you see will have experienced a miscarriage. Many women look at me in disbelief when I tell them this fact. You may have no idea that your friend or neighbour has had to cope with the problem of miscarriage until you too experience one. This is because miscarriage is still a taboo subject for many people. It is almost always accompanied by sadness and distress and it can be very difficult to discuss these feelings or to offer words of comfort to a woman who is experiencing them. I hope that this chapter will help you to understand just how common miscarriage is.

Recognising a pregnancy

I know that many women find it surprising when I tell them that doctors still do not know exactly how many pregnancies end in miscarriage. It may seem a very straightforward question, but the answer is difficult to obtain. This is because it is only possible to be accurate about the outcome of pregnancies that are recognised clinically.

By clinically recognised, I mean those pregnancies in which the patient and her doctor know that she is pregnant. This may be as a result of a pregnancy test or an early ultrasound scan. Of course, after the woman has missed a few periods and has obvious symptoms of pregnancy such as nausea, tender breasts, weight gain and tiredness, the diagnosis is much simpler. And when an ultrasound scan has visualised a pregnancy sac in the uterus, the diagnosis of pregnancy is clinically confirmed.

Gathering statistics – the problems

Doctors generally accept that 15% – or one in six of all clinically recognised pregnancies – end in miscarriage. It is useful to remember that this figure may be higher or lower depending upon how the numbers are collected. For example, if the number of miscarriages is calculated from those women who show up at an emergency department with bleeding in early pregnancy, the figure rises. On the other hand, when the number of miscarriages are counted by looking at women who are already booked into an antenatal clinic for pregnancy care, the figure will be lower, because any miscarriages that have occurred before the woman attends the antenatal clinic will be missed.

Some groups of women have a higher risk of clinically recognised miscarriage. For women over the age of 40 years, the figure is about 25% – one in four. For younger women with no previous history of miscarriage and no medical problems, the risk of miscarriage may be as low as 5%.

Unseen pregnancies

However, we now realise that a large number of pregnancies are lost at such an early stage in development that the woman has no specific symptoms and physical signs of being pregnant. These very early miscarriages are called subclinical or 'occult' miscarriages. The reason for using these words is that the miscarriages are occurring during the period of time between fertilisation of the egg by the sperm, the implantation of the tiny embryo into the womb lining and the clinical identification of the pregnancy. These events are usually hidden from our view (hence 'occult') and so it is difficult to realise that they are happening, let alone that they may go wrong.

Before we had access to the very sensitive pregnancy tests that are now available, the vast majority of these very early losses went unrecognised. Indeed, for many women they still go unrecognised, since usually only those women who have had problems becoming pregnant or have suffered previous miscarriages, would perform a pregnancy test before they have missed a period or before 5 weeks have elapsed since the last period. When a pregnancy test is positive, but the menstrual period occurs a few days later, we call the pregnancy a 'biochemical' one. The tiny embryo has started to make some HCG (human chorionic gonadotrophin, or pregnancy hormone) which can be detected in the mother's urine or blood, but because the embryo does not implant properly in the womb lining, the pregnancy cannot continue, and the pregnancy test becomes negative again. Some women might notice that their menstrual period has been delayed for a few days, or may detect a slightly increased blood loss. It is just as likely, however, that they consider the period to be entirely normal.

I think you will be interested to hear the results of a recent study performed by a group of well-respected researchers in this field. They recruited normal fertile women who were trying to become pregnant and followed them carefully over a period of 6 months. With the help of hormonal blood tests these researchers identified the day on which the woman ovulated and, by taking repeated urine samples and measuring the level of HCG hormone, were able to pinpoint the day of implantation for each of the pregnancies that these women went on to conceive. When they analysed the outcome of these pregnancies they were able to show that in most successful pregnancies the tiny embryo implants 8 to 10 days after ovulation (which corresponds to day 22 to 24 of a normal menstrual cycle). The risk of very early miscarriage (before 6 weeks) increased dramatically when the day of implantation was delayed. For example, when implantation occurred before the ninth post-ovulatory day the early loss rate was 13%. But after day 11 the early miscarriage rate was a staggering 82%. This elegant study helps to remind us that there is a very specific window of implantation during which the endometrial (womb) lining is receptive to the tiny embryo.

Theoretically there are several reasons why pregnancies that follow the late implantation of the embryo fail to develop successfully. Unhealthy embryos may develop more slowly or the actual implantation process may be defective, resulting in later or weaker production of HCG. Whichever, it is likely that a tight window of implantation is a special human design feature which helps to ensure that damaged embryos do not progress very far.

Even if we were able to document every biochemical pregnancy that occurs, this would still not be an accurate estimate of the wastage involved in human reproduction. The fate of a fertilised egg is an unhappy one. As many as 15% of the eggs from healthy fertile women are lost before they are fertilised. A further 15% of fertilised eggs degenerate (fall apart) before they are able to implant in the womb lining. Of those embryos that do implant, at least 30% are unable to progress into a recognisable pregnancy. If we collect all these figures together, we come up with the amazing figure that 60% (nearly two-thirds) of all conceptions or potential pregnancies are lost.

Furthermore, the majority of these losses are so early that we usually do not know about them. Unless the woman is undergoing special monitoring to see whether she has become pregnant as a result of infertility treatment, we will not know how many tiny embryos fail to implant successfully in the womb lining or whether they start to implant and produce HCG pregnancy hormone but then miscarry. So when we study the number of miscarriages that occur in any population or in any group of women, it is important to start off by trying to distinguish between the separate contributions that are made by both clinical and subclinical pregnancy losses.

I hope that the reader is now in a position to realise the true size of the problem of miscarriage. Although we talk most frequently about the 15% of clinically recognised pregnancies that we actually see being miscarried, these are just the 'tip of the iceberg' of pregnancy losses. Underneath the surface of the water, a much larger number of pregnancies are miscarried, often without the woman or her doctor realising that she has been pregnant. Most doctors working in this field believe that 1 in 3 conceptions never develop far enough to be recognised.

THREE

DIFFERENT TYPES OF MISCARRIAGE AND PREGNANCY LOSS

We have already seen that a miscarriage can occur at any stage in pregnancy from the time of the first missed menstrual period until 24 weeks of gestation. Not surprisingly, such a wide time span means that there are many types of miscarriage with many different causes, and many women feel confused by the variety of terms used to describe the miscarriages. The different causes are discussed in later chapters. In this chapter, we will look at the terminology used to describe the various types of miscarriage and the methods that are used to identify them.

Early miscarriage

A miscarriage is called 'early' if it occurs before the thirteenth week of pregnancy. The thirteenth week marks the end of the first trimester (the first three months) of pregnancy. Long before ultrasound was available, doctors were aware that the majority of miscarriages occurred in this early stage – after this date miscarriage is fairly uncommon.

Now that an early pregnancy can be so clearly visualised on the ultrasound scan, we know that most early miscarriages have occurred by eight weeks of gestation, well before the 13-week point. Many of the miscarriages which were thought to have occurred between eight and 13 weeks in the past, can now be identified as having occurred at an earlier date. The pregnancy has ended but the physical process of miscarriage and expulsion from the uterus has been delayed (see below, 'missed miscarriage'). As we will see in this chapter, most of the terms used to describe pregnancy loss actually represent different stages in the physical process of early miscarriage.

Late miscarriage

The miscarriage is termed 'late' if it involves the loss of a baby of 13 weeks' size or more. This is an important point to recognise, because in some cases of pregnancy loss, the physical process of miscarriage may not happen until the second trimester, for example at 16 weeks. Ultrasound scans are very important in these cases, because they enable the doctor to determine the size of the fetus, and hence the probable causes of the loss. Without a US scan, it is possible to mistakenly conclude that a woman has had a late miscarriage, when in actual fact her pregnancy could have been 'lost' at an earlier stage.

The causes of late miscarriage are quite different from the causes of early miscarriage. In addition the symptoms and signs that accompany late miscarriage are usually different. For example, a late miscarriage may be heralded by ruptured membranes (breaking of the waters) which is not usually noticed in early miscarriages, and the pain experienced may resemble labour contractions because the baby being miscarried is so much larger. All cases of late miscarriage should be carefully investigated in an attempt to find an underlying cause. True late miscarriages are relatively rare. It has been estimated that only 1% of pregnancies miscarry after 13 weeks of gestation.

Sporadic miscarriage

When a pregnancy miscarries due to an occasional or isolated occurrence, it is called a sporadic miscarriage. These are pregnancies that are lost because of a 'one-off' genetic abnormality in the baby, or because the mother has caught a severe viral infection during the early weeks of pregnancy. It is unlikely, though not impossible, that the cause of the miscarriage will recur. This is why sporadic miscarriages are sometimes referred to as bad luck or chance episodes of pregnancy loss. I always try to avoid these descriptions in the clinic because they sound so insensitive to someone who has just lost her baby.

Sporadic miscarriage is the commonest complication of pregnancy. It has been estimated that 25% of women experience a sporadic miscarriage.

Recurrent miscarriage

In contrast to sporadic miscarriage, recurrent miscarriage is uncommon, affecting no more than 1% of women. Various definitions are in use, but the most widely accepted is the loss of three or more consecutive pregnancies. Although three miscarriages in a row can be due to bad luck or chance (as we will discuss in more detail in Chapter 6), it is also possible that an underlying cause may be responsible for the repeated miscarriages which, if identified, may be treatable (see Chapters 7–12).

It is useful for the reader to understand that over the last few years, some doctors (and their patients!) have chosen to define recurrent miscarriage as two or more miscarriages. There is nothing wrong with this definition but it is important to appreciate that it means that the scale of the problem of recurrent miscarriage would need to include not 1% but nearly 5% of all couples who are trying to achieve a live take-home baby.

Threatened miscarriage

A threatened miscarriage can occur at any stage in pregnancy until 24 weeks. However, the problem is much more common during the first three months of pregnancy. The first symptoms are usually vaginal bleeding and/or mild stomach pain. On physical examination, the doctor may identify some tenderness in the lower abdomen, usually just above the pubic bone, but this is not always present. Gentle examination often reveals some blood in the vagina, but no tissues (products of pregnancy) are seen. Most importantly, the neck of the womb (cervix) remains closed and the size of the womb (uterus) is consistent with that expected from the date of the last period.

The diagnosis of threatened miscarriage is made with the help of an ultrasound scan. In very early pregnancies (before six weeks) the scan will probably only be able to visualise the presence of an intact pregnancy sac containing amniotic fluid and a small 'fetal pole' – a nubbin of embryo tissue which, as it grows, will become recognisable as the tiny baby. After six weeks the scan can usually show a heartbeat, particularly if a vaginal scan is performed. Sometimes the scan may show up a small blood clot at the edge of the placenta, which identifies the source of the bleeding, but more often nothing abnormal is seen.

Miscarriage is a process, not a single event, and the loss of the baby is by no means inevitable in all cases. Once bleeding has started there are several possible outcomes. The bleeding may resolve spontaneously in a few days and not recur again. The bleeding may continue, or stop and start over several days or weeks. It is only when abdominal pains follow that the process moves in the direction of inevitability. Even then, the process can still stop and the pregnancy continue safely. Threatened miscarriage is very common. It has been estimated that an episode of bleeding occurs in as many as half of all pregnancies. Happily, in the majority of cases the pregnancy continues normally, but if you notice any bleeding, you should contact your doctor straight away.

Inevitable miscarriage

In some cases of threatened miscarriage, the process continues and unfortunately becomes what we call an 'inevitable miscarriage'. The important difference is that the cervix starts to open or dilate. Once this happens, the miscarriage is 'inevitable' because the cervix cannot close up again. In these cases, the vaginal bleeding is usually accompanied by pain, caused by the opening of the cervix and the passage of the pregnancy sac, containing the baby, into the canal of the cervix. The pain is cramping in nature, which reflects the fact that the muscles of the uterus are contracting in an attempt to expel the pregnancy. The bleeding usually becomes more severe and the pregnancy sac may break, releasing the amniotic fluid or 'waters' surrounding the baby.

The diagnosis is obvious when a vaginal examination is performed and the cervix is found to be opening. In this situation, an ultrasound scan is not useful because even if a live baby can be visualised, the process of miscarriage cannot be halted. The inevitable miscarriage may be incomplete or complete.

Incomplete miscarriage

If some of the pregnancy tissues are retained in the uterus, the miscarriage is described as 'incomplete'. The findings on examination depend upon when the miscarriage became inevitable. If this was recently, then the cervix may still be open and tissues seen in the cervical canal or in the vagina. If the miscarriage process became inevitable some time ago, the cervix may have started to close again. An ultrasound scan is useful if there is concern that the miscarriage is incomplete. Usually the tissues left behind are pieces of placenta and membranes from the pregnancy sac, and this situation has to be dealt with straight away, to prevent bleeding from the uterus. Under anaesthetic, the doctor will usually carry out a 'D & C' (dilatation and curettage) or an 'ERPC' (evacuation of retained products of conception) to remove the tissues. This is a routine procedure lasting only a few minutes, and the recovery is fast.

Complete miscarriage

If the fetus and all the placental tissues are expelled spontaneously by the uterus, the miscarriage is called 'complete'. The symptoms of this are heavy bleeding and the passing of blood clots and tissue. Some women may even be able to recognise a pregnancy sac or fetus. As soon as the uterus is empty, the bleeding usually subsides as the uterus contracts down to its normal size and the cervix closes up again. If there is any doubt that the miscarriage is truly complete, an ultrasound scan is useful to see whether any pieces of tissue have been left behind. The doctors will usually wait some time before carrying this out, because if the scan is performed too soon after the miscarriage, small blood clots in the uterus might be mistaken for tissue, but they will be passed without complication if left alone for a short while.

It is difficult to estimate the true numbers of complete early miscarriages that occur. This is because they usually do not require medical intervention and quite often people do not report them if they happen in very early pregnancy. Of course, if you have any cause for concern, you should consult your doctor – even if the pregnancy is progressing safely, being worried will do you no good.

Septic miscarriage

Any type of miscarriage that is complicated by infection is called a septic miscarriage. Fortunately, this is a rare complication these days because incomplete early miscarriages are usually dealt with speedily to prevent infection of any retained tissues. Furthermore the introduction of legal termination of pregnancy in this country has greatly reduced the risk of infection, which used to be a common sequel to 'back-street' abortions.

However, if you have miscarried recently, and experience a recurrence of bleeding, develop a smelly discharge, a temperature or fever, or constant abdominal pain, it is likely that you have some endometritis (inflammation of the womb lining). This can be swiftly treated with antibiotics and, if necessary, the removal of retained tissues from the uterus, to prevent infection in the pelvis and the risk of secondary infertility.

There is no evidence to suggest that infection is more common after a complete late miscarriage. Because some late miscarriages may be caused by infection (see Chapters 4 and 10), your doctor will look carefully for any signs of infection at the time of the miscarriage, particularly when the late miscarriage occurs after the waters around the baby have broken. In this situation, organisms normally present in the vagina can travel up into the uterus and cause endometritis and infection, so if this happens, make sure you are checked for infection.

Anembryonic miscarriage

This is the term used to describe a pregnancy which appears to consist of a pregnancy sac containing placental tissue but no embryo (fetal pole). Obviously it is only possible to make this diagnosis with accuracy after an ultrasound scan has been performed (or after a pathologist has examined the complete pregnancy sac under a microscope, which is rarely possible). Anembryonic miscarriages are one of the most common types of early miscarriage, a fact that doctors were unaware of until ultrasound was routinely available.

The old-fashioned name for anembryonic pregnancy was 'blighted ovum'. This name reflected previous thinking that the cells required for the embryo to develop were either absent, rudimentary or grossly deformed from the beginning of the pregnancy, usually because of a major genetic abnormality in the embryo. More recent research studies suggest that the apparently empty pregnancy sacs did contain an embryo at one time, but that the embryo was reabsorbed very early in its development.

Since anembryonic miscarriage occurs at a very early stage, it is unusual for a woman to suspect that there is any problem until she has had an ultrasound scan. Having identified that the pregnancy cannot continue, the doctors may suggest an ERPC to clean out the uterus, although some women prefer to let the tissues pass away of their own accord (see Expectant management of miscarriage, later in this chapter).

Embryonic miscarriage

An embryonic miscarriage is the term used to describe a pregnancy that fails after an embryo with an active fetal heartbeat has developed. From a practical point of view this means that the embryo must be larger than 5mm in length when seen on the ultrasound scan, which approximates to a six-week pregnancy. The reason for this definition is that we can be confident that an embryo of six weeks' size has developed heart activity in order to reach this size. The importance of distinguishing between embryonic and anembryonic miscarriage is that the underlying cause may be different. Embryonic miscarriage is much less common and suggests that some event has occurred to stop the progress of the pregnancy after the embryo has developed fetal heart activity. In anembryonic miscarriage, the development of the pregnancy is halted at a very early stage.

Missed miscarriage

A missed miscarriage or missed abortion are the terms used to describe the situation in which the fetus/embryo dies in the womb but no clinical signs of miscarriage follow. These words are not very helpful to the uninitiated patient and hence a recent study group held at the Royal College of Obstetricians and Gynaecologists recommended that the terms missed miscarriage and blighted ovum be replaced by early embryonic death or early fetal demise. It is not understood why the uterus fails to expel some failed pregnancies. In some cases women do recall a brief episode of light vaginal bleeding and sometimes mild cramping pain, which are then resolved. In retrospect, some women can then pinpoint the time at which subjective symptoms of pregnancy, such as nausea and breast tenderness, disappeared. However, this is not always the case and some women may be unaware that they are no longer pregnant. This situation, as you can imagine, can be quite distressing. 'How could I not have realised that my baby had died?' is a question I am asked frequently in this situation. I always try to remind people that only the benefit of experience can bring about the correct diagnosis, and this is as true for doctors as for pregnant mothers.

If a vaginal examination reveals that the uterus is much smaller than would be expected from the menstrual dates, then a missed miscarriage is likely. This is confirmed if the ultrasound scan demonstrates a baby of greater than six weeks' size, with no heart activity. If the pregnancy died some time ago, the scan may also show that the fetus and membranes are being resorbed and cannot be visualised clearly. If no action is taken, the uterus will usually expel the pregnancy in time. In practice, however, a lot of women prefer to have the pregnancy removed surgically, in order to 'end the pregnancy' formally.

Ectopic pregnancy

A pregnancy which starts to develop outside the uterine cavity is called an ectopic pregnancy. The vast majority of ectopic pregnancies occur in the fallopian tubes, but occasionally may be found on the ovary or in the abdominal cavity. The ectopic pregnancy dies because there is not enough room for the pregnancy to grow (i.e. in the wall of the fallopian tube) or because the placenta cannot implant properly (i.e. on the surface of the ovary). Although some ectopics undoubtedly 'miscarry' completely without complication (tubal miscarriage or abortion), there is a risk that the pregnancy might continue to grow and even rupture through the walls of the fallopian tube. This is why your doctors will take immediate action if they suspect an ectopic pregnancy.

Since an ectopic pregnancy may mimic a 'normal' miscarriage – that is, one which takes place in the uterus (intrauterine miscarriage) – and because prompt action is important if one should occur, a few points need mentioning here. The general symptoms of an ectopic pregnancy are the same as of early pregnancy, accompanied by a positive pregnancy test and lower abdominal pain, which almost always starts before any vaginal bleeding has occurred. This pain may become severe, suggesting that the fallopian tube is being stretched and/or internal bleeding has started. Sometimes these symptoms appear to settle down and then restart a few days later as the ectopic enlarges in size.

If you notice any of these symptoms, you should contact your doctor immediately. The first step will usually be to send you for an ultrasound scan. This will demonstrate that there is no pregnancy sac within the uterine cavity, although the lining of the uterus may be thickened. Sometimes it is possible to see fluid in the bottom of the pelvis, behind the uterus, if bleeding has already occurred. The scan may suggest that there is a poorly defined mass outside the uterus (the ectopic) but it is often very difficult to visualise the pregnancy clearly or see a fetal heartbeat. If there is any doubt about the diagnosis, the doctor may carry out a laparoscopy – which is carried out under anaesthetic, and involves the insertion of a microscopic 'camera' into the abdomen, just below the navel. Once a diagnosis has been made, the ectopic will be removed by surgery. More and more hospitals are developing the surgical expertise required to deal with an ectopic pregnancy by laparoscopy, and avoid the need for an open operation. This has significant advantages to offer: less trauma to the tissues, a shorter stay in hospital and quicker long-term recovery.

It may be possible to avoid surgery altogether if the ectopic is small, has not ruptured, and the HCG levels are low (less than 2000IU), by giving the woman an injection of methotrexate. This is a cytotoxic drug which destroys very actively dividing cells, such as those in the early placenta. When successful, the methotrexate causes the pregnancy to stop developing and gradually it shrivels away. However, this treatment is not always successful – we usually quote a 4% failure rate – so it is very important that any woman who is treated in this way agrees to undergo regular HCG blood tests for a few weeks to ensure that the levels have fallen satisfactorily. In theory, this drug treatment, which avoids surgery to the tube, could mean that the woman's future fertility is safeguarded. But at the present time our experience with this technique is limited and we do not have enough follow-up data on these women to be able to say that drug treatment is a better treatment option for early ectopics.

Ectopic pregnancies are quite common. In this country it is estimated that one in 200 pregnancies implants outside the uterine cavity. Although the reasons why some pregnancies are ectopic are not fully understood, it is well recognised that there are several groups of women who are at greater risk. Damage to the fallopian tubes caused by infection or previous abdominal surgery increases the chances of the fertilised egg implanting in the scarred portion of the tube. Hence, if you have had any infertility problems, there is an increased risk of an ectopic, since you may also have damaged tubes.

For similar reasons the risk is increased if you have had a previous ectopic pregnancy, or used an intrauterine contraceptive device, which can lead to low-grade infection of the uterine cavity and fallopian tubes.

It is not entirely clear to me why the incidence of ectopic pregnancy is higher in women with recurrent miscarriages. However, when we looked at the women attending the recurrent miscarriage clinic at St Mary's Hospital, we noticed that over 2% of the women had experienced an ectopic pregnancy in the past, compared to the 0.5% incidence expected in the general population. Some recurrent miscarriage sufferers have also had problems becoming pregnant, which accounts for a certain number of cases, but this is not the whole story, since most of the fertility problems in this group of women are due to disordered ovulation, and not to damage of the uterus or fallopian tubes.

Hydatidiform moles

Hydatidiform moles are the most common type of placental tumour. There are complete moles and partial moles. Complete moles are rare in Caucasian women, occurring no more frequently than one in 1500–2000 pregnancies, although they are very much more common in women in South-East Asia. Complete moles are derived entirely from the cells of the father, due to an accident that occurs at the time of fertilisation. No embryo is present in the pregnancy sac, but the placental tissues develop rapidly in an uncontrolled fashion. On the ultrasound scan these placental cells resemble bunches of grapes because they became swollen with fluid.

Persistent bleeding and severe nausea are usually associated with the presence of these moles, and the size of the uterus is usually larger than would be expected for the menstrual dates.

The important difference between complete and partial moles is that a complete mole may develop into an invasive cancer in a small percentage of cases. Specialist treatment and follow-up is needed, which in this country is concentrated in a few specialist centres with extensive experience in the management of this rare condition.

Partial moles are much more common and usually mimic the appearance of an inevitable or incomplete miscarriage. The partial mole contains a fetus/embryo which has three sets of chromosomes instead of the usual two. The placental cells do swell and proliferate but not to the same degree as occurs in a complete mole. It can be difficult to distinguish between a partial mole and a normal miscarriage on the basis of the ultrasound findings alone. Quite often, women with partial moles experience no unusual symptoms, and the diagnosis is only made by the pathologist after removal of all the tissues from the uterus (ERPC), which emphasises the importance of always trying to send evacuated pregnancy tissues for laboratory analysis when available. Very rarely a partial mole may develop into an invasive mole, but no cases of actual cancer have ever been reported. Nonetheless, any woman who has a partial mole is carefully followed up at special hospitals with experience in managing these unusual types of early pregnancy loss.

Medical management of miscarriage

For the last 50 years the standard method of emptying the uterus after the diagnosis of a failed pregnancy has usually been surgical – involving an anaesthetic and a brief operation. The successful development of medical (drug) treatments to terminate pregnancies has meant that we can now use these methods to empty the uterus for women who have suffered a miscarriage, and avoid the need for a surgical procedure. In brief, the woman is first given a drug that blocks the effect of progesterone (the hormone that is essential for the continuation of pregnancy) and after 36–48 hours she then takes a second drug (a prostaglandin) that encourages the uterus to contract and expel its contents.

The success rates of this treatment have been very varied, ranging from 13 to 100%. However, most units would agree that when the women are selected carefully, medical treatment will be successful in about 80% of cases. It is very important that the woman returns for a follow-up visit to ensure that the medical evacuation is complete. Some women will need to have a subsequent operation for heavy bleeding, or an incomplete miscarriage. This method appears to be acceptable to many women and in some cases preferable to the surgical alternative, although it must be noted here that if the pregnancy tissues need to be sent for genetic analysis the testing is less likely to be successful. Only pregnancies that have not progressed beyond nine weeks of gestation are suitable for this type of treatment and there are several contraindications to using it, such as women with heart, kidney and severe chest disease.

Expectant management of miscarriage

Over the last few years many doctors have questioned the need to surgically or medically empty the uterus after the diagnosis of a failed pregnancy. Historically, it was believed to be risky to leave the mother with retained tissues in her uterus. Junior doctors were all instructed about the potential dangers of life-threatening uterine bleeding and severe pelvic infection. However, these complications of infection and haemorrhage are actually quite common after surgical evacuation has been performed. Indeed, some experts in this field argue that infection is more common after surgical evacuation because dilating the cervix may interfere with the normal cervical barrier against infective organisms, allowing them to ascend into the uterine cavity. Further, that the curettage, or scrape, then contaminates the whole of the uterine cavity and may also increase the chances of the infection reaching the woman's bloodstream and causing a generalised illness. Added to these potential risks are the need for an anaesthetic and the possibility of surgical complications such as perforation of the uterus during the procedure.

These issues have led many doctors to reassess the situation and reconsider the option of expectant management – and just leave the miscarried tissues to come away of their own accord. Several studies have looked at the feasibility of this and the results so far have been encouraging. Not surprisingly, the success of expectant management appears to depend on the quantity of tissue in the uterine cavity, and ultrasound measurements of the retained products are important in the assessment of which pregnancies are most suitable. Experience to date suggests that the highest success rates are achieved when the miscarriage is incomplete and that 80% of these women will have an empty uterus on US scan within three days. However, the figure may be as low as 25% for women who present with a missed miscarriage. I think it is reassuring to note that although women who have chosen expectant management continue to have vaginal bleeding for a few days longer than women who have a surgical or medical evacuation, their blood counts do not appear to be lower. The reports so far also suggest that there is no difference in the time taken to return to normal menstrual periods or to become pregnant again. However, it is important for the reader to appreciate that all of the studies on expectant management published so far have only included small numbers of women and that we must wait for the results of much larger randomised studies before we can draw valid conclusions about the safety and potential benefits of this treatment.

The role of the pathologist

Throughout this book I will keep referring to the importance of involving a pathologist in the investigation of miscarriage. Even if the quantity of miscarried tissue is very small it is always worth trying to obtain a genetic analysis and asking the histopathologist to look at the structure of the placental tissues and membranes under the microscope. The pathologist can confirm that the pregnancy was intrauterine and that no signs of an ectopic or molar pregnancy are present. It may also be possible to identify the gestational age at which the pregnancy failed. This is particularly useful when no US scan reports are available. Specialist pathologists can also make an assessment of the degree of placental development and give us an idea of how well (or otherwise) the placenta was attached to the uterine lining. In some cases of infection, histology will be able to accurately determine the underlying cause of the miscarriage. In women with prothrombotic disorders (blood-clotting problems – see Chapter 12) it may also be possible to tell whether the placenta was fibrosed (shrunken) or contains any areas of infarction due to lack of blood flow.

Even more useful is the fact that the microscope slides can be stored for many years, if required, and this is potentially very valuable. As we improve our understanding of the causes of miscarriage it may be possible to go back to these slides and carry out newly discovered tests on the stored tissues. Many of the latest medical advances rely on extracting the DNA (genetic code) from tissues and it is now becoming possible to do this from tissues even when they have been fixed in formalin, embedded in paraffin and stored for some years. As new genetic disorders are identified we will be able to go back and literally 'probe' the miscarriage tissues to find these molecular abnormalities. The role of the pathologist with an interest in pregnancy loss is a very important one. Gone are the days when all they could tell us was whether there was a pregnancy present. The new molecular techniques promise to open up another whole dimension in our understanding of the causes of pregnancy loss.

Summary

There are many different types of miscarriage, and thanks to the widespread availability of ultrasound, we now have much more knowledge about the development of the young embryo and the stages at which this process most commonly goes wrong. We now understand that the vast majority of miscarriages occur very early and well before eight weeks of gestation. Further, that when the scan identifies a fetal pole measuring more than six weeks' size fetal heart activity must have been present before the pregnancy loss occurred.

Not only can the scan identify the stage at which the pregnancy failed, it can also be used to determine the stage that an ongoing miscarriage process has reached. When vaginal bleeding occurs in early pregnancy, the scan can differentiate between a threatened, inevitable, incomplete and a complete miscarriage. In skilled hands the scan can also exclude an ectopic pregnancy. Although ultrasound will never replace the value of a skilled doctor's examination, in early pregnancy it is the fastest and most accurate way to confirm whether the pregnancy is ongoing or has ended. Most importantly, the sight of a beating fetal heart after an episode of bleeding in pregnancy can provide a mother-to-be with more concrete reassurance than hours of verbal reassurance.

At the present time we do not know whether surgical, medical or expectant management provides the woman who has just miscarried with the best chances of a speedy recovery and the minimum of short- and long-term complications. The success of each treatment appears to depend on the type of miscarriage and the stage in the process that the miscarriage has reached when the woman seeks medical advice. It is likely that we will need to continue to have all three types of treatment available in the future but most doctors are hoping that we can move towards fewer surgical interventions. A large randomised trial comparing the results of surgical, medical and expectant management is now under way (the MIST study) and the results of this study are eagerly awaited. Since more than half of all emergency gynaecological operations are surgical evacuations for miscarriage, a non-surgical approach has very important implications for the quality of patient care and Health Service funding.

PART TWO

UNDERSTANDING THE CAUSES

FOUR

SPORADIC MISCARRIAGE

Why did I miscarry?

In the previous chapter we looked at the different types of miscarriage that can occur. We noted that sporadic miscarriage is the commonest complication of pregnancy and that as many as 25% of all women suffer a single episode of miscarriage. We also noted that recurrent miscarriage is very uncommon and only 1% of couples ever suffer this particularly distressing problem. My reason for emphasising this point again is that the factors which cause sporadic and recurrent miscarriages are different. The aim of this chapter is to look at the reasons why miscarriages occur sporadically. In later chapters of this book we will look in more detail at the reasons why miscarriage may occur repeatedly.

A sporadic pregnancy loss is often described as an isolated episode of bad luck or nature's way of getting rid of a pregnancy that was 'no good'. For many women this seems a poor and possibly unacceptable explanation for the distressing event that they have just suffered. It is important to understand here that often the doctors do not know why the miscarriage occurred, because there are no obvious pointers to its exact cause. Not surprisingly, a woman might assume that her miscarriage was caused by a specific event that occurred in her pregnancy, but in the majority of cases, this is impossible to prove.

Genetic abnormalities in the baby

What we do know is that a genetic abnormality in the embryo or tiny baby is the commonest cause of sporadic miscarriage. Genetic disorders which may result in sporadic miscarriage can be divided into three main headings: chromosomal abnormalities, gene defects and congenital malformations which have a genetic origin, such as spina bifida.

Chromosomes are long strands of genetic material which are housed in the nucleus of our cells. The chromosomes contain the coding for the different genes which make up an individual. There are a total of 46 chromosomes arranged into 23 pairs in each cell of the body. Each pair of chromosomes can be recognised by its size and shape and is numbered. For example, chromosome pair number 1 is the largest and chromosome pair number 22 is the smallest. Chromosomes 45 and 46 (pair 23) are the chromosomes which determine the sex of an individual. Each chromosome contains thousands of genes (about 5,000 per chromosome). Each gene is a single unit of 'information' inherited from the parents, and it occupies a specific position on the chromosome. The genes contain numerous small segments of DNA (genetic material) each of which provides a code for a specific characteristic or a particular cell function.

Chromosomal abnormalities

An embryo is created when an egg is successfully fertilised by a sperm. The egg and the sperm each contribute one set of 23 chromosomes from the mother or the father to the embryo. Before, during and after the process of fertilisation these two sets of chromosomes undergo a complex series of divisions and rearrangements. If one of the chromosomes is abnormal, or if during the process of dividing and rearranging, too many or too few chromosomes are left in the fertilised egg, an abnormal embryo or fetus may develop. The vast majority of these embryos miscarry at a very early stage in the pregnancy, because most chromosomal abnormalities are incompatible with life. However, a few continue through pregnancy, resulting in the birth of an abnormal baby or a baby that dies soon after birth. It is not difficult to understand why an abnormal fetus is at risk of being expelled from the uterus. It is much more difficult to explain why some abnormal fetuses fail to be expelled and how the pregnancy can continue developing,

As many as 50% of all early miscarriages are caused by chromosomal abnormalities in the fetus. It is important to understand that apart from a small proportion of inherited conditions (called parental translocations – discussed later), nearly all the chromosomal defects seen in sporadic miscarriages arise out of the blue (de novo). There are many types of chromosomal abnormality but the most common defects are trisomies, monosomies and polyploidies.

Trisomies

When the cells of the fetus contain three copies of one type of chromosome instead of the usual two, the defect is called a trisomy. Trisomies account for over half of all the chromosomal defects in sporadic miscarriages. The most frequent trisomy involves chromosome number 16 and since it is incompatible with life, no liveborn babies ever have this condition. Some frequently occurring trisomies have been given special names after the doctors who first described the condition.

Down's syndrome is probably the best known and affects chromosome pair number 21. The syndrome is named after Dr John Langdon-Down who was the first person to describe the problem in 1866. All Down's children are mentally handicapped but the severity of the handicap is variable. These children share certain physical features, particularly the slanting oriental eyes (that have led to this trisomy being called 'mongolism') and the presence of a single skin crease on the palms of the hands and feet. In addition the eyes are small, the tongue protrudes and the bridge of the nose is shallow, which often means that the child is snuffly and and very susceptible to colds and chest infections. Babies with Down's are floppy and are more likely to be born with an abnormality of the heart or intestine.

In Patau's syndrome, three copies of chromosome 13 are present. This trisomy is usually fatal within a few days of birth. Tiny eyes, too many fingers and toes and severe heart defects are characteristic. In Edward's syndrome (trisomy 18) the physical malformations include a small receding jaw, low-set ears, and the hands are clenched, whilst the feet have a curved sole described as 'rocker bottom'. Severe mental retardation is usual and most of these babies die within the first year of life. Other chromosomes often involved in trisomies are numbers 22, 15, and 2.

Most trisomies are due to abnormal division (meiosis) in the egg which occurs before fertilisation. This explains why trisomies are much more common in older women, because they are more likely to ovulate eggs which are abnormal. The best example of this maternal age effect is seen in Down's syndrome (trisomy 21). The chance of having a baby with three copies of chromosome 21 increases sharply after the age of 35 years. Although the majority of trisomy 21 fetuses are miscarried, some do go on to deliver at term and it is estimated that one in 30 babies born to mothers aged over 45 years has the condition. This is one of the commonest chromosomal abnormalities seen in live births.

If you have had the misfortune to miscarry because of a trisomy, you do have a slightly higher risk of suffering another one for the same reasons, even though the chromosome affected may be different. If it is known that your miscarriage occurred because of a trisomy, your doctor will probably advise you to have an amniocentesis or other type of prenatal test in a future pregnancy, to make sure that your next baby is not affected.

Monosomies

When one of the chromosomes is completely missing, the defect is called monosomy. The commonest type of monosomy is only found in girls and involves one of the two X chromosomes, which is why it is called monosomy X or Turner's syndrome. Monosomies are the cause of 15% of all miscarriages but only a tiny number of these pregnancies with one sex chromosome survive to be liveborn. It is estimated that one in 2,500 live births have monosomy X. These girls with Turner's syndrome are short (their growth is seriously affected), have no menstrual periods and are infertile.

Polyploidies

In this condition, the embryo contains one or more extra sets of 23 chromosomes, and accounts for about 20% of all the sporadic miscarriages caused by chromosomal abnormalities. Where one extra set appears, the defect is called triploidy and it is not affected by maternal age. It may result from an egg being fertilised by more than one sperm. Some triploidies are miscarried very early, before the embryo has developed, whereas other triploidies result in the growth of quite large babies and are often accompanied by abnormalities of the placenta (see Chapter 3 – partial hydatidiform moles). These babies never survive to be delivered. Tetraploidies (4 sets of 23 chromosomes) are a much less common type of polyploidy and usually the development of the pregnancy is arrested very early.

Structural rearrangements

These are changes in individual chromosomes, which may arise de novo in the egg or sperm, or may be inherited from one parent who carries a genetic defect in one of their chromosomes. These are a more likely cause of repeated miscarriages and are discussed in Chapter 7.

Other chromosomal abnormalities

Some men have an extra X sex chromosome (bringing the total to 47) which is known as Klinefelter's syndrome. In other cases, the addition of an extra X or Y chromosome may produce such a mild abnormality that the diagnosis is not made until after puberty or is never made, unless the woman or man happens to have their chromosomes examined for some other reason.

Sometimes an individual may be carrying two different cell lines made up of different chromosome numbers. This is called mosaicism. Mosaic cells occur when a cell divides abnormally some time after fertilisation. Every time this mosaic cell divides, it will produce further mosaic cells. Mosaic cells may also occur as an artefact (an induced artificial abnormality) during the processing and preparation of cells in the laboratory. Unless the mosaicism affects the germ cells (the eggs or the sperms) they frequently go undetected and are not a cause for concern. Certainly, mosaic cells are rarely found in miscarriage tissues.

Overall, the incidence of chromosomal abnormalities found in babies at birth is approximately 0.6% (six abnormalities per 1,000 babies born). If we look at the number of chromosomal defects in babies that are stillborn, the number increases tenfold to 6% (six abnormalities per 100 babies born). This is the tip of the iceberg; the vast majority of chromosomally abnormal pregnancies are miscarried early. It is believed that 50–60% of sporadic miscarriages are chromosomally abnormal. This represents a 100-fold increase when compared to live births.

Although chromosomal defects are common, we remain very ignorant about what causes them. We know that some trisomies are increased in older women and we suspect that radiation, some chemicals and a variety of other environmental factors may cause some defects. But the cause of most chromosomal abnormalities remains a mystery and this is an area which needs much research in the future.

Diagnosing chromosomal abnormalities

This can be difficult to achieve. Although the technology is available to look at miscarried tissues and determine the chromosomes present in them, there are many pitfalls which may prevent you from knowing for certain whether your miscarriage was caused by an abnormality of the chromosomes. The first problem is that in many pregnancies that are miscarried, the fetal tissues are not available to be examined. I hesitate to say that they are lost because this implies that someone has misplaced them. But lost they frequently are, most often in the heavy bleeding that occurs, or down the toilet.

The second problem is that the tissue needs to be very fresh if the analysis of the chromosomes is to be successful. Many pregnancies that miscarry are not immediately expelled from the uterus. If the tissues are removed surgically from the uterus by an ERPC (see Chapter 3) they may be sent to the laboratory for analysis, but if the pregnancy died some time ago, it may not be possible to 'resurrect' the cells to grow. This may sound rather macabre, so it is important for the reader to understand exactly what the laboratory tries to do to these tissues. They have to separate out the fetal tissues (including the placenta) from all the other tissues (such as maternal blood cells and pieces of the womb lining or decidua) that are present in the pot of products that they receive. Having identified the fetal and placental tissues, they have to try and encourage them to start regrowing. This is called tissue culture and it is time-consuming work which requires a lot of expertise.

The scientists in the laboratory who perform this work are called cytogeneticists (*cyto* is the Greek word for cell). They are experts in looking at the genetic make-up of cells. When cytogeneticists are asked to work on miscarriage tissues there are several factors which may make their job difficult and in some cases impossible to perform. The first is that there may be so few cells from the miscarried pregnancy that setting up a culture of 'living' cells may not be possible. This problem is often made worse because the tissues that are received in the laboratory always contain maternal tissues from the womb lining. It is very common for these maternal cells to grow rapidly in the culture that is set up and overrun the fetal cells, making the analysis difficult. On many occasions the final report may state that although the chromosomes present in the culture are female, it is suspected that they originate from the mother and not from the miscarried pregnancy. Of course, if the chromosomes are male or very abnormal (see possible types discussed earlier in this chapter) then we can be confident that the tissues cultured really have come from the baby.

Another common problem is that the miscarriage tissues may have become infected by organisms ('bugs') in the womb after the pregnancy has died, or during the course of the surgical evacuation organisms, which normally live in the woman's cervix or vagina, may have contaminated the specimen. Infective organisms grow extremely well in a good tissue culture and may damage the fetal tissues to such an extent that no chromosomal analysis is possible.

One last point needs to be mentioned here. I am sad to have to tell you that there are still some doctors and nurses who do not understand that if the miscarriage tissues are put into formalin (which is a preservative fluid used to prevent tissues from decomposing before they are examined under the microscope) no chromosomal analysis can be carried out. The formalin 'fixes' the tissues, killing them as it does so. Trying to make the cells grow in culture after they have been exposed to formalin is a hopeless task.

So if you are hoping to have your miscarriage examined genetically, it is probably worth asking the doctor how the tissues will be stored during their transport to the laboratory. Your gentle question may just be the reminder that is needed to ensure that your tissues are put into special cytogenetic fluid (called transport medium). Many laboratories now put some antibiotic into this fluid to reduce the risks of infection. If this is not available, then it is best for the tissues to be sent 'dry' in a sealed container or in some normal saline (salt water of a concentration that does not damage the cells).

I know that many couples I meet feel very upset that cytogenetic analysis of their miscarriage is not usually performed until they have suffered three losses. This does sound very heartless when you have just lost your baby and are desperately trying to understand the reason for the miscarriage. But if we were to do genetic analysis on every miscarriage that occurs, the expense would cripple the Health Service which is already hopelessly overstretched! So we have to try and use our resources to the best effect. As discussed earlier in this chapter, the majority of sporadic miscarriages are due to a chromosomal abnormality in the fetus, which will not recur. This is why we are forced to reserve genetic analysis for those women who have suffered repeated miscarriages (see Chapter 7).

Gene defects

Our genes are arranged in pairs along the chromosome and they may be dominant or recessive. If one or both members of the pair of genes present on the chromosome are dominant, they produce a recognisable effect in the body. A single copy of the dominant gene can override the action of the non-dominant gene. In the case of recessive genes, a noticeable effect is only produced if both members of the pair are present. Most diseases which are genetically inherited are carried by recessive genes. Recessive genes are very common, but they will only give rise to a specific disease in the baby if both parents carry the recessive gene and pass it on to their baby. A good example of this is seen in cystic fibrosis. One in every 22 people carries the recessive gene for cystic fibrosis. However, the chance of two of these individuals both passing on their recessive gene to the baby that they produce is one in 400.

It is likely that future research will identify many specific gene defects that cause miscarriages, but at the present time our knowledge is limited. The human genome project is fast mapping each of our 23 chromosomes and soon we will be able to pinpoint the location of many genetic mutations (abnormalities). However, we do know of some gene defects that will give rise to an abnormal baby with a serious disease such as cystic fibrosis, sickle cell anaemia or thalassaemia. Some gene defects are sex-linked. This usually means that they are carried on the X chromosome of the mother who, because she has a second normal X chromosome, does not suffer from the disorder. However, she has a 50% chance of passing on her gene defect to her children, but only her sons will develop the disease. This is because their second sex chromosome is a Y and they do not have the balancing benefit of a second X chromosome. Examples of this situation are Duchenne muscular dystrophy and haemophilia. The study of gene defects is fascinating and very complex, but detailed explanations are beyond the scope of this book. Further examples of gene defects that may lead to recurrent miscarriages are included in Chapter 7.

Congenital abnormalities

When doctors talk about congenital abnormalities, they mean that the baby is born with a structural or functional defect or malformation. Congenital malformations are sometimes, but not always, inherited. When there is a genetic origin for the malformation, it is usually because several abnormal genes are acting together. Usually, a collection of factors is responsible for the problem, but no one factor alone can be held responsible. This means that the inheritance of the congenital abnormality may not follow any well recognised pattern. Nonetheless, couples who have already had a baby with a specific congenital abnormality have a high risk of conceiving another child with the same abnormality. The risk may be as high as one in 20.

A good example of a congenital abnormality is spina bifida. Spina bifida is one type of neural tube defect in which the baby's spinal cord is not properly covered by the bony spine. Where the delicate spinal cord is unprotected, it is in great danger of damage and these babies, if they survive, may have very severe neurological problems including paralysis. Spina bifida is a common problem and has a strong genetic link. But it is when the genetic tendency is exaggerated by a factor in the environment, such as poor maternal nutrition (in particular a deficiency in folic acid and other vitamins) that the spinal defect occurs.

As many as 40% of neural tube defects are miscarried and a further 20% are stillborn babies. In total, neural tube defects account for about 5% of all sporadic miscarriages. In the vast majority of cases of neural tube defect, the abnormality cannot be predicted from the woman's or her family's previous history. This is why it is important that all women who are trying to become pregnant are advised to take folic acid tablets, not just those women who have already suffered a neural tube defect. Fortunately, the sophisticated ultrasound scans that are now available to most pregnant women are capable of detecting 99% of all cases of neural tube defect. I know that this does not remove the pain of being diagnosed as carrying a baby with this problem, but it does allow you and your partner the option of terminating a badly affected pregnancy, if this is your choice.

A major congenital malformation affects four in every 100 newborn babies. These abnormalities are responsible for one in four of all the babies that die soon after delivery. Although 40% of congenital malformations are due to recognised genetic factors, there are other important causes. Damage to the baby before birth may be caused by infections, particularly viruses (about 5%). Drugs taken during pregnancy account for about 2% (perhaps the most notorious example is thalidomide, which caused limb malformations called phocomelia); exposure to chemicals, irradiation and some metabolic disorders (uncontrolled diabetes) are also culprits. Although a large proportion of congenital abnormalities are still unexplained, it is likely that many of them will be shown to have a genetic origin in the future.

Abnormalities of the uterus and cervix

Abnormalities of the uterus and cervix may also cause miscarriages. The abnormality may be congenital (for example, the mother may have been born with a double uterus or an incompetent cervix) or may appear later on (an acquired abnormality). Examples of an acquired abnormality are uterine fibroids (benign growths in the wall of the uterus) or the development of adhesions within the cavity of the uterus after an infection or surgical procedure.

In early pregnancy, the presence of any of these abnormalities may hinder the embryo from implanting properly in the uterine lining and give rise to a miscarriage. In later pregnancy, the size of a fibroid or the restrictive shape of the uterine cavity may prevent the baby from having enough space to grow to its full size. This situation may result in a late miscarriage or the onset of premature labour.

It is important to understand that anatomical abnormalities of the uterus are extremely common. They are so common, that I often find myself wondering whether they should be called 'abnormalities'. Perhaps it would be more sensible to consider them as a variation of the normal shape of the uterus. Certainly, a large number of quite major structural abnormalities of the uterus never cause any trouble at all for a woman during her pregnancies. I can remember many occasions when I have only recognised that a woman has a double uterus (sometimes called a bicornuate uterus) or a uterine septum (sheet of tissue protruding down into the cavity from the top (fundus) of the uterus) after delivering her normal baby at full term! If this same woman had experienced miscarriages, instead of normal pregnancies, she would probably have had tests that would have shown up the abnormality.

If you find this difficult to believe, then I must tell you about a charming 75-year-old lady I performed a hysterectomy upon a few years ago. She was having the operation done because she was suffering from prolapse. The muscles supporting the uterus had weakened and she complained of 'something uncomfortable coming down below' every time she went for a walk. At the operation I discovered that she had two completely separate uterine bodies joined together by one cervix. When I explained this to the lady after she had recovered she asked me what problems this might have caused. I told her that this type of abnormality is associated with infertility, miscarriages, premature labour and babies that are born small in size. She looked at me in utter disbelief. She then went on to tell me (in a gentle manner, suggesting that I was obviously a bit simple) that she had never had a miscarriage. Furthermore, that her six sons had all weighed more than eight pounds and had had to be induced to deliver when they showed no signs of going into natural labour at 42 weeks!

Space does not allow me to continue with more stories like this one. However, I hope the reader has got a feel for the fact that uterine abnormalities do not necessarily give rise to problems in achieving a successful pregnancy. This is why I believe that it is only useful to look for these abnormalities in women who have experienced several pregnancy losses, whether they be early or late miscarriages. (Chapter 8 deals with the relationship between these abnormalities and recurrent miscarriages.)

Infections in the mother and in the baby

One in 20 pregnant women will experience an infective illness during their pregnancy. If this sounds an alarming figure you will be relieved to hear that the majority of these infections are completely harmless. Only a minority of maternal infections during pregnancy are capable of causing damage to the fetus or the newborn baby. When the fetus is infected whilst still in the uterus, the infection is called 'congenital'. If the baby is infected at the time of delivery, the infection is 'acquired' in the 'intra partum' period. Some infections are only passed to the baby by close contact or breast feeding after birth and these are 'postnatally acquired' infections.

There are many different possible outcomes to a pregnancy that is complicated by an infection in the mother. The infection may cause an early or a late miscarriage. It may be responsible for the woman going into premature labour or suffering a stillbirth. Some infections will result in congenital abnormalities in the baby, which may be obvious at birth or not be recognised until early childhood. Some infections during pregnancy will be so mild that no specific symptoms are noticed by the mother. Often these mild infections are a source of great anxiety to pregnant women, who fear that their baby is being harmed, and since they have no symptoms, they can do nothing to prevent this risk.

Let me reassure you that the most likely outcome of an infection during pregnancy is an entirely normal baby. Although the word 'infection' may conjure up all sorts of alarming thoughts, particularly if you are pregnant now, it is important for me to stress that most are harmless. Infections during pregnancy are the cause of less than 3% of all congenital abnormalities.

I think it is true to say that almost every viral, bacterial or parasitic infection ever described in medical textbooks has also been claimed as the cause of sporadic miscarriage. Most bacterial and parasitic infections can be successfully treated if they are correctly identified. Some viral infections can be prevented by vaccination. Since treatment may be possible, it is particularly important that we try to identify the infectious organism in the hope that we might be able to prevent some cases of miscarriage.

To do this successfully, we need to know at what point during pregnancy the mother is most likely to catch and pass on the infection and what effect it will have, if any, on her baby. For example, rubella only affects the baby in early pregnancy, whereas cytomegalovirus can infect the baby at all stages in pregnancy. Chickenpox causes problems early and at the time of delivery, but the middle of pregnancy is not a problem time. The route by which the infection is passed to the baby is also important. During pregnancy, any infectious agent must be capable of passing through the placenta if it is going to infect the baby. During labour the organism may be transmitted by the mother's blood or vaginal fluid secretions.

In this chapter we will look at a variety of bacterial, viral and parasitic infections which may cause sporadic miscarriages. Infective causes of recurrent miscarriage are discussed later in this book (see Chapter 10). I spend a lot of time in the miscarriage clinic answering queries about infections that cause problems in very late pregnancy and in the newborn baby. Strictly speaking these infections should not be included in a book about miscarriage. However, I am going to mention some of them at the specific request of many of my patients!

Viral infections causing sporadic miscarriage

Viral infections during pregnancy are extremely common. The best example is the common cold. During a nine-month pregnancy the chances of a woman developing a cold are very high and usually the baby suffers no ill effects.

Rubella

Many viral infections result in the production of antibodies in the mother, during her first infection, to protect her against future infections with the same virus. A good example of this is rubella (German measles). This infection is important because it has very damaging effects on the fetus if the mother develops the infection in early pregnancy. Many early pregnancies that are infected by rubella miscarry. The virus crosses the placenta and can cause blindness, deafness, heart defects and mental retardation in the fetus. The earlier in pregnancy the woman becomes infected, the more severe the abnormalities in the baby may be. So severe, in fact, that a termination of pregnancy is offered to women who catch rubella in the first 14 weeks of pregnancy. After this date, the fetus may still become infected, but it is unusual for rubella to cause significant damage.

Once a woman has had rubella infection, she is no longer at risk of transmitting the infection to her baby because of the immunity she develops. Rubella antibodies can be measured in her blood and the presence of these antibodies is looked for in every pregnant woman in the UK when she first attends the antenatal clinic. If the pregnant woman has no immunity, she will be advised to avoid contact with the virus (young children are the most common source of the infection) and will be offered vaccination soon after she has delivered her baby. Since 1988 all children in this country have been vaccinated against rubella (together with measles and mumps – MMR injection) during the second year of life or at the time of preschool entry at 4–5 years. This vaccination policy was aimed at eradicating rubella from the community rather than just targeting young women who may become pregnant and has been so successful that we have now been able to abandon routine vaccination for teenage girls at school. In most cases the vaccination is successful but in a few cases antibody production is weak or shortlived. When this occurs, a further vaccination is needed.

If you have suffered the miseries of having German measles as a child or as an adult (when it is usually much more unpleasant) you will almost certainly be immune. I emphasise this point because at least once a month I meet a tearful woman in my antenatal clinic who has been in contact with German measles and is frightened that her baby will be affected. Frequently her distress is because she cannot recall having had German measles in the past. If you find yourself in this situation, please remember that some women have been exposed to rubella but develop such a mild infection (subclinical) that they do not realise they have had it. A simple blood test will tell you whether you are immune. Rubella is not a cause of recurrent miscarriage.

Genital Herpes
There are two main types of herpes virus infection. Type 1 is responsible for cold sores of the lips and mouth. Type 2 is responsible for the ulcers that develop on the vulva, vagina and cervix and are referred to as genital herpes. If a woman develops her first genital herpes infection during pregnancy and it is severe, miscarriage may result. However, the greatest risk for the fetus is when the mother develops a primary genital herpes lesion near the time of delivery. If the virus is being excreted from the lesion (ulcer) it can infect the baby after the membranes have ruptured and during the passage down the birth canal. Although only 10% of babies are infected, the consequences can be very severe, including death of the newborn baby from infection of the tissues surrounding the brain and the spinal cord (encephalitis and meningitis). This is why doctors advise delivery by caesarean section for women who develop a primary genital herpes around the time of delivery. After delivery, the paediatricians will treat the baby with antiviral drugs (such as acyclovir) to ensure that no problems develop.

Infection with the herpes virus produces an antibody response in the mother but this does not protect her from another attack of herpes. However, if you are pregnant it will be comforting to know that the fetus can only be infected during the course of your first herpetic infection and is unaffected by any recurrences that you may experience. I stress this point because I meet many worried mothers who think they should have a caesarean delivery when they develop another attack of herpes near to the time of their delivery. This is not necessary and your baby will not be at risk if the attack is a secondary one. Exciting new research has suggested that it may become possible to vaccinate babies against herpes infection while they are still in the womb, but at the present time this method has only been tried in animals. As with rubella, herpes is not a cause of recurrent miscarriage.

Chicken-pox

The chicken-pox virus is highly contagious, which means that chicken-pox infection is very easily caught. As a result, the vast majority of children (90%) have had chicken-pox before they reach adolescence and infection in pregnancy for the first time is rare. This is another infection which causes great anxiety for pregnant women so I am going to include some details here, even though they are not strictly related to miscarriage problems.

I am puzzled by the fact that I have never been able to find any information about the effects of chicken-pox on the pregnancy when the infection occurs before eight weeks of gestation. I quizzed one of my virology colleagues about this recently, who explained that infection in the very early weeks of pregnancy is not thought to be associated with problems in the baby later on. This is probably because babies infected very early are miscarried early, but no one has any proof about this.

If you catch chicken-pox for the first time between eight and 20 weeks of gestation, there is a possibility that the baby will become infected. This congenital infection may give rise to abnormalities affecting the limbs, eyes, skin and brain – the congenital varicella syndrome. The baby may also be growth retarded. It is important to emphasise, however, that the risk is small and that no more than

3–5% of babies will be affected to any degree. If you find yourself in this worrying situation, it is likely that your obstetrician will suggest that you have regular ultrasound scans during the pregnancy to look for problems such as calcification in the baby's head, fluid accumulating in the baby's body cavities (hydrops fetalis) and increasing fluid in the amniotic cavity or pregnancy sac. In the vast majority of cases there will be no problem and the scans will provide you with reassurance.

If you catch chicken-pox after 20 weeks your baby will not be affected by the congenital varicella syndrome. However, towards the end of your pregnancy, the situation is potentially more worrying. The ability of the chicken-pox virus to cross the placenta and infect the baby increases as the pregnancy advances. As many as 50% of babies become infected if the mother catches chicken-pox one to four weeks before delivery. The newborn baby can develop a very severe infection (with pneumonia and encephalitis) because its immune system is not mature enough to deal with the chicken-pox virus. Before this puts you into a panic, let me reassure you strongly that these problems are easily avoided by giving the baby a special injection soon after delivery. (The injection is called Zoster Immune Globulin (ZIG) because the proper name for chicken-pox virus is varicella zoster.)

If you think you may have caught chicken-pox in pregnancy but you do not develop the typical rash and symptoms, make sure you tell your doctor quickly. A blood test will usually be able to establish whether you are immune or not and, if there is any doubt at the time of your delivery, your baby will be given some ZIG to be on the safe side. Chicken-pox is not a cause of recurrent miscarriage because the mother is immune to future infections.

Parvovirus

This is a virus which appears to be confined to humans. The symptoms of infection with parvovirus B19 are very similar to those of German measles (rubella). Frequently, the infection is so mild that it goes unrecognised. Parvovirus is spread by respiratory droplets (coughing and sneezing) and fomites (any substance which is capable of absorbing and retaining infectious particles – for example, bedding, clothes, carpets and curtains). Although 40% of pregnant women are susceptible to parvovirus infection because they have not previously been infected, it is not a common problem during pregnancy. Parvovirus is capable of causing late miscarriage and intrauterine death, which is usually associated with 'hydrops' – when the baby accumulates lots of fluid in all the cavities of its body, including the abdomen, chest and ventricles of the brain. However, 80% of pregnancies in which parvovirus infection occurs result in normal live births. Congenital abnormalities are not associated with this infection, so there has never been any suggestion that termination should be offered to mothers who develop this infection during pregnancy.

Other viruses causing sporadic miscarriages

Influenza infection in early pregnancy may be followed by miscarriage, but it is just as likely that the miscarriage is caused by the very high fevers that the mother develops, rather than the 'flu virus itself. Technically speaking, influenza cannot be a cause of recurrent miscarriage since the strains of the virus are constantly changing. This is one of the reasons why 'flu vaccines do not always prevent further outbreaks of 'flu.

Infection with the mumps virus is said to occur less frequently in pregnancy, but when it does occur, the risk of miscarriage is high. Similarly, hepatitis A, B and C have all been accused of causing miscarriages. Hepatitis B virus cannot cross the placenta and the baby only becomes infected at or after the time of delivery, so I think that the few reports that have suggested it causes miscarriage are inaccurate and circumstantial. My practical experience from the miscarriage clinic suggests to me that both mumps and hepatitis are very rare in pregnancy. Certainly, the contribution they make to the problem of miscarriage is small.

Rubeola (measles), variola (polio) and vaccinia (smallpox) viruses have all been the cause of sporadic miscarriages in the past. However, vaccination is now eradicating these diseases so successfully that smallpox and polio are becoming extinct. Measles vaccine has not been available for so long, so it will take longer for this disease to be eradicated worldwide. Polio vaccination given during pregnancy has no harmful effect on the fetus and certainly does not cause miscarriage.

Viral infections which may cause recurrent miscarriages

Some viral infections, such as cytomegalovirus (CMV), can be reactivated. This means that a second episode of CMV infection can be triggered off, under certain very rare circumstances. Some viruses persist in the mother's body and remain infective even after she has developed antibodies to them. The classic example of this is the human immunodeficiency virus (HIV). Since both of these viruses are possible causes of recurrent miscarriage, they are also discussed in Chapter 10.

Bacteria and other organisms causing sporadic miscarriage

Bacterial infections during pregnancy are quite common but usually they do not affect the baby seriously, if at all, until around the time of delivery. Some may cause premature labour, for instance, the beta haemolytic streptococcus and bacterial vaginosis. (Since these infections may occur repeatedly, they are also discussed in Chapter 10.)

Listeria

Infection with listeria monocytogenes during pregnancy is not common but it may have serious consequences for the baby. Typically, the mother has a short, influenza-like illness in the second or third trimester of pregnancy. The usual symptoms are fever, aching muscles, general malaise, nausea, diarrhoea and abdominal pain. Listeria is a well-recognised, but uncommon, cause of late miscarriage.

The bacteria are present in animals and contaminated soil. They infect humans when they are eaten in contaminated foodstuffs, especially unpasteurised dairy products. In non-pregnant women the infection is often very mild and goes unnoticed, but during pregnancy the infection can be more severe. It seems that listeria find the placenta a particularly comfortable place to multiply. Antibiotics (ampicillin) will cure the infection but the best way to avoid complications to the baby during pregnancy is prevention. If you are pregnant, make sure that you never eat unwashed salad and vegetables and avoid soft cheeses and meat pâtés. If you are in any doubt about whether the product is made from unpasteurised milk, then do not risk eating it.

Brucella

Brucella bacteria are an important cause of infertility and miscarriage in cattle. Different types (species) of brucella affect cattle, goats and hogs. The bacteria invade the placenta, which contains an alcohol called erythritol, and this stimulates the brucella to grow. Brucellosis is now rare in the UK because the disease has been virtually eradicated from our cattle. Brucellosis is sometimes referred to as 'undulant fever' because the symptoms are night fevers which come and go, along with cough, headache, muscle pains and weight loss.

Very occasionally farm workers may become infected because they are exposed to infected cattle. There is also a tiny risk of catching brucella if you eat unpasteurised dairy products. The human placenta does not contain erythritol, which means that the risk of infection is very small, even if you are exposed to infected cattle. If you work on a farm or in a veterinary surgery, simple precautions can reduce the risk of infection. Do not help with lambing or calving. Do not milk cows or sheep that have recently given birth. Nor should you handle miscarried lambs or calves or their afterbirths (placentae). If your partner cannot avoid these contacts, make sure that you do not come into contact with soiled clothing. Careful personal hygiene is all that is needed to prevent person-to-person infection. It is extremely unlikely that you will suffer a miscarriage because of brucella infection.

Chlamydia

Chlamydia are small, infective organisms that are halfway between bacteria and viruses. There are two important types of chlamydia. Chlamydia trachomatis is spread by sexual contact and causes cystitis, a sore vagina and conjunctivitis in the newborn baby. It is a common cause of tubal damage leading to infertility, but it does not cause miscarriage.

Chlamydia psittaci causes miscarriage in sheep and it has been suggested that it may cause miscarriages in farm workers and vets, but this has never been proven conclusively. Infection can cause cough, fever, headache and general 'flu-like symptoms. If you think there is a risk of being exposed to chlamydia psittaci during your pregnancy, then follow the advice given in the brucella section, on page 50. This is a very rare cause of sporadic miscarriage.

Salmonella

Salmonella is one of the commonest causes of food poisoning, giving rise to sickness and diarrhoea which can be severe. The maternal fever may occasionally cause a miscarriage. Although it may not have any effect on your unborn baby, it is sensible to try and avoid this illness while you are pregnant. Salmonella infection is associated with eating undercooked poultry and eggs. All you need to do to avoid this problem is to follow some simple precautions. Always wash your hands before preparing these foods. Do not let raw meat juices touch or drip on to any other foods in your fridge. Make sure that any poultry or eggs you eat have been thoroughly cooked to ensure that the bacteria are destroyed. Avoid eating mayonnaise and mousses, both of which contain uncooked egg yolks or whites.

Parasites

Toxoplasma

The parasitic organism (bug) toxoplasma gondii causes toxoplasmosis. Toxoplasma can sometimes cause miscarriage in early pregnancy and damage to the baby in late pregnancy. It is mainly associated with cats, but sheep can also be infected. Infection with toxoplasma gondii may occur if you eat unwashed vegetables, poorly cooked infested meat or inhale eggs from cat faeces.

The disease itself causes vague 'flu-like symptoms in the mother, with a low-grade fever and swollen glands, particularly in the neck. Fatigue, headache, a rash, enlargement of the spleen and eye problems are less common. Many women do not recognise that they have had the illness. Toxoplasmosis is more prevalent in communities that have lots of cats or where meat is eaten rare (e.g. France). Recent estimates suggest that two per 1000 pregnancies will be infected with toxoplasmosis in the UK each year.

If the mother acquires her primary (first) infection during pregnancy, she will transmit the infection to her baby in about 40% of cases. I need to emphasise that the fetus can only become infected during the course of the mother's primary infection, which is why toxoplasma infection cannot be a cause of recurrent miscarriage. The baby is most likely to become infected when a non-immune mother is infected near the time of delivery, and may develop congenital toxoplasma or a subclinical infection.

The baby is more severely affected when the infection occurs around the time of conception or during the first trimester of pregnancy. Only 10% of babies will be infected at this early stage in pregnancy but the risk of injury to the baby is high. The injuries include early and late miscarriage, later intrauterine death or live-born babies with severe neurological problems. Hydrocephaly (water on the brain), cerebral calcification and impaired vision are all possible, but only 10% of infected newborn babies have symptoms and we do not really understand what the later problems may be. However, we do know that congenital toxoplasmosis is a significant cause of mental retardation and blindness worldwide.

The blood tests to diagnose whether you have had toxoplasma in the past or recently are not entirely straightforward. Many false positives and negatives have occurred. However, in the simplest of terms, your blood will be tested for what we call 'IgG toxoplasma antibodies'. IgG is the name given to the class of antibodies which appear in our blood after we have developed immunity to the infection. If it is positive, then you are immune to toxoplasmosis and there is nothing more to worry about.

If the test is negative, this means that you are not immune to toxoplasmosis and may be at risk during pregnancy. The problems come when a woman is retested at a later stage in pregnancy and found to have developed the IgG antibody, which indicates that she has become infected during her pregnancy. Then the laboratory has to go back to the first blood sample and see whether they can find any 'IgM antibody' in it. IgM antibodies are the first antibodies to be made in the immune response and so their presence in the blood sample suggests that the infection is recent. To check that these results are accurate, a 'dye test' then has to be performed which requires live toxoplasma parasites and therefore has to be sent to a special laboratory.

As soon as the maternal infection has been confirmed, the woman will be given the antibiotic spiramycin, because this can reduce the risk of the baby becoming infected by as much as 60%. If the baby is thought to have been infected, the only way to confirm the diagnosis is by taking a sample of the blood from the baby's cord using ultrasound to guide the needle into the uterus (cordocentesis). If the toxoplasma parasite can be found in fetal blood or amniotic fluid, then the mother is at risk of having a baby with serious damage. Some women will want to have a termination at this point, whereas others may want to wait and see whether future ultrasound scans suggest any complications.

About one third of women build up some immunity to toxoplasma without even realising they have come into contact with it. Nonetheless if you are pregnant, it is a good idea to try and minimise your chances of being exposed to the risk. Wash your hands carefully after handling cats or kittens and avoid contact with strays. Worm your pet cats regularly. Avoid contact with cat litter. Try to find someone else to remove the soiled litter from the tray every day. If you have to do it yourself, wear rubber gloves and make sure that you wash the gloves and your hands afterwards. Always wear gloves when gardening to protect your hands from contaminated soil. Avoid eating any raw or undercooked meat and make sure that you wash vegetables and salads carefully to remove any soil from them.

The purpose of pre-pregnancy and antenatal screening for women who are susceptible to toxoplasmosis is to reduce the risk of a mother acquiring an acute infection during pregnancy. If she does become infected, it is important to identify her quickly so that the risk of the baby developing congenital infection can be reduced. A recent working party at the Royal College of Obstetricians and Gynaecologists concluded that routine antenatal screening of all pregnant women in this country to detect and warn women who were not immune to toxoplasmosis would not be 'appropriate'. Although this infection causes much anxiety, it is important to remember that the numbers of affected pregnancies are quite small. Furthermore, your antenatal clinic can arrange for you to have your blood checked to see whether you are immune, even though routine screening is not offered to everyone.

Malaria

In countries where malaria is rife, pregnant women are at risk of miscarrying because of the high fevers that usually accompany the infection. Pregnant women are more likely to catch malaria and the infection is often more severe. It is thought that this is because of the altered immune response in pregnancy. Having said this, it is important to remember that the malarial parasite rarely crosses the placenta and gains access to the baby. If it does, the baby is better protected than the mother from becoming infected, because the red blood cells contain fetal haemoglobin (haemoglobin F) which is much more resistant than adult haemoglobin.

It is best to avoid malaria zones when you are pregnant. If this is not possible, then make sure that you take your tablets to prevent becoming infected and continue taking them after you have left that country, for as long as is recommended. New anti-malarial drugs are continually coming on to the market and you should talk to your doctor about which drugs are safe in pregnancy. Chloroquine will not harm your baby, nor will Proguanil if you take folate supplements at the same time. Mefloquin and Maloprim should be avoided in the first 12 weeks of pregnancy. If you have taken these drugs already, do not panic. The most important thing to remember is that a malarial infection is far more likely to cause problems for you or your pregnancy than the drugs you have taken to prevent infection. If you are in doubt about any anti-malarial drug, I suggest you ring up the information centre at the London School of Hygiene and Tropical Medicine (see useful addresses). Their experts will advise you.

Hormonal causes of sporadic miscarriage

There is no doubt that the state of a woman's hormones at the time of conception and in early pregnancy may be a cause of pregnancy loss. Getting pregnant and staying pregnant is dependent on the correct balance of reproductive hormones. There are a multitude of different ways in which the balance can go wrong.

In order to understand this, we need to look carefully at the hormonal events which occur during a normal menstrual cycle leading up to a pregnancy. Soon after the menstrual period, the follicle stimulating hormone (FSH) is secreted by the pituitary gland. This hormone acts upon the ovary. The ovaries contain thousands of eggs which are present at birth. Each egg is surrounded by a group of cells which, as the egg develops, form a small fluid-filled sac, or follicle. FSH stimulates the follicles to start growing. As the follicles develop, the cells which surround the egg start producing oestrogen. This hormone stimulates the growth of the womb lining (endometrium) and the tissues of the breasts.

The rising level of oestrogen in the blood stimulates the brain, telling it that the follicle is mature and ready to ovulate. The brain signals to the pituitary gland to reduce the amount of FSH that it is producing. The pituitary gland also releases a short sharp burst of the hormone LH (luteinising hormone). This burst of LH (called a pulse) triggers the release of the egg from the follicle, which occurs about 36 hours later.

Ovulation usually occurs when the follicle has grown to about 20mm in diameter (the size of a one pound coin). The egg then passes down one of the fallopian tubes. The space in the follicle which used to be occupied by the egg then becomes filled with blood. The blood forms a clot which is then 'organised' into fibrous tissue. The secretion of LH continues at a lower level and this encourages the remaining cells in the ruptured follicle to form the corpus luteum (Latin for 'yellow body'). The cells produce a bright yellow pigment which stains the whole of the ruptured follicle.

The corpus luteum starts to produce progesterone hormone. Like oestrogen, progesterone has effects on the uterus, breasts and the hypothalamus and pituitary glands in the brain. In the uterus, progesterone makes the cells receptive to a pregnancy by producing the nutrients needed to support a developing embryo.

The corpus luteum is programmed to break down after 14 days if it does not receive the 'message' that a pregnancy has occurred. LH production from the pituitary gland falls after ovulation and without this hormone stimulus to the ovary, the corpus luteum withers and the levels of progesterone fall. The loss of progesterone stimulus to the uterus means that its blood-filled lining starts to disintegrate and menstrual bleeding results. The levels of both oestrogen and progesterone fall, causing a new cycle of follicle growth to start.

If the egg is fertilised by a sperm, this usually occurs in the fallopian tubes and then the fertilised egg (embryo) travels to the uterus, where it implants in the lining of the uterus (endometrium) and grows as a pregnancy. The embryo starts to produce human chorionic gonadotrophin (HCG). The corpus luteum recognises the presence of the HCG as a signal not to break down and to continue producing progesterone. The womb lining does not disintegrate and the menstrual period does not occur. A healthy, active corpus luteum is essential for the pregnancy to continue. If it is damaged and the production of progesterone is poor during the first eight weeks of pregnancy, a miscarriage will result.

The reader will not require more than common sense to recognise that this complex hormonal jigsaw puzzle can go wrong at many different places. If the ovary does not respond well to FSH, the follicles will not grow and the eggs they contain will not mature and be released. If the LH levels in the early part of the cycle are too high and there is no proper LH surge, ovulation may not occur or it may occur too early or too late. These ovulation problems are an important cause of infertility and are frequently seen in women with polycystic ovaries (see Chapter 11). If an egg that is poorly matured is released, the production of progesterone from the corpus luteum may be so poor that the luteal phase (the second half of the cycle after ovulation) is too short and the uterine lining so poorly developed that an embryo cannot implant successfully.

Many cases of miscarriage are claimed to result from a 'deficient luteal phase'. This may be true, but it is important to understand that the success of this phase depends upon a complex sequence of hormonal events that are already in place by the time that the luteal phase starts. If the hormonal events of the first part of the cycle are in any way impaired, the die has been cast. If progesterone levels are low in the luteal phase, this means that the corpus luteum is not functioning properly. If progesterone levels are low in the early weeks of pregnancy, this means that the placental cells surrounding the embryo are not producing sufficient HCG to stimulate the corpus luteum to produce enough progesterone.

I know that many women and their doctors hope that by giving injections of progesterone or HCG, they will be able to prevent a miscarriage. This is a convenient idea but it does not work. This treatment is a good example of 'closing the stable door after the horse has bolted'. Injections of these hormones cannot make a flagging corpus luteum or a flagging placenta come alive again. All they will do is increase the levels of HCG or progesterone in the mother's blood for a short period of time. This may delay the time at which the bleeding and the miscarriage appear to start, but it will not change the overall course of events. The factory producing the necessary hormones to ensure the continuation of pregnancy is not working properly and so miscarriage is inevitable.

In many cases of sporadic miscarriage, the hormonal imbalance which leads to miscarriage is a one-off event and is not likely to be repeated. In those women who have suffered repeated miscarriages, and in particular those women who have polycystic ovaries (see Chapter 11), the hormonal problem will be present in most pregnancies they conceive. These women need careful investigation and need to be offered treatment where it is available and appropriate for their problem.

For many years the medical textbooks have stated that other types of hormonal disorders such as diabetes and thyroid problems are a cause of miscarriage. As a result, many doctors have suggested that their miscarriage patients should undergo investigations to see whether they have a previously unrecognised diabetic tendency (glucose tolerance tests) or problems with the way their thyroid gland works (thyroid function tests). I strongly believe that these tests are a waste of both time and money. Women who have these types of hormonal disorders do not go and visit their doctors for the first time with a miscarriage. If you have an overactive or an underactive thyroid, you are much more likely to meet me for the first time in my infertility clinic. A hormone disorder which affects the functioning of every cell in the body (and the thyroid does) will make it very difficult for you to get pregnant in the first place.

However, after you have been diagnosed as having a thyroid problem and been started on the right treatment, you will probably find that you can become pregnant quite quickly and you will not be at any greater risk of suffering a miscarriage than your next-door neighbour who has an entirely normal thyroid gland.

The same is true for diabetes. If you are already a diabetic or suddenly develop this disease, then you will have a variety of medical problems which hopefully will be diagnosed promptly and looked after by a physician. It is true that a woman who has poorly controlled diabetes has a greater risk of miscarriage. She also has a considerably greater risk of producing a baby that has a congenital abnormality. However, when her diabetes is under control she will have no particular problems in becoming pregnant and she will not be at any greater risk of miscarrying. It is very unusual to meet a woman in the miscarriage clinic who has unrecognised diabetes or thyroid disease. Nor is it likely that performing glucose tolerance or thyroid function tests in all miscarriage sufferers will identify women who are 'on the brink' of developing either of these disorders. The perceptive reader will realise, as I say this, that I have used these tests in the past. Yes, I was taught that the tests 'should' be performed. With more experience in looking after women with miscarriage, I have now abandoned them as a routine investigation.

Immunological causes of sporadic miscarriage

Although these mechanisms may be involved in a few cases of sporadic miscarriage, the overall contribution is small. Many women ask me whether asthma, hay fever, eczema and other allergic skin disorders increase the risk of miscarriage but there is no evidence to suggest that this is the case. However, there are some women who have thyroid antibodies (see Chapter 12 for more details) who may be at risk of developing an underactive thyroid gland in the future. In this particular situation it is sensible for the woman to have her thyroid function tests checked on a regular basis to make sure that she does not need to be given thyroxine replacement treatment.

Of course, it is possible that a woman with antiphospholipid syndrome (see Chapter 12) may miscarry her first pregnancy because of this problem, but many studies have shown that this syndrome is more of a problem in women who have miscarried three or more pregnancies. I think it is sensible to reserve the special tests needed to diagnose this problem for recurrent miscarriage sufferers.

Summary

In this chapter we have looked at a wide selection of possible causes for sporadic episodes of miscarriage. Although the broad categories I have used can all make contributions to the problem, it is important for me to emphasise that the most important factors are genetic abnormalities in the baby and infections that occur in the mother. As we will see in later chapters of this book, this is not the case for recurrent miscarriage.

Sensible steps to take to avoid a sporadic miscarriage

- start taking folic acid tablets three months before becoming pregnant
- adopt a sensible healthy diet
- stop smoking
- drink alcohol in moderation
- avoid taking drugs – whenever possible
- if you suffer from diabetes, thyroid disease, epilepsy or high blood pressure, consult your doctor, who may suggest that you

alter the type or dose of the drugs you are taking. Make sure that these medical problems are well controlled before you conceive
- keep a record of your menstrual periods so that you do not expose a tiny embryo to X-rays or a drug which may have potential side effects for a tiny baby
- avoid or minimise contact with farm animals and pets
- avoid travel to malarial zones and countries where the risks of food poisoning or gastroenteritis are high
- ensure that meat is well cooked, vegetables are carefully washed and avoid unpasteurised milk products and pâtés
- ensure that you are immune to German measles infection – and if you are not immune, get vaccinated without delay

Further useful information is included in Part Four – 'Getting ready for the next pregnancy' and 'Coping with the next pregnancy'.

FIVE

WILL I MISCARRY AGAIN? THE RISK OF RECURRENCE

If you have had a miscarriage, this will probably be one of your chief concerns. Let me start by reassuring you that the chances of having another miscarriage are far smaller than your chances of having a successful pregnancy. Hopefully, you will have been looked after by doctors who have explained to you that many cases of early miscarriage are due to bad luck. By bad luck, I mean that the cause of the miscarriage was a random one and is unlikely to occur again.

Many couples I see find it very difficult to believe that their miscarriage was due to bad luck. They want to know what went wrong with the pregnancy. In Chapter 4 we looked at the many different causes of sporadic miscarriage and discussed how it is often impossible for the doctor to know exactly why the miscarriage occurred.

In early miscarriages, this bad luck is often because the fetus has the wrong number of chromosomes, or because the mother had a viral infection in the first few weeks of her pregnancy which affected the baby's development. If you have had a late miscarriage, this may be because the baby was abnormal but did not miscarry in the early stages of the pregnancy. It may have been that the baby was normal but you caught an infection (for example, listeria) which was passed on to the baby and caused the miscarriage. Of course, it is just possible that exactly the same thing may happen again in your next pregnancy, but it is highly unlikely. It is much more probable that these problems will not occur again and that your next pregnancy will be trouble-free.

Often women who have experienced a first miscarriage will ask me if there is something wrong with them that will make them miscarry again. This is a very understandable and, I think, a very sensible question. It is very unlikely, however, that there is anything wrong with you which would cause future miscarriages. Although much of this book deals with the causes of repeated miscarriage, it is very important to stress that they are quite rare. However, they cause so much distress that much medical research has been carried out, in order to explain why a small number of couples (no more than 1% of all couples in the population) suffer recurrent miscarriages. Throughout this book I am defining recurrent miscarriage as the loss of three or more consecutive pregnancies. As we noted in Chapter 3, some doctors prefer to include couples with a history of two or more miscarriages in their definition, in which case the scale of the problem increases and 3–5% of all couples who are trying to have a baby are potentially affected.

Problems with recurrence studies

When I first became interested in the field of miscarriage in the mid-1980s, I looked hard for information that would help me to give couples advice about their risks of miscarrying again. I could find very little data that was useful, because most of what had been written was retrospective. This means that a group of women and their pregnancies are studied and analysed after the outcome of their pregnancies is known.

The problem with this sort of study is that the results may be very misleading. For example, if we study the labour ward register of delivered babies and identify a group of women who have had miscarriages in the past, our study may conclude that the risk of having several miscarriages is very low, because all the women included in this study will have achieved a successful pregnancy. Those women who have miscarried again will not appear on this register. On the other hand, if we study the operating theatre register of women who have undergone ERPCs after a miscarriage, and look back at their previous pregnancies, our study may conclude that the risk of another miscarriage is very high. This is because there will be some women included in this study who have not yet achieved a successful pregnancy. Nor will this study be able to identify the women who have miscarried in the past, but gone on to have a healthy live baby, because they did not have to undergo an ERPC.

The reason for me describing these issues in such detail is that I think it is enormously important for the reader to understand the shortcomings of retrospective research studies and the value of prospective studies, whatever the subject of the research may be. At the end of reading all the studies that were available in the mid-1980s, the only conclusion I reached was that the risk of a woman miscarrying again after a previous miscarriage was somewhere between 15 and 75%!

The Cambridge miscarriage study

Since this conclusion was of no use to me or the patients I was trying to advise, I set about designing a prospective study that would be able to work out the numerical risk of miscarriage for any woman who was trying to become pregnant. To do this, I had to recruit women to my study before they became pregnant, so that their pregnancy could be followed all the way through. This was no small task, since it can be very difficult to get women to declare that they are thinking about becoming pregnant before they actually fall pregnant. I was helped greatly by my hospital colleagues in Cambridge where I was working at that time (I must mention Peter Braude and Paula Trembath in particular) and also by the local radio and the GPs who helped me to advertise for recruits.

The study proved so informative because the women in this Cambridge population all had their babies and their miscarriages at a single hospital, so that with hard work and dogged determination, it was possible to follow over 400 women during a time period of several years.

The first aim of the study was to find out how many pregnancies ended in miscarriage. We had recruited all the women before pregnancy, in the hope that we would not fall into the pitfalls of previous population miscarriage studies (as described in Chapter 2).

We did not miss any of the very early miscarriages, where the women did not need to come into hospital and were dealt with at home. Nor did we end up concluding that miscarriage is more frequent than it really is, because we did not include any woman who came into hospital with bleeding or miscarriage unless we had known about her before she became pregnant. As a result, we were confident about the accuracy of our finding: in a general population of women, 12% of all pregnancies will end in a clinically recognisable miscarriage.

The second aim of the study was to see whether we could find any reasons why these 12% were likely to miscarry. We found no connection between the risk of miscarriage and the previous use of the contraceptive pill or a previous termination of pregnancy (see below). Nor were there any general medical disorders in this group of women which put them at greater risk of miscarriage in the pregnancy we followed. We did notice, however, that women who were heavy cigarette smokers appeared to be at greater risk of miscarriage. So too were the women who had had difficulties in becoming pregnant. However, this group seemed to be composed mainly of those women who had experienced a miscarriage and then developed problems in conceiving. The effect of infertility on the risk of miscarriage is discussed in detail in Chapter 13.

The third aim of the Cambridge population study was to assess the risk of miscarriage for a woman who had never been pregnant before, for women who had had a miscarriage and for women who had had a live baby in the past. We were able to show that it is possible to put a figure on the risk of miscarriage in future pregnancy by looking carefully at the outcome of a woman's previous pregnancies. We were able to draw up a table of percentage risks, in the hope that other doctors and their patients would find these numbers helpful when faced with the problem of a recent miscarriage (see Table 1).

Although many previous studies had suggested that miscarriage is more common in first pregnancies (primigravid women), we found that the risk of miscarriage is very low in first pregnancies, about 5%. Among women who had enjoyed a successful pregnancy or pregnancies in the past, the risk of miscarriage was also very low. This low risk of miscarriage was also found in those women whose last pregnancy had been completed successfully, even if she had experienced miscarriages in the past.

TABLE 1: THE CAMBRIDGE MISCARRIAGE STUDY
Effect of past pregnancy history upon the risk of miscarriage (n=407).

History	No of patients miscarrying	Total number of women	% Risk of miscarriage in study pregnancy
Last pregnancy miscarried	40	214	19
Only miscarriages in the past	24	98	24
Only pregnancy miscarried	12	59	20
Last pregnancy successful	5	95	5
All pregnancies successful	3	73	4
Only pregnancy successful	3	62	5
Previous termination of pregnancy	2	32	6
Primigravidae	4	87	5

The Cambridge study also showed that a woman's risk of miscarriage increases when she has suffered a miscarriage in the past. After one miscarriage, the risk of a second miscarriage was 20%, which is significantly higher than the miscarriage rate for a woman who has enjoyed a live birth in her first pregnancy or who has never been pregnant before. Before you become distressed by this fact, let me remind you that this figure of 20% miscarriage still means that 80% of the pregnancies in women who have had a single miscarriage in the past will be successful.

It is true that the risk of a further miscarriage does rise as the number of previous miscarriages increases. We found that the risk of miscarriage after two previous losses was 24% and after three consecutive losses, the risk increased to 43%. Once again, it is important to remember that these figures still mean that the majority of future pregnancies will be successful.

Furthermore we were also able to show that if you have had a successful pregnancy in the past, then your risk of miscarriage is lower, even if this live birth was followed by several miscarriages. After two successful pregnancies, the future risk of miscarriage never went above 20%, which is the same level of risk as a woman who has only ever had one miscarriage.

The risk of miscarriage after termination of pregnancy

There was one more group in whom we found a low risk of miscarriage – women who had undergone an uncomplicated termination of pregnancy in the past. I would like to emphasise this point because I know that some miscarriage patients who have had a termination years ago are full of guilt and remorse that the termination may in some way be the cause of the later miscarriages. They may even fear that the miscarriages represent some form of divine retribution for the fact that they voluntarily terminated a pregnancy. I am sure that this is not the case and I hope that you feel heartened by the data in this Cambridge population study, which demonstrated that early, uncomplicated terminations of pregnancy do not increase the risk of miscarriage in the future.

Terminations of pregnancy, however, do have a definite effect on a woman's reproductive health. Approximately one in every 200 women who voluntarily terminates a pregnancy will find that she cannot conceive again. This is usually because of infection at or soon after the termination, which damages the fallopian tubes. Of course, in years gone by when the methods of dilating the cervix and evacuating the uterus were less sophisticated, I think it was true to say that a termination could also have an adverse effect on a woman's risk of miscarriage. The method of termination may have weakened the cervix, leading to incompetence of the cervix in the future. However, this is rarely the case nowadays. A termination of pregnancy is always a sad event and it is quite likely that you will continue to feel emotionally distressed about it for some time. If you are unfortunate enough to then experience a miscarriage, do talk to your doctor about your feelings and try to remember the results of the Cambridge miscarriage study (see Table 1).

Maternal age and the risk of miscarriage

The risk of miscarriage increases as a woman becomes older and, since a woman who has experienced a miscarriage and wants to embark on another pregnancy cannot shed any years, I think it is sensible to consider that maternal age is a risk factor for recurrence. We have known for many years that this increase in risk is directly related to the age of the woman's eggs (ova). We are born with all the eggs that we will ever have available to ovulate, whereas men produce new sperm on a regular basis. As the eggs grow older they become more fragile and when they undergo the special cell division called meiosis that occurs before fertilisation, the chance of too many or too few chromosomes ending up in the cell increases. As a result, older women are more likely to ovulate a chromosomally abnormal egg, which when fertilised by the sperm gives rise to a genetic abnormality in the tiny embryo. The clearest example of this maternal age effect is seen in Down's syndrome (trisomy 21). After the age of 35 years the chance of a woman conceiving a baby with Down's syndrome increases sharply – indeed, if you plot a graph of maternal age along the X axis and number of miscarriages along the Y axis, the graph appears like a tick (✓) or the letter J (which is why many geneticists refer to the J-shaped curve) with the upward change in direction occurring at 35 years.

As we saw in Chapter 4, chromosomal abnormalities are the commonest cause of sporadic miscarriage and account for at least half of all early pregnancy losses. So any factor that increases the risk of chromosomal abnormality obviously makes an important contribution to the problem. However, before any reader who is over 35 years of age starts to feel depressed, let me share with you the results of two studies which I think help to make the problem of maternal age a little less daunting. The first is a study carried out in Italy some ten years ago, in which the doctors followed the outcome of pregnancy in nearly 3000 women in a local community. They showed that the overall risk of miscarriage was 15% (which agrees with the studies of sporadic miscarriage mentioned in Chapter 2). When they went on to calculate the rate of miscarriage by the woman's age, they found that women less than 35 years of age had a much lower miscarriage rate (6%) and in the women over the age of 40 years the figure was 25%. Furthermore, they were able to genetically analyse all of the miscarriages and found that in the 40-year-olds the incidence of chromosomal abnormalities was over 80%.

Where is the comfort in that? I suspect you are asking. Well, try to remember that the vast majority of older women (75% of them in fact) did not miscarry and went on to have a baby. The second study is one that we carried out in the recurrent miscarriage clinic at St Mary's several years ago. We too followed the pregnancy outcome of a large number of recurrent miscarriers and grouped the women by their age. Happily, I can tell you that the risk of miscarriage did not increase significantly when the woman reached 35 years, in fact it only increased when she was in her forties. And even though all of the women attending our clinic have had at least three previous miscarriages, 55% of the 40-plus-year-olds went on to have a live take home baby. So please don't despair when you hear that miscarriage increases with age. You cannot change your age, but you can take a positive attitude towards your next pregnancy and remember the above points. The outlook is probably not nearly as gloomy as you feared.

Recurrence – recent study results

I think you will also be heartened to hear of the results of a more recent study that has been carried out at the recurrent miscarriage clinic at St Mary's Hospital. We looked at the number of miscarriages experienced by several thousand couples coming to our clinic. We then grouped the women by the numbers of miscarriages that they had had in the past and looked at the outcome of their next pregnancy. We noted that the live birth rate was always higher than 60% until we reached the women who had suffered more than five miscarriages, where the figure started to fall slowly. Indeed, this high likelihood of successful pregnancy, even after miscarrying on three or four occasions, leads some doctors to question whether detailed investigations and treatment are justified for this problem. I have never shared this viewpoint, but I do think the reasoning behind it can be a source of comfort on occasions!

SIX

RECURRENT MISCARRIAGE

Definitions

The most frequently used definition of recurrent miscarriage is the loss of three or more consecutive pregnancies before the baby has reached viability. Some doctors consider couples who have had two miscarriages to be suffering from recurrent miscarriage. I prefer to use the definition of three losses because, as we have seen in previous chapters of this book, miscarrying twice in a row is much more likely to be due to chance than miscarrying three times in a row.

The other reason I choose this definition is that most of the good miscarriage research has been centred upon women with three losses. It is noticeable that when studies have included women with two losses, the 'waters become muddied' and I sometimes suspect that they have been included to boost the numbers of patients in the study. This does not mean that I consider your two miscarriages to be unimportant. On the contrary, I think they are so important that I do not want to risk confusing why they have occurred with the reasons why a woman with three or more miscarriages has lost her pregnancies. The reasons are likely to be different ones.

Incidence of recurrent miscarriage

You may be surprised, and possibly horrified, when I tell you that the incidence of recurrent miscarriage in the population has never been established accurately. There have been lots of studies looking at how many couples are affected by the problem, but they have been bedevilled by all the usual pitfalls of collecting data in a retrospective way. As I mentioned in Chapter 5, if we collect the number of patients who have experienced three miscarriages by looking at the labour ward register, we are likely to underestimate the problem of recurrent miscarriage. On the other hand, if we collect the figures from the operating theatre register for women who have undergone an ERPC to empty their uterus after a miscarriage, we are likely to overestimate the problem.

I know of no large population study that has examined women with a history of two miscarriages and been able to give a percentage figure for the chances of her having a third or a fourth. The reason for this is that the problem of recurrent miscarriage is quite rare. If we were to set up a national register of miscarriages, it might be possible to come up with a percentage risk, but for any one clinician working in the field, the numbers of women in their local population who experience three or more miscarriages is small. In my miscarriage clinic I see patients from all over the UK, but even this large group does not allow me to work out the overall risk. Couples who have had several miscarriages followed by a successful pregnancy are not usually referred to the clinic. It is the couples who have persistent problems that I see and by definition these are not a representative group. I believe that they are the exceptional cases and not the rule.

What we do know is that compared to sporadic miscarriage, which is very common, recurrent miscarriage is a rare problem. Sporadic miscarriage affects 25% of all women and 15% of all clinically recognised pregnancies miscarry. If we calculate the chances of having three miscarriages in a row from a purely mathematical or statistical point of view, we should be able to work out how many women will miscarry three times in a row because of bad luck. The statistical chances of having two miscarriages is 15% to the power of two and this works out to be 2.3 %. The statistical chance of having three miscarriages in a row is 0.34% – three to four cases per thousand women.

This figure is certainly lower than the most optimistic doctor would probably estimate. If we take an average of all the figures that have been estimated for the incidence of recurrent miscarriage we end up with a figure of about 1% – one per hundred women. This is a significantly larger figure than the one we predicted from the mathematical calculation above (0.34%). It suggests that in addition to random or bad luck cases, a proportion of women miscarry repeatedly because of a specific problem.

Characteristics of women with recurrent miscarriage

If some women with recurrent miscarriages are the victims of bad luck and others have a systematic cause, then the most important aim of a recurrent miscarriage clinic is to try and sort out which women belong to which group. This is not always as easy as it sounds and the next few chapters of this book are dedicated to the ways in which we can try to unravel this problem.

To help us try to distinguish between the two groups, it is useful to look at some general characteristics or pointers about these women and their individual reproductive histories. These pointers cannot identify the cause of the miscarriages on their own, but I often find that they help me determine how to begin my investigations. A good example is the genetic makeup of the miscarried pregnancy. If this was abnormal, it points towards the miscarriage being sporadic. If the chromosomes were normal, we know that this suggests that the woman has an underlying cause for the miscarriages. Recurrent miscarriers have a much greater likelihood of miscarrying a chromosomally normal fetus.

The age or gestation at which the pregnancy miscarried is another useful pointer. Very early miscarriages are often due to genetic abnormalities in the baby or hormonal problems. If the baby has reached a size of eight weeks or more and a beating fetal heart has been seen on the ultrasound scan, a miscarriage after this stage suggests that something has attacked the pregnancy causing it to miscarry. It is still possible that the baby did have a genetic abnormality, but since the majority of chromosomally abnormal pregnancies are lost early the likelihood of a chromosomal abnormality decreases as the weeks of pregnancy increase. Of course there are exceptions to this general rule. Some trisomies (see

Chapter 4) may not miscarry until much later in pregnancy and in some cases of trisomy 21 (Down's syndrome) and monosomy X (Turner's syndrome) the baby is born live.

Similarly, a miscarriage that occurs after a fetal heartbeat has been identified is unlikely to be due to an hormonal cause. Although many hormones are needed throughout pregnancy to ensure the well-being of the baby, it is usually only in the early weeks of pregnancy that a hormone deficiency is capable of single-handedly causing the pregnancy to miscarry (see Chapter 11).

In Chapter 3 we defined late miscarriages as pregnancies that are lost after the baby has grown to a size of 13 weeks or more. This is the accepted definition, but the more miscarriage patients I see, the more I think that this definition will change in the future. Pregnancies lost after fetal heart activity has been visualised may be due to chromosomal abnormality, but there is an increasing chance that it may be due to autoimmune or pro-thrombotic causes (see Chapter 12) and sometimes because of an infection (see Chapter 10). Any woman who has visited the recurrent miscarriage clinic at St Mary's will recall how much of the first visit was spent carefully discussing the details of all her previous pregnancies. We will have quizzed you (gently, I hope!) about the findings of any US scans that were performed in the hope that we can work out exactly what size the baby had grown to before the miscarriage occurred. Any baby that measures the equivalent of seven to eight weeks' gestation must have had a fetal heart. This knowledge will point us towards looking at autoimmune, pro-thrombotic and infective causes as a priority. You will also remember how keen we were to know whether genetic testing or histology was performed successfully on your lost baby.

Another pointer which may suggest that the woman is a recurrent miscarrier is the length of time it took her to get pregnant. Conception delays of more than 12 months are much more common in recurrent rather than sporadic miscarriers. In Chapter 13 we will look at the miscarriage rate in women who have experienced infertility before their miscarriage. It is true to say that difficulties in becoming pregnant affect as many as one in six couples in the general population, but a degree of infertility is present in one in three couples who miscarry repeatedly. In these cases, an hormonal factor is a likely cause. In addition, recent research in autoimmune disorders is suggesting that some cases of subfertility and subsequent repeated miscarriages may be due to antiphospholipid antibodies (see Chapter 12).

Recurrent miscarriage sufferers are also more likely to experience a premature delivery or deliver a baby at the right time who is small for dates or has growth retardation. Once again, this pregnancy history suggests that there may be an infective or autoimmune disorder as the root cause of the problem. In days gone by, a woman with a history of repeated pregnancy losses, premature deliveries and growth-retarded babies was labelled a 'bad breeder'. These old wives' tales were accurate observations, but there were no underlying reasons put forward. The exciting step forward, I believe, is that we are now beginning to understand that all these pregnancy problems are points on a spectrum, or a scale of reproductive disease. Whether you have suffered infertility, early or late pregnancy losses, there is a common thread linking your problems. The factors that make a woman a good or a bad breeder are enormously important and we are starting to understand that the outcome of any woman's pregnancy is largely dictated by events that occur well before the miscarriage or later pregnancy complications occur. Most importantly, the factors which control the implantation of the pregnancy have far-reaching effects on the course of the pregnancy.

The underlying causes of recurrent miscarriage

The term 'recurrent miscarriage' suggests that there is a single underlying cause for the miscarriages. But this need not be so. Some women will suffer recurrent miscarriages because of a single persisting cause. Others will miscarry repeatedly because they have the misfortune to have several different problems. I think this is one of the most difficult things for miscarriage sufferers to understand and to cope with.

If we can identify that you are miscarrying because of problem X and we are able to offer you treatment for problem X, this still does not protect you from miscarrying from problem Y. Worse still, after recognising that you have both problem X and problem Y, this will not protect you from having another miscarriage because of a sporadic cause, such as a chromosomal abnormality of the baby, which can occur 'out of the blue' and by chance. This is why I use every opportunity possible in this book (and with every couple I see in the miscarriage clinic) to stress the importance of ensuring that the tissues from any future miscarriage are analysed genetically.

My reason for emphasising this, is that the results may have important implications for how your next pregnancy should be managed. If your miscarried pregnancy has an abnormal karyotype (chromosomal makeup) the likelihood is that this miscarriage was a sporadic event and unrelated to the previous recurrent miscarriages. In this situation, the treatment you had for this pregnancy should probably be tried again. On the other hand, if the miscarried pregnancy has a normal karyotype, this suggests that the miscarriage is not sporadic and must be considered as a treatment failure. In this situation it is probably unethical to try the same treatment again and an alternative approach needs to be considered, if it is available.

I think the best way to look at the different causes of recurrent miscarriage is to examine the groups we identified in Chapter 4, which was devoted to the causes of sporadic miscarriages. These same groups apply to recurrent miscarriages, but the proportion of cases in each group is different. For example, the majority of sporadic pregnancy losses are the result of chromosomal (genetic) abnormalities in the baby, which occur out of the blue. In women with recurrent miscarriages, genetic problems in the baby are much less frequent. Inherited genetic problems from one of the two parents are a well-recognised cause, but they are present in no more than 5% of couples.

Viral infections are another important cause of sporadic miscarriage, but most viruses do not affect a woman and her pregnancies repeatedly. Instead, other types of infection with bacteria may be important. And whereas structural abnormalities of the uterus and cervix may occasionally cause a sporadic pregnancy loss, they are more usually identified in women who have repeated episodes of miscarriage. Similarly, environmental, hormonal and autoimmune problems seem to cluster in women with recurrent miscarriage, although they may occasionally be responsible for a sporadic miscarriage.

Having said all this, I think it is important to reflect on the fact that whole chromosomes contain many, many genes and that looking at the number and the shape of chromosomes alone, is a crude method of assessing whether a genetic problem is present. In fact, I will go so far as to say that genetic research in the field of miscarriage is still in the dark ages. My hope is that when the international collaboration that has developed in order to map the human genome has successfully reached its goal, we will be able to sit down and look at how this fantastic mountain of knowledge can be used to help us understand the causes of miscarriage more effectively. Of one thing I am already quite certain. The twenty-first-century understanding of miscarriage will not be centred on abnormal chromosomes. It will need to focus on genetic abnormalities and mutations that predispose to abnormalities in the hormonal, infective and immunological mechanisms that control the development of a successful pregnancy. So instead of looking at hormone X, infective agent Y, or antibody Z, we will be examining how a gene mutation leads to the woman being unresponsive to hormone X or more susceptible to an infection with agent Y or the presence of antibody Z.

In Chapters 7 to 12 of this book we will look in detail at the established causes of recurrent miscarriage. A chapter for each of the six categories of miscarriage is needed, so that you, the reader, will be able to recognise how and why the numbers of miscarriages in these groups differ from sporadic miscarriages and also understand why some causes are more important than others. Here again we need to remember that the currently recognised checklist for the causes of miscarriage will undoubtedly have to be rewritten in the very near future. For example, we used to think that the antiphospholipid syndrome (see Chapter 12) should be classified as a maternal disorder. A better understanding of reproductive immunology then prompted us to move this important cause of recurrent miscarriage into the immune section. During the last two years we have started to realise that the phospholipid syndrome is an acquired type of prothrombotic abnormality that makes women more susceptible to miscarrying and that there are a whole lot more prothrombotic abnormalities, many of them inherited (genetically determined), which seem to be additional causes of recurrent miscarriage. Where should we put these newly identified defects? In the genetic section, in the immune section, or should we start up a new category on the checklist called prothombotic abnormalities? At the present time it is difficult to decide, so for the time being I have left them in Chapter 12. But the reader needs to understand that this area of medical research is changing so fast that by the time this edition of *Miscarriage* is in print, another handful of genetically determined prothrombotic disorders will have been discovered. My job will be to perform the studies, aiming to find out whether they are truly causes of miscarriage, and if the answer is yes, whether we can develop treatments to combat them.

SEVEN

RECURRENT MISCARRIAGE – GENETIC CAUSES

Genetic abnormalities in the baby are one of the most important causes of sporadic miscarriage (Chapter 4). Structural chromosomal abnormalities are also a cause of recurrent miscarriage, but the contribution they make to this problem is smaller.

There are two ways in which a baby might repeatedly end up with abnormal chromosomes. The first is recurrent aneuploidy, which means that in several different pregnancies, the total number of chromosomes is abnormal, either too many or too few. The second is due to abnormalities in one of the parents' chromosomes, which are repeatedly passed on to the baby in each successive pregnancy. These are usually structural abnormalities or rearrangements in one of the parents' chromosomes, called a translocation.

Recurrent aneuploidy

The baby may have abnormal chromosomes because of an event that occurs 'out of the blue', before or after fertilisation of the egg. This is called non-disjunction and results in the wrong number of chromosomes being present in the tiny embryo. Good examples of this are Down's syndrome (called trisomy 21), where the baby ends up with three copies of the number 21 chromosome instead of two, and Turner's syndrome (or monosomy X), where there is only one X chromosome. Many miscarriages are due to polyploidy – too many extra sets of the 23 chromosomes. This is why we use the term 'aneuploid' as an overall description for any pregnancy that does not have the correct (euploid) number of 46 chromosomes.

Although these 'out of the blue' chromosomal abnormalities are most usually associated with sporadic miscarriage, there are some couples who seem to be at risk of repeated sporadic events. They produce chromosomally abnormal eggs or sperm, not as a result of a translocation (see below), but because they have a tendency towards non-disjunction. The tendency may be inherited or induced because of environmental factors. At the present time we do not understand all the mechanisms that cause this problem, although we do know that the risk of trisomies increases with maternal age, while polyploidies are not affected by this factor.

Trisomy is the most common type of recurrent aneuploidy. However, this does not mean that the chromosome involved in the trisomy is always the same. I will always remember the recurrent miscarriage patient I looked after, who had suffered a trisomy 21 miscarriage and then went on to have a trisomy 13 and then a trisomy 7. When she asked me which chromosome would be affected next time, I was completely lost for words and felt nearly as desperate as she did. There was nothing I could do to sort the problem out for her. Happily, I can tell you that she has now had a healthy baby and has recently contacted me to tell me that she is pregnant again. We advised her to have an amniocentesis test to see whether this baby is normal and the report has just come back confirming that she is carrying a normal baby boy.

If you are a recurrent miscarriage sufferer, all this information about recurrent aneuploidy has probably made you feel gloomy. So I must go on to explain that in fact, the risk of you having another miscarriage after miscarrying a chromosomally abnormal pregnancy is very low. Lower, in fact, than your risk of miscarrying again after you have suffered a chromosomally normal miscarriage. If this sounds confusing, let me put it another way. Chromosomally normal miscarriages are less random than abnormal ones. This is another reason why trying to find out the genetic makeup of the pregnancy that you miscarry is so useful. If the baby was chromosomally normal, this points to the fact that some other cause was responsible for the miscarriage and needs to be looked for.

Of course, the only way to diagnose whether the miscarriage was genetically normal or abnormal is to ensure that the miscarried tissues are analysed. In Chapter 4 we discussed in detail the problems and pitfalls of chromosomal analysis and it might be useful for the reader to recap on some of these points.

Chromosome abnormalities in the parents

In some couples who have experienced recurrent miscarriages, an abnormality in one of the parents' chromosomes may be the cause. Although it is an important cause to identify, this problem is found in no more than 5% of couples with recurrent miscarriage and is extremely rare in couples who have had a single sporadic miscarriage (about 0.3%: three cases per thousand couples). The defect can be in either parent.

The most frequent chromosomal abnormality found in the parents is a balanced translocation. Translocation describes the situation which occurs when a fragment of one chromosome becomes attached to the broken end of another. The cause of this condition is not understood, but it is sometimes associated with exposure to radiation. The translocation is 'balanced' because the abnormality affects only one of the chromosome pairs. This means that the abnormal one is 'balanced' by the normal chromosome, which is why the parent with the translocation appears to be entirely normal. Indeed, the parent with the chromosome abnormality will only be identified if the couple experience repeated miscarriages and the chromosomes are analysed.

The majority of balanced translocations are reciprocal. This means that the translocation involves an exchange of genetic material between one of the two chromosomes making up a pair, with one of the two chromosomes making up a completely different pair. As we saw in Chapter 4, there are 23 pairs of chromosomes and so there are many different types of reciprocal translocation that can occur. Although the individual with the balanced translocation appears normal, when he or she produces eggs or sperm, some will be normal but others will inherit the abnormality. No longer is the abnormality balanced by the second normal chromosome in the pair. If a normal egg is fertilised by a normal sperm, the resulting embryo will be normal. But if one of the abnormal eggs or sperm takes part in a fertilisation, the resulting embryo will inherit the translocation. This may result in the embryo becoming a balanced translocation carrier, like its mother or father, and this is compatible with normal life. On the other hand, it may become unbalanced, and this usually leads to a miscarriage or an abnormal baby.

Robertsonian translocations are much less frequent and they only affect chromosomes 13, 14, 15, 21 and 22. These five chromosome pairs have a different shape to the others. If you think of a chromosome pair as two strands tied together in the middle (this middle point is called the centromere) you will be able to imagine that there is an upper short arm and a lower long arm to each of the two chromosomes in the pair. Chromosomes 13, 14, 15, 21 and 22 have very short upper arms. In a Robertsonian translocation, the upper short arm of two chromosomes are lost and the long arms fuse together at the midpoint. This means that one of the chromosomes ends up being very small indeed and when it divides at a later date, it is lost completely.

There are some other types of parental chromosomal abnormalities, called inversions and mosaics. Inversions are just like they sound, a piece of chromosome is turned upside down in its position but this only rarely leads to problems. They are usually considered to be a variant of normal. As I mentioned in Chapter 4, some individuals are made up of two different cell lines with different chromosome numbers. This is called mosaicism, but unless the mosaicism affects the eggs or the sperms, they are usually never detected and are not a cause for concern.

If all of these chromosomal variants are counted, the percentage of abnormalities in couples with recurrent miscarriage rises to about 10%. However, it is important to emphasise that it is only the translocations which cause serious problems. I always quote the figure of 5% when I am talking to recurrent miscarriage couples about the chances of one of them having a chromosomal abnormality. If couples who have had babies with severe congenital disorders are tested for chromosomal abnormalities, the figure may be as high as 20%.

Diagnosing parental chromosomal abnormalities

If you have had recurrent episodes of miscarriage, your doctor will probably suggest that you and your partner have your chromosomes analysed. All that is required for this is a sample of blood from both of you. The blood sample needs to be put into a special bottle containing a small quantity of anticoagulant. This is because the test needs to be performed on white blood cells, which can only be separated from the other cells in the blood sample if the blood is prevented from clotting.

I emphasise this point because I so frequently see couples who have tried to have this test performed and are told that the blood sample was unsuitable because it had been put into the wrong bottle, which had allowed it to clot. If either you or your doctor are unsure which bottle should be used, it is best to telephone your local hospital or the nearest cytogenetics laboratory and ask them for advice. The chromosome test, which is also referrred to as peripheral blood karyotyping or parental karyotyping, usually takes four to six weeks to be reported, because it has to be sent to a specialised cytogenetics laboratory which has all the techniques required to prepare the white blood cells for genetic analysis. Patients often ask me to 'speed up' the results of the test, but this is simply not possible, because the careful processing of the cells and analysis of the chromosomes takes time and cannot be hurried. The test is very accurate and, of course, because it determines your individual chromosome pattern, it will never change. I mention this point because I quite often talk to couples who ask me to recheck their chromosomes because they were done some time ago. If the blood sample has been taken the right way, it is only very occasionally that the test fails to give a result and if this does occur, the laboratory will request another sample of blood from you.

It is important that both partners are tested because it is equally likely that the male or the female partner carries the translocation. It is also important to realise that even if you have had a healthy baby in the past, this does not mean that you and your partner's chromosomes are normal. Earlier in this chapter we noted that an individual with a balanced translocation can 'pass on' the normal or the abnormal chromosome in their eggs or sperms. So it is quite possible for you to have a normal baby together and then have several miscarriages. It is also possible that your baby inherits the balanced form of the translocation and you may never know about it, unless you experience problems in the future which result in you, your partner or your baby (now an adult!) being tested.

Of course, if you have had several healthy babies followed by, or interspersed with miscarriages, the chances of one or other of you having a translocation is very unlikely. However, I identify several couples each year in the recurrent miscarriage clinic who do have a translocation which has been missed, because their doctor thought that their previous healthy baby meant that a chromosomal abnormality could not be present.

Genetic counselling

If you do find that you or your partner has a chromosomal abnormality, it is important that you have the opportunity to talk to a genetic counsellor. They are medical doctors who have specialist training in genetic disorders. They will be able to explain the problem to you in very clear terms, sometimes drawing diagrams or showing you pictures which will help you to understand the abnormality and the problems it could lead to if a baby were to inherit it.

The geneticists I work with always send the couples a letter after the hospital appointment, which summarises all the points they discussed. I think this is particularly useful, since it is often very difficult to take in all of this genetic information at the first sitting! A letter will give you and your partner the opportunity to digest all the information at leisure and go over points that you remain unsure about. Most doctors are quick to refer their patients for genetic advice when they uncover an abnormal karyotype result, but do not hesitate to ask for help if this avenue is not suggested to you immediately.

The genetic counsellor will also be able to give you a figure for your risk of conceiving a baby which will be affected by the problem. This is important because not all chromosome abnormalities carry the same risk of recurrence. Some abnormalities are more likely to result in an early miscarriage, whereas others may lead to later miscarriages or a baby that is born with severe problems. It is also important to remember that the outcome of your next pregnancy may be entirely normal. Often the appointment with the genetic counsellor can result in you feeling much more optimistic than you had thought possible.

I am reminded of a couple I saw recently in the miscarriage clinic. The man had a balanced translocation and had done some reading about his problem. When I explained to them that I was arranging for them to see a genetic counsellor, he told me that he thought this was a waste of time. 'Fifty per cent of my sperm are going to be normal and the other 50% will be abnormal, which means that every other pregnancy will be lost.' I tried hard to explain that this was not the case, but I did not have the right vocabulary or approach to help him understand that the outlook was not as gloomy as this. We came to a compromise that he would go to the appointment, so that he could then confirm for other couples that it really was a waste of time.

A few weeks later he returned to tell me excitedly that his translocation meant that he and his wife were unlikely to have more than 25% of their future pregnancies complicated by miscarriage, and that their risk of having an ongoing pregnancy with an abnormal baby was as low as 10%. I was delighted, not only with the news, but also because my patient had become a mini-expert, which provided him with comfort and confidence. I tell this story against myself, not the patient, in the hope that you, the reader, will realise that the geneticist can offer you very specialised, individual advice and is enormously skilled at being able to deliver the information.

Sadly, not all translocations have such a good prognosis. Some rare types of Robertsonian translocations involve the chromosomes in such a way that any liveborn baby has a severe abnormality and all other conceptions end in a miscarriage. Finding out this information will always be distressing, but it will give you an opportunity to discuss other ways to achieve a pregnancy. Artificial insemination with donor sperm may be acceptable to some couples, and nowadays the option of donor eggs or even surrogacy (see Chapter 13) may also be a possibility.

The genetic counsellor may suggest that other members of your family have tests to see whether they are carriers of the same translocation. You may have inherited the translocation from your mother or father. Occasionally, the translocation will be a new one, but this will only be established if the rest of your family are screened. It may be that one of your sisters or brothers inherited the same abnormality, or they may have inherited normal chromosomes. All the advice that you need for future pregnancies needs to be offered to them too, so encouraging other members of your family to have these tests will help them greatly.

If you do have a translocation, it is important that you are offered the option of having antenatal diagnosis in any future ongoing pregnancy. Antenatal diagnosis is the term used to describe a variety of diagnostic tests that are available to establish the chromosomes of your baby during your pregnancy. The aim of these tests is to identify a baby which has inherited an unbalanced translocation, which may lead to severe abnormalities if the pregnancy continues to term. These tests are discussed in detail below.

Gene defects – new research

We have thousands of genes and of course this means that potentially there are many gene defects (mutations) that could lead to miscarriage. Since our individual genetic code is inherited, it is reasonable to conclude that any genetic mutation which is linked to sporadic pregnancy loss (see Chapter 4) is also a possible cause of repeated miscarriages. This is a fascinating and fast-moving area of research. New genes are being identified on a daily basis and knowledge of the entire code for human genes is nearly completed. Our understanding of single gene defects such as those that give rise to sickle cell disease, Duchenne muscular dystrophy (discussed in Chapter 4) will soon be expanded to include an understanding of the complex interaction of many groups of genes that collectively control our bodily functions. For example, recent reports have identified genetically determined abnormalities in a crucial enzyme that controls the way that our cells deal with free radicals. These free radicals are the toxic chemicals produced every second of our lives as oxygen is metabolised in our bodies. It is ironic to realise that, although we need to breathe oxygen to feed our brain and other body organs, the waste product of this oxygen consumption is actually very toxic to our bodies. If the enzyme (called glucose 6 phosphate dehydrogenase, or G6PD for short) that helps to clear these waste products is not functioning properly, then we start to accumulate free radicals which lead to all sorts of abnormalities, including cancer.

The good news is that the research is also starting to identify that the use of anti-oxidants may help to reverse this toxic build-up. Further, that there are many natural anti-oxidants in the form of vitamins and minerals such as vitamin C, vitamin E and zinc and magnesium that may prove to be helpful in combating the damaging effects of free radicals. However, I need to add a gentle word of warning here. Before any of the readers of this book rush out to buy large doses of vitamins and minerals from the local chemist, they need to reflect on the fact that we do not know whether the use of these compounds in early pregnancy is safe and a good deal of careful research will need to be performed before we can recommend this potential treatment.

Antenatal diagnosis

There are several tests available to identify whether your baby has normal chromosomes. To diagnose a chromosomal abnormality it is necessary to take a sample of amniotic fluid, placenta or fetal blood from the baby to analyse. I stress this point because many women I meet believe that the wide variety of blood tests and specialist US scans that have recently become available can make an accurate diagnosis. This is not true. These blood tests are very useful, but they can only offer you a probability that your baby is chromosomally normal or abnormal. They cannot give you a yes or no answer. The only tests that can tell you definitely what chromosomes your baby is carrying are invasive tests, which sample tissue from the baby. These are amniocentesis, chorionic villus sampling, cordocentesis and fetoscopy.

Amniocentesis

If you decide to have an amniocentesis test, a sample of the amniotic fluid around the baby will be removed from the uterine cavity using a long, thin needle. This test will be done with the help of an ultrasound scanner, which accurately locates the position of a deep pool of liquor around the baby and allows the doctor performing the test to avoid touching the placenta and the baby. The special needle is introduced through the mother's abdominal wall and the fluid is sucked up into a sterile syringe and then taken to the laboratory for analysis. It is unlikely that the doctor will use a local anaesthetic in your skin if you have this test, for the simple reason that the anaesthetic is usually more uncomfortable to inject into the skin than the thin amniocentesis needle.

After the fluid has been withdrawn, the doctor will scan the pregnancy carefully to ensure that the baby is all right and will probably advise you to take it easy for the rest of the day. There is a risk of miscarriage following an amniocentesis of about one in 200. In hospitals where many tests are performed regularly by experienced doctors, the miscarriage risk may be only one in 300. The time of greatest risk is within two weeks of having the amniocentesis performed. Having said this, if you experience a complication after this two-week date, I think it will be difficult for me to ever convince you that the amniocentesis test had nothing to do with it. When discussing the risks of amniocentesis, it is also important to remember that only pregnancies which have potential problems are going to undergo this test. Later complications may not be directly related to the needling procedure and may have been going to happen anyway.

The sample of amniotic fluid will be taken to the cytogenetics laboratory. The fluid is spun hard to collect all the cells together in a pellet. These cells come from the baby's skin. They have floated off the surface of the skin into the amniotic fluid, in the same way that our skin cells float off into the bathwater. Many patients wonder why it takes three to four weeks to get a chromosome result. The reason is that these fetal skin cells have to be encouraged to grow in tissue culture, which takes time and much expertise. After culturing the cells, they then have to be specially prepared and brought to a stage where they are actively dividing (called the metaphase stage) in order to perform the chromosomal analysis. Sometimes the cells cannot be encouraged to grow or are very slow in growing, which can delay your result.

This is one of the reasons why amniocentesis is not performed until 14 to 16 weeks of pregnancy, although some doctors do offer the test at an earlier date. Before this date, the number of fetal skin cells may be insufficient to set up a culture and obtain a chromosome result. Another reason for delaying the test until after 14 weeks is that removing fluid from the amniotic pool before that time may result in problems with the development of the baby's lungs. The downside to amniocentesis is that you will not have the results before about 18 weeks. This means that if the baby has an abnormality and you decide to have a termination of pregnancy, you will have to undergo an induced labour to deliver the baby vaginally (see Chapter 16). The upside is that the risk of miscarriage is low and that amniocentesis is very accurate. It is extremely rare for the results to be wrong.

New developments in amniocentesis and chromosomal analysis

For those readers who feel particularly distressed by the thought of a three-week wait for the results of their amniocentesis cell culture, there is an exciting new technique which has recently become available in some specialist centres, called amnio PCR. Using a powerful molecular biology technique – the polymerase chain reaction (PCR) – the DNA (genetic code) present in the fetal skin cells can be multiplied enormously in order to provide sufficient quantities to allow the diagnosis to be made quickly, within a couple of days. At the present time trisomies 21, 18 and 13, together with other frequently occurring trisomies and all of the sex chromosome abnormalities, can be reliably identified with this technique. However, the less common chromosomal abnormalities and mosaicism (two different cell lines) may not be identified immediately. To reliably identify these rarer defects, which probably arise in no more than two per 1000 women undergoing antenatal diagnostic testing, the cytogenetic experts will probably want to proceed to the older and more established methods of culturing the cells.

FISH, or fluorescent in situ hybridisation, is another new technique which is becoming more widely available in cytogenetics laboratories to quickly test samples for chromosomal abnormalities. This method labels (tags) pieces of DNA from a specific chromosome with fluorescent coloured markers. These are then placed on the amniotic cells or any other cells that are being tested (such as fetal blood cells – see Cordocentesis, below) where they glow (fluoresce) with a specific colour which is easily seen under the laboratory microscope. The beauty of this technique is that the cells being examined do not have to be nurtured to the point where they are actively dividing (the metaphase stage) to see whether the correct number of chromosomes are present. The signal will glow from any cell at any stage of its cell cycle and so this rapidly speeds up the diagnosis of any suspected abnormality. For example, if Down's syndrome is present we would see three signals (one for each of the three copies of chromosome 21) but if the baby is normal we would only see two signals.

Chorion villus sampling

In this technique, a small sample of the placenta is removed through a needle inserted into the uterus via the mother's abdominal wall. For an amniocentesis, the placenta is avoided and the fluid in the amniotic sac is sampled. In chorion villus sampling (CVS for short) the amniotic sac is avoided and, under ultrasound control, the placenta is sampled. Since the baby and the placenta both develop from the same cells, the chromosomes in placental cells are the same as in cells from the baby.

CVS can be performed much earlier in pregnancy than amniocentesis, usually between eight and 11 weeks. The tissue obtained is fresh living placenta, which means that culture and chromosomal analysis is much quicker than from the fetal skin cells cultured from an amniocentesis sample. If you have a CVS test, you will probably receive a provisional test result within ten days. Since this test can be performed before 12 weeks, this means that a pregnancy with a severe chromosomal abnormality can be diagnosed in time for a suction termination of pregnancy to be performed. CVS is also used when a specific gene defect is suspected because the tissues can be used for molecular techniques which speed up the results dramatically.

Although the results are available quickly, there are some disadvantages with the CVS test. The first is that the risk of miscarriage seems to be slightly higher. About 1% of all pregnancies that undergo a CVS miscarry. Although this slight increase may be due to the fact that the test is performed earlier in pregnancy and the pregnancy may have been going to miscarry anyway, it is still a concern for both the woman and her doctor. The second problem is that there is some evidence that when the CVS is done very early, the baby may develop an abnormality in the growth of its limbs. The third problem is that sometimes the placental tissues may contain mosaic cells (see earlier) and this can lead to a confusing diagnosis which suggests that the baby has a chromosomal abnormality when, in fact, there is no abnormality. In this situation you will probably be advised to have a later amniocentesis test to check the results. On balance, I think it is reasonable to say that you should be cautious about undergoing a CVS in very early pregnancy.

Cordocentesis

This procedure involves taking a sample of blood from the baby's umbilical cord. It is rarely undertaken and only by very skilled operators in specialised units. The value of this test is that it obtains fetal blood which can be directly and rapidly analysed for chromosomal abnormalities. A needle is inserted into the mother's abdominal wall and, guided by the ultrasound machine, finds the cord and removes a small sample of blood. This test is performed after 18 weeks, when the blood vessels in the cord are large enough to be clearly visualised. The risk of miscarriage is the same as the risk for CVS – about 1%. It is the quickest way to obtain a chromosomal analysis and is very useful when an abnormality in the baby is suspected during the routine screening ultrasound scan performed at 20 weeks in many obstetric units.

Fetoscopy

In this investigation a thin, lighted telescope is inserted through the cervix and into the uterus to look at the baby. Some rare liver and skin abnormalities in the baby can be diagnosed with this method and samples of tissues obtained for analysis in the laboratory. It is only performed in very exceptional circumstances and it carries with it a risk of miscarriage of about one in 50.

Ultrasound screening

Ultrasound scans have become enormously valuable in the diagnosis of abnormalities in the baby during pregnancy. The machinery and the quality of the pictures obtained become better each year. However, it is important to emphasise that ultrasound can only pick up structural abnormalities that are present in your baby. Many women I meet are under the false impression that a normal nuchal translucency scan (NTS) at 11–13 weeks or a normal anomaly scan at 20 weeks guarantees her a normal baby. This is not true.

The ultrasound can only see abnormal anatomy. Experienced scanners are able to see tiny pointers that make them suspect that there may be a problem, and they will probably then advise you to have an invasive test to check the baby's chromosomes. But many congenital abnormalities do not have any obvious anatomical or structural markers in the baby. A good example is Down's syndrome. Many babies with Down's syndrome have recognisable heart, kidney and gut abnormalities on the US scan and we are now able to look at the skin creases on the baby's hands and assess the eyelids, which may give us a clue that the baby is affected. Some babies with Down's syndrome have no obvious signs and will not be detected until after the birth.

Cerebral palsy is another good example. There is no antenatal test that can detect cerebral palsy. For decades we have thought that cerebral palsy was the result of a traumatic labour. We now know that many infants with cerebral palsy have developed this problem during the course of the pregnancy but we have not yet been able to identify the trigger(s). We recognise that cerebral palsy is more common in babies born prematurely, but the exact mechanism is not understood.

Over the last few years there have been several 'scare' stories reported in the newspapers suggesting that repeated ultrasound scans during pregnancy may cause damage to the developing baby. Laboratory experiments have suggested that US waves may cause changes in the membranes (covering layers) of cells that potentially could affect the development of the embryo and later growth of the fetus in utero. There are no scientific data to support these assertions and, importantly, a large Swedish study has recently been published which has concluded that there is no association between multiple pregnancy US scans and the later occurrence of childhood leukaemia. Several other large studies looking at the follow-up of babies scanned on many occasions during complicated pregnancies have demonstrated that there are no serious developmental abnormalities in these babies. Indeed, the only difference that I am aware of between pregnancies that are scanned regularly and those that are not, appears in a recent Scandinavian study, which reported an increase in the number of left-handed babies born to the mothers who had received multiple scans. The fear here was that the sound waves had in some way interfered with the development of the baby. Some people may argue that being left-handed is an advantage in life – it is certainly not a disadvantage!

Many women now opt to have an early scan between 11 to 13 weeks of gestation which measures the size of the fetus and the nuchal translucency (the fluid present behind the neck of the fetus – the nuchal fold). The thickness of the nuchal fold is then fed into a computer program along with the exact age of the pregnancy in weeks and days and the mother's age. The computer then calculates the adjusted risk for this woman having a chromosomally abnormal baby, based on all the information it has been provided with. Once again this is a probability and not a black-and-white answer. The only sure-fire way of establishing that your baby has normal chromosomes is to undergo an invasive procedure such as amniocentesis. The NTS is best at detecting Down's syndrome (trisomy 21) but it is also available to detect other major trisomies.

Although not a guarantee that your baby is normal, I think the NTS scan is particularly helpful for women who have suffered recurrent miscarriages. They are usually, and understandably, fearful that an invasive procedure may result in a further miscarriage or later pregnancy complication. I have looked after many patients in the last few years who have been unsure what to do because they are older than 35 years, and recognise their increased risk of fetal abnormality, but do not want to place themselves at greater risk of miscarriage from amniocentesis. The NTS scan is a good halfway house. In expert hands it is a good predictor of abnormality and normality and many of my patients end up concluding that they would prefer to have an NTS scan and only proceed to have an amniocentesis if the results suggest that they are at significant risk of carrying a baby with a major chromosomal abnormality.

Maternal serum screening

This is the name given to the special antenatal blood test which you will probably be offered at about 15–16 weeks of pregnancy. It provides you with a probability (risk assessment) of whether or not there is an increased chance of your baby having a chromosomal abnormality such as Down's syndrome or an open neural tube defect (such as spina bifida). There are a variety of tests on the market measuring two, three or more substances in your blood. The double test is the best known and measures alphafetoprotein and free beta HCG. In babies with Down's syndrome the aFP tends to be lower and the HCG higher. Just as with the nuchal translucency scans (see above) your age and the exact gestation of your pregnancy are then used to calculate your risk of Down's syndrome. The double test is carried out in Birmingham and detects two out of three cases of Down's and four out of five cases of neural tube defect. The triple test, undertaken at Bart's Hospital, London, adds another hormone, oestriol, to the calculation and the Bart's test further includes two other substances called inhibin A and pregnancy-associated protein A (PAPP-A).

When the screening test shows a significant chance of having a baby with Down's syndrome it is called screen positive and you will be given the option of having an amniocentesis (see earlier). If the test shows an aFP level indicating an increased risk of an open neural tube defect, a detailed scan will be arranged to look carefully at the baby's head and spine. When you undergo a maternal serum screening test I think it is really important that you remember three things: 1) that a screen positive test does not necessarily mean that the baby has Down's syndrome or a neural tube defect. It only indicates that you are in a higher-risk group and that you need to be offered a further diagnostic test. 2) Although women with screen negative results are unlikely to have a baby with either of these problems, sadly, a few women will. 3) If you decide to have a serum screening test you need to have thought carefully about what you will do if the test is positive. You will be offered an amniocentesis and if you decide to accept and the baby is found to be affected, you will be faced with the choice of whether or not to continue with the pregnancy.

As I mentioned previously, there is no right or wrong answer to these difficult questions. You and your partner will need to make a decision that is right for you. These serum screening tests are very helpful but they can only provide you with a numerical risk. If you need to know for certain that your baby does not have Down's syndrome, or any other chromosomal abnormality, then the amniocentesis or other invasive tests will be required.

Preimplantation diagnosis

Diagnosing a genetic disorder in a tiny embryo is a new and very exciting development which has been pioneered at the Hammersmith Hospital. It is now possible to determine the sex of a baby and several specific genetic diseases (for example, cystic fibrosis) by removing a cell from an embryo. Of course, the only way to obtain an embryo is for the woman to undergo an IVF cycle. The embryo created by fertilisation of an egg in the laboratory can then be sampled before the embryo is transferred into the mother's uterus. This cell is then carefully broken up to release the DNA (the genetic code) and, using specialised molecular biology techniques, the genetic code can be identified. If the abnormal genetic code is found, the embryo will not be transferred back to the mother. We hope that in the future it will be possible to use these techniques for couples who have miscarried repeatedly due to balanced translocations, identifying whether the baby has inherited the normal, balanced or unbalanced chromosomal element from the parents.

I feel compelled to make a further comment before completing this brief overview on preimplantation diagnosis. Several patients who I have cared for recently have attended the clinic clutching copies of articles that they have found on the Internet about the use of preimplantation diagnosis, which have alleged that this technique reduces the miscarriage rate in couples who have suffered recurrent pregnancy losses. This is an inaccurate viewpoint and is sadly very misleading to many desperate couples trying to achieve their ambition to have a live, healthy baby. When I read these scientific papers I can understand why my patients have come to their conclusions. The data need to be scrutinised much more closely and interpreted a lot more cautiously if we are to prevent false hopes being dashed.

When a couple undergo preimplantation diagnosis they are effectively being screened for chromosomal and other genetic abnormalities in one of the cells taken from an embryo that they have produced as a result of IVF and related specialist treatments. The purpose is to avoid replacing any embryo that is found to be abnormal back into the woman's uterus. It is true that, as a result of this selection procedure, the number of miscarriages that result from those embryos that manage to implant and go on to develop into recognisable pregnancies is low. This is because the commonest cause of miscarriage is a chromosomal abnormality in the fetus. But it is essential that any couple who opt to undergo this complex treatment realise that there is an enormous difference between the number of embryos produced and the number of embryos that progress to become an established pregnancy.

Preimplantation genetic diagnosis is not a cure for miscarriage. It is a highly specialised technique that prevents miscarriages occurring due to chromosomal anomalies in the tiny embryo, because it removes these affected babies from the potential pregnancy pool. It will never be able to increase the live take home baby rate. This may sound harsh to the reader but I am confident that it is not as harsh as the reality that some couples find themselves experiencing unwittingly. Namely, that they have undergone an expensive, emotionally and physically exhausting procedure and have not understood that the chances of achieving a healthy baby have not been increased in real terms. I must conclude by stating that I am a great supporter of the advantages that preimplantation genetic diagnosis can provide when the technique is offered to couples with an established risk of conceiving repeated genetically abnormal pregnancies that can be identified accurately. This technique can prevent these couples from ever conceiving pregnancies that are destined to bring further distress and disappointment, but for recurrent miscarriers who do not carry a specific genetic disorder this is not a treatment that will solve your problems.

Summary

Recognised genetic abnormalities in the baby are common in women with sporadic miscarriages and less common in women with repeated miscarriage. A chromosomal abnormality in one of the parents is present in no more than 5% of couples who experience recurrent miscarriages. It is extremely important to identify these couples, because the management of their future pregnancies will be altered by this knowledge. They need to be offered antenatal diagnosis in any ongoing pregnancy. It is important to remember that even if your reason for repeated miscarriages has been identified and treated, you are not protected from a sporadic miscarriage caused by an 'out of the blue' chromosomal abnormality in the baby. The most useful way forward is to ensure that any future pregnancy which miscarries is analysed genetically. Knowledge of the chromosomal makeup of the baby will provide you and your doctors with information that will make important contributions to your medical management. It is also likely to be a source of comfort to you and your partner.

EIGHT

RECURRENT MISCARRIAGE – ANATOMICAL CAUSES

Much has been written in medical textbooks about the reproductive problems which may result from abnormal development of the ovaries, fallopian tubes, uterus, cervix and vagina. When
the structure of these organs is abnormal, they are called 'congenital
abnormalities'. The human uterus, cervix and vagina develop from
two separate tubes of tissue which normally fuse together in the
midline. As a result, most women have two ovaries, two fallopian
tubes and a single uterus, cervix and vagina. If this fusion is
incomplete, a wide variety of abnormal types of anatomy can result.
Abnormalities of these female organs can also be acquired after birth
(for example, fibroids) or following an operation on the uterus or
cervix (for example, intrauterine adhesions), whereas other abnormalities can be a mixture of congenital and acquired causes (cervical
incompetence). Whatever the abnormality is or what has caused it,
the methods we use to identify or 'image' these anatomical problems
are common to all the different types. At the end of this chapter we
will look at these techniques and their practical usage.

Congenital abnormalities of the uterus

No one knows exactly how many women have a congenital abnormality of their uterus. Some studies have suggested that as few as
one in a thousand women (0.1%) are affected. Other studies have
concluded that as many as one in ten women (10%) have an
abnormality. The true incidence is somewhere between these two

figures and depends upon the population of women studied. This uncertainty is another good example of how the specialist interest of the doctors investigating women with recurrent miscarriages influences the results. For example, if all women with a history of repeated premature labours or late miscarriages are investigated, it is likely that the number of uterine abnormalities found will be much higher than the figure for women with repeated early miscarriages.

The most frequent uterine abnormality is a bicornuate uterus. This means that the two tubes of uterine tissue (called horns) have not fused together and instead of the rounded dome shape, the uterus has the appearance of two horns joined together at the cervix. Very rarely, the abnormality is so severe that there are two cervices (uterus didelphys) and two vaginas (bicollis). Occasionally only one uterine horn is present, communicating with a single fallopian tube, and this is called a unicornuate uterus. An arcuate uterus, in which the normal dome of the uterine cavity is flattened, is quite common. So too is the presence of a septum in the uterus. If you can imagine a domed ceiling with a curtain hanging down from the centre, then you will understand what a septate uterus is. The curtain can be long or short in length and so we refer to septate and subseptate abnormalities of the uterus.

If you have a bicornuate uterus, it is possible that the baby will not have enough room to grow to its proper size and that you will experience a premature labour or late miscarriage. A bicornuate uterus is also one of the reasons why the baby may be a breech presentation (sitting with his or her bottom above the cervix instead of pointing head downwards). Having mentioned the problems that a bicornuate uterus may cause, I must also tell you that there have been many times when I have only recognised that the woman has a bicornuate uterus after an entirely normal delivery or a routine caesarean section at term. My most memorable case was the pair of healthy twins I delivered at 36 weeks, each twin delivering out of their own uterine horn.

In the past, open surgery to correct a bicornuate uterus was recommended. This entailed a major pelvic operation during which the two horns of the bicornuate uterus were opened and stitched back together to form a single uterine cavity. Although supporters of this treatment claimed that the women they operated upon had a high live birth rate in future pregnancies, it was later realised that about one third of these women never became pregnant again. The scar tissue and pelvic adhesions caused by their surgery resulted in them becoming infertile. I feel strongly that this is much too high a price to pay for a treatment which has never been demonstrated to offer benefit in a proper controlled trial. Fortunately, open surgery has fallen out of favour and I know of no clinicians who now offer this treatment to women with a bicornuate uterus and a history of recurrent miscarriage.

Some doctors believe that a septum in the uterine cavity is a major cause of infertility and repeated miscarriages. The septum is usually thin and has no proper endometrial covering, so it is argued that the embryo cannot implant properly on this surface, which may result in the woman experiencing difficulties in becoming pregnant. Alternatively, the embryo may start to implant on the septum, but because of the poor blood supply and thin endometrium, the pregnancy cannot continue and an early miscarriage is likely. I am sure that this is a valid explanation for a few cases of miscarriage, but it has always struck me that it goes against the laws of probability to assume that every embryo makes a beeline for the septum rather than choosing another more promising site to implant in the uterus.

Certainly there have been numerous papers published on the incidence of uterine septae in women with a history of infertility and of recurrent miscarriage. The figures quoted have varied greatly, because once again they reflect the specialist interests of the doctors involved. However, one very important Spanish study has helped to put the problem into perspective. These doctors found that the incidence of septae in women who were undergoing laparoscopic sterilisation after completing their families was in the region of 3%. This is not significantly different from the incidence of septae found in women being investigated for infertility. Furthermore, in a study performed at the recurrent miscarriage clinic at St Mary's a few years ago, we also found that 3% of our patients had an intrauterine septum. These results emphasise the importance of always including appropriate control groups when trying to establish the incidence of a particular disorder in women presenting with a history of repeated pregnancy loss.

If you have a septate uterus, the doctors may suggest that they cut out (or 'resect') the septum with the help of an operating hysteroscope. This is a fine telescope which is inserted through the cervix into the uterine cavity. At the tip of the telescope is a small hooped cutter which is used to carefully resect the septum in small pieces. I confess to the reader that it was only very recently, when looking up some old research papers, that I discovered how ancient this technique of septal resection is! The first septal resection was carried out blindly by a Dr Ruge in 1884 long before fibre optic telescopes or proper anaesthetics were available. Nearly a hundred years later, in 1974, Dr Edstrom performed the first septal resection under direct vision using one of the newly designed operating hysteroscopes. The current-day procedure is usually performed quickly under a light general anaesthetic and requires no more than a day or overnight stay in hospital. I have certainly used this technique for some of my miscarriage patients, who appear to have been cured by this simple operation and gone on to have successful pregnancies.

I hope that some readers of this book will question this unscientific statement and want to know about the pregnancy outcome of those patients whose septum I did not resect. They did very well too, so I am not convinced that hysteroscopic surgery is always necessary in this situation. I tend to reserve resections of a septum for those of my patients who have experienced difficulties in becoming pregnant as well as repeatedly miscarrying. Certainly an open pelvic operation (see earlier) is likely to cause more harm than good and should definitely be avoided. Of course, what is really needed is a well-designed, multicentred, properly controlled, randomised trial in which future pregnancy outcome is compared in recurrent miscarriers with a septum who undergo resection treatment and those who have no surgical intervention. Several units have tried to start such a trial but it has proved very difficult to recruit patients – they all want to be in the treatment group despite the fact that there is no clear evidence to suggest that it is going to resolve their problems.

Diethylstilboestrol

A variety of congenital uterine abnormalities, particularly a T shaped uterine cavity, are found in some of the daughters of women who were treated with diethylstilboestrol (DES) in pregnancy. DES is a synthetic oestrogen and ironically it was first prescribed in the late 1940s for women who were threatening to miscarry! It did not stop the miscarriages, a fact that was known as early as 1953, but it was only when it was realised in the 1970s that this drug caused problems in the daughters of the women who had been treated that it was withdrawn from the market. The problems ranged from an increased risk of developing autoimmune diseases such as lupus and rheumatoid arthritis to the development of vaginal tissue abnormalities, called vaginal adenosis. The most serious problem was the occurrence of a rare type of vaginal and cervical 'clear cell' cancer. DES-related abnormalities are very rare these days because only a few daughters exposed to the drug are still of childbearing age. Hopefully it will only be a few more years before the problem becomes extinct.

Fibroids

Uterine fibroids are very common, and may cause both infertility and miscarriage. In fact, fibroids are the most common benign (non-cancerous) growth in women and as many as 50% of women will eventually develop one or more fibroids. Fibroids can vary in size from a small pea to a large melon and vary in number from one to a hundred. The amazing thing about fibroids is that no one really understands how they develop. Since they are the cause of many obstetric and gynaecological problems, I always think it is strange that we still do not know how to prevent them from growing in the uterus.

They are rare before the age of 20 years, and do not develop after the menopause, which points to the fact that their growth is influenced by our reproductive hormones. There is obviously a genetic tendency to develop fibroids, since they are often found in several women in the same family and are much more frequent in Afro-Caribbean women. Fibroids can grow in any part of the uterus. If they are in the wall, they are called intramural fibroids. If they are on the outside of the uterus, they are called subserous, or pedunculated if the fibroid is attached to the outside surface of the uterus by a stalk. When the fibroids protrude into the uterine cavity, they are known as submucous fibroids and occasionally these may form a polyp attached to the endometrial lining by a stalk.

Many women with fibroids become pregnant without any delays and experience no complications during their pregnancies. However, some fibroids can enlarge the uterus and distort the uterine cavity to such an extent that they cause serious reproductive problems. Submucous fibroids are the worst offenders and if they grow near the opening of the tubes into the uterine cavity, or occupy a large surface of the uterine cavity, the woman may present with infertility. The endometrial lining over the surface of submucous fibroids has a poorer blood supply and this is probably what makes it difficult for an embryo to implant (infertility) or to continue to develop successfully (miscarriage).

In later pregnancy, fibroids in any position may cause problems. They grow along with the rest of the uterus under the influence of the hormones of pregnancy. Many of the problems they cause are beyond the scope of this chapter, but a few points need to be mentioned here. Sometimes their growth outstrips their blood supply and the fibroid starts to degenerate – this is most commonly experienced between 20 and 28 weeks of pregnancy. Fibroid degeneration in pregnancy can be very painful and the inflammation that it causes may make the pregnancy go into labour prematurely. When they are very large, the fibroids may limit the growth of the baby. If the fibroids are positioned low in the uterus, near the cervix, they can cause difficulties with the delivery. The risk of these complications is one of the reasons we try to remove large fibroids before pregnancy.

If you are found to have a fibroid polyp, the doctors will advise you to have it removed from the uterine cavity. Fibroid polyps can usually be dealt with during a D&C operation. The decision to remove a submucous fibroid will depend upon the position and size of the fibroid and also whether you have had problems getting pregnant or repeated miscarriages. It may be possible to resect the fibroid with the help of an operating hysteroscope (see earlier), which is undoubtedly the best approach. An open pelvic operation is always more complicated and carries with it many more problems in the post-operative period, the most serious of which is not being able to conceive due to scar tissue and adhesions.

The most appropriate method of dealing with intramural fibroids and subserous fibroids will also depend on their size and position. If you are advised to have it removed, the operation is called a myomectomy (a 'myoma' is a fibroid). It involves an open operation, cutting through the muscular wall of the uterus in order to shell out the fibroid, which is surrounded by a tough fibrous capsule. The operation can be very bloody and much care is taken to try and reduce the bleeding during and after the operation by very carefully stitching the muscle walls together. Open surgery for fibroids is best done by experienced fertility doctors, in order to reduce future complications.

New treatments for fibroids

In the future it may be possible to avoid open surgery for fibroids in women who want to preserve their fertility. An exciting new technique has been developed which uses special needles inserted into the fibroids through the skin. Special laser fibres are passed through the needle, which heat the fibroid tissue to such a temperature that it coagulates and eventually disintegrates. The whole procedure is monitored carefully and is only possible with a new type of scanning technique, called interventional magnetic resonance imaging. The beauty of this technique is that the patient is not hidden away in a claustrophobic tube but is positioned between the two rings of the magnet (which is why it is sometimes referred to as the double doughnut). This means that the operator has easy access to the patient, can perform the laser ablation procedure and at the same time watch the tissue destruction on the real-time imaging screen. There are only a handful of these IMR machines available across the Western world and, at the time of writing this chapter, the only machine in the UK is sited at St Mary's Hospital, London. I have been enormously impressed by the results that we have achieved with this technique. When we started the pilot study we were worried that the laser heat might in some way damage the endometrium (womb lining) or lead to the development of intra-abdominal adhesions by damaging the surface of the uterus. Hence, we only recruited women who had already decided to have a hysterectomy to undergo this pioneering treatment, so that we would have an opportunity to examine the tissues in the pathology laboratory at a later date.

The results are very encouraging. Not only does the laser treatment reduce the size of the fibroids significantly, but it does not appear to cause any endometrial or surface problems. Perhaps the best test of the method is that the heavy bleeding and pelvic pain that these women were experiencing with their fibroids was so dramatically reduced that more than half of the original study group decided not to go ahead with their hysterectomy operation! We still have more studies to undertake but the advantages of this technique are enormous. It can be performed as a day-case procedure, involves little or no anaesthetic or pain-killing drugs, and there is virtually no recovery time – a rather different story from the usual six weeks off that women are advised to take after an open surgical myomectomy. To date we have not experienced any short- or long-term complication of the laser procedure. However, the real test will be whether it is safe to use in women who have not completed their families – and indeed this is the next stage of the trial.

Uterine artery embolisation (blocking off) has been tried by several centres over the last five years. In brief, a radiologist inserts a catheter into an artery in the woman's groin and feeds it up and along until the uterine artery is reached. Then particles of polyvinyl are inserted into the vessel and the procedure repeated on the other side of the uterus. The short-term results from this treatment suggest that the fibroids reduced greatly in size, but as more procedures have been performed the list of unacceptable complications has lengthened. Most women complain that the post-operative pain is very severe and requires intravenous painkillers for some days. A few pregnancies have been reported following embolisation but some women have become menopausal as a result of the embolisation. Life-threatening infections have been reported, along with several deaths. I do not recommend this treatment as an alternative to myomectomy and it compares very poorly with the laser ablation technique described above.

If the very newest development called MR guided focused ultrasound, lives up to its promise, we may be able to burn away fibroids without having to insert needles through the skin. The high energy US is focused on a small area after it has passed through the skin and heats the tissues until they shrivel up. The process is followed with the MR imaging which allows us to see exactly how much of the fibroid has been treated and gives a clear picture of the tissues before the heat is applied and causes irreversible damage. The procedure is carried out as an outpatient treatment and our experience so far is that the patients do not require any analgesia.

Intrauterine adhesions

These are also referred to as synechiae and are fine bridges of fibrous tissue which cause the walls of the uterus to stick together. These adhesions stop the endometrium from thickening at the appropriate time in the woman's menstrual cycle. In mild cases, this may prevent an embryo from implanting successfully. In more severe cases, the woman may stop having periods altogether although she will often experience pain and discomfort at the time when the period should have come. Intrauterine adhesions almost always follow a surgical procedure in the uterine cavity, such as a D&C or an ERPC after a miscarriage, termination of pregnancy or following a manual removal of the placenta. As such, they are another type of acquired uterine abnormality.

Adhesions in the uterus are really very common. In fact, the more you suspect that they may be present, the more you find them. I frequently meet women who have no periods but experience cyclical abdominal pain for several months after a miscarriage which has required a surgical evacuation (ERPC). Experience has taught me to do nothing in the short term and wait for a few months – the problem usually resolves spontaneously. The traumatised uterine lining starts to regenerate and the periods come back with no adverse consequences. When the problem continues, it is advisable for the woman to have the adhesions divided under a light anaesthetic using a hysteroscope (see earlier). If there are a lot of adhesions in the cavity, your doctor will probably insert a plastic coil into the uterus after dividing the adhesions with the hysteroscope. The coil (intrauterine device, or IUD) ensures that the walls of the uterine cavity stay apart, giving the endometrial lining time and space in which to regenerate. Some doctors also advise a short course of antibiotics, together with some steroid and oestrogen tablets, all of which can help the uterine lining to heal more quickly.

Fortunately, uterine adhesions are almost always responsive to treatment and do not usually cause long-term problems. I mention this because many women I meet in the miscarriage clinic worry about how many ERPCs they have undergone due to repeated miscarriages. Let me reassure you that it is much better to have a carefully performed ERPC (even if you do have the bad luck to develop some adhesions) rather than risk infection of the remaining tissues in the uterus. Infection can cause much more severe problems and is a very real cause of future infertility.

Cervical incompetence

The cervix needs to remain closed during pregnancy to allow the fetus and placenta to develop to a size that will allow a viable baby to be delivered. However, if the muscles of the cervix are weak, the cervical canal may start to open during the second trimester of pregnancy, most usually at or around 20 weeks. This situation is called cervical incompetence and may occasionally be due to a congenital abnormality of the muscles of the cervix. In days past, cervical incompetence was not infrequently caused by forceful wide dilatation of the cervix at the time of a D&C or a termination of pregnancy. Nowadays, doctors are very conscious of this potential problem and frequently use drugs to prime or soften the cervix to make it more pliant before starting the uterine evacuation. They are also careful not to dilate the cervix more than 10–12mm when they are operating on the uterus. Occasionally, damage to the cervix may result from a difficult vaginal delivery where the cervix is torn by forceps or a particularly large baby.

The cervix also needs to remain closed so that the membranes surrounding the baby are not exposed to the vaginal environment. The vagina contains many bacteria which normally do not cause any harm to the pregnancy because the cervix is closed. However, if the muscles of the cervix start to open, the bacteria present in the vagina may then cause inflammation of the membranes which are protruding into the vagina. The woman may experience an increase in her normal vaginal discharge and a feeling of heaviness in the vagina as the cervix shortens and starts to dilate. The inflammation causes the membranes to weaken and sometimes to burst, releasing liquor from the pool around the baby. When the waters break, it is usually only a matter of time before the uterus starts to contract. The reason for this is twofold. Firstly, the membranes release a variety of chemicals when they rupture, which encourage the uterine muscles to contract. Secondly, the bacteria present in the vagina now have easy access to the uterine cavity and within a very short period of time the fetus and placenta become inflamed and infected, which further encourages the uterus to expel its contents. Once infection has set in, it is not possible to save the pregnancy, even with the use of antibiotics. An infection in the uterus is a very serious problem for the pregnant woman, and she needs to be delivered promptly to ensure that she does not develop a life-threatening systemic (generalised) infection.

For some women, there may be no symptoms or signs such as vaginal discharge, broken waters and uterine contractions. Instead, with very little or no warning, the cervix may suddenly open and expel the pregnancy from the uterus. Most commonly, the woman suddenly feels that she wants to open her bowels and on reaching the toilet realises that what she is feeling is the baby miscarrying through the open cervix. The placenta may deliver spontaneously, but more often it is retained in the uterus and has to be removed manually with the help of an epidural or general anaesthetic. I have always thought that nature is particularly unkind in this situation – the woman fails to keep the baby in the uterus, but then has to go through manual traction to get rid of the placenta.

Classical cervical incompetence is described in the textbooks as a 'painless' and sudden opening of the cervix. It has been considered an important cause of late miscarriage for decades. My practical experience is that a painless opening of the cervix during the second trimester of pregnancy is a relatively rare event. If I take a careful history from a woman who has suffered a late miscarriage there are almost always pointers that the opening of the cervix was accompanied by painful uterine contractions or broken waters. Furthermore, I regularly see patients in my recurrent miscarriage clinic referred to me as cases of 'cervical incompetence', but further questioning reveals that the baby had died in the uterus during the second trimester of pregnancy and it was necessary to use drugs to induce the uterus to contract and expel the dead baby – a very different set of affairs to the spontaneous opening of an incompetent cervix.

I am not suggesting that cervical incompetence does not exist, but I do want to state that it is quite rare. More importantly, you need to realise that if causes other than this weakness of the cervical muscles are not looked for, it is unlikely that we will find the root cause of your problem. In the past I think that cervical incompetence has been used as a dustbin diagnosis into which all previously unexplained late miscarriages have been thrown. An infection in the vagina which ascends (travels up) into the uterine cavity is undoubtedly a cause in some cases, and in Chapter 10 we will look at this problem in more detail. However, I firmly believe that many cases of late miscarriage, previously considered to be another example of cervical incompetence, are due to the antiphospholipid syndrome of pregnancy (see Chapter 12). This is an autoimmune disorder, which can be difficult to identify in some women, but undoubtedly is the cause of a wide variety of pregnancy losses. In the miscarriage clinic at St Mary's, we spend a lot of time looking for these antiphospholipid antibodies in the patients referred to us with late miscarriages. Many of these women have been told that they have an incompetent cervix, but after careful questioning and a study of their medical records, we frequently find that there is more to the story than a weak cervix. I think every woman who suffers a late miscarriage or a premature delivery should be screened not once, but repeatedly, for evidence of the antiphospholipid syndrome. My reasoning is quite simple. Treatment for this problem is extremely effective and can transform a high risk of miscarriage into a high chance of a live birth.

Surgical treatment of cervical incompetence

True cervical incompetence is rare in my opinion, but this chapter would be incomplete without describing the treatment method of 'cerclage' – where a stitch is inserted into the cervix to stop the cervix from dilating. Several operations have been tried to achieve this aim, the most famous of which have been named after their inventors, Mr Shirodkar and Mr McDonald. Essentially, the technique is the same. Under a general anaesthetic, the cervix is examined with a speculum inserted into the vagina. A strong mersilene tape or thick nylon stitch (which cannot dissolve like other types of suture material) is inserted into the cervix with a special needle at the 12 o'clock position and brought out at the 3 o'clock position. Further stitches around the circumference of the cervix bring the needle back to the 12 o'clock position, where a strong knot is tied. Personally, I prefer the nylon sutures, which I find easier to insert without having to pull too hard on the cervix.

The success of the suture depends upon how high up the cervix the operator can insert the stitch. Indeed, the original Shirodkar method involved careful dissection of the bladder off the front of the cervix in order that the stitch could be placed even higher. If you undergo cervical cerclage, you will probably be given some medication to quieten the uterus if it becomes irritable as a result of manipulating the cervix. You will be advised to rest in hospital for a few days before going home again. You may experience quite a lot of vaginal discharge during the remainder of the pregnancy, because of the presence of the suture material (a 'foreign body'). Having said that, I have recently had the opportunity of operating with a colleague who inserts the stitch very high and then buries the knot under the bladder or below the peritoneum, and these women do not seem to be troubled by discharge at all.

Of course, not all stitches are successful and sometimes the trauma of inserting it may cause the cervix to start bleeding, the uterus to start contracting, or the waters to break. In this situation, the stitch must be taken out without delay to avoid the risk of strong contractions ripping the stitch out of the cervix as it dilates. Similarly, if an infection develops or is suspected, the stitch should also be removed quickly, because it will encourage further infection, which can ascend into the uterus with serious consequences for the mother (see earlier). If the procedure is uncomplicated, then the stitch will remain in place until about 37 weeks, when it needs to be removed to allow a normal labour to progress. Removing the stitch is much less of a problem than putting it in, and is usually managed without an anaesthetic.

Most doctors plan to insert the suture at about 14 weeks of gestation, although I know that some doctors advise that the cervical suture should be inserted before pregnancy. I have never thought this approach to be very sensible, since it means that any pregnancy that dies in the first trimester cannot miscarry without removing the stitch. As you will remember from previous chapters in this book, early miscarriage is much more common than late miscarriage and so the risk of this complication is quite high.

During the late 1980s the Medical Research Council (MRC) of England mounted a large multicentre trial of cerclage treatment. Sadly, the results were disappointing. The MRC study demonstrated that women who did have a suture inserted delivered their babies a few weeks later than the women who did not have a cervical suture. As a direct result of the longer gestation time, the weight of the babies in the suture group was higher. It was concluded that for every 13 sutures inserted, one baby would be prevented from delivering prematurely. However, the number of live 'take home' babies did not increase. Furthermore, the suture group spent considerably more time during their pregnancies in hospital and required more medication for infection and other complications than the control group of women who had no suture. I think it is important for the reader to have these details about the MRC trial results because I frequently hear them being misquoted. I can see no value in a treatment method that requires 13 procedures to be performed to increase the gestational age of one baby, if that one baby does not leave hospital alive and well.

Nonetheless, as I mentioned above, I have been exploring the use of high cervical sutures recently and although it is too early to jump to conclusions, the early results are encouraging. I find myself wondering whether the improved success (when compared to the MRC results) that we have noted recently is due to the fact that the length of the cervix is markedly increased when the sutures are inserted higher. You will note that I mention length rather than how tightly closed the cervix becomes after the stitch is in place. I suspect that a longer cervix not only prevents the membranes around the baby from being exposed to infective organisms in the vagina, but also makes the successful ascent of these organisms into the uterine cavity less likely for purely mechanical reasons.

Recently, there have been reports of the use of a cervical stitch inserted by the abdominal route either before or during pregnancy. This method involves a major operation to open the abdomen and identify the top of the cervix from above. Not surprisingly, the advocates of this technique claim an excellent success rate, although it is important for the reader to note that this method has never been assessed in a controlled trial.

Cervical cerclage has always been a very controversial issue in the management of recurrent miscarriage and it continues to be so since a randomised treatment trial of sufficient numbers is unlikely to be completed for women with repeated late miscarriages. Armed with the facts, you, the reader, will now be in a position to make up your own mind about this treatment if it is ever offered to you.

Methods of diagnosing anatomical abnormalities

There have been many techniques used to identify anatomical abnormalities. Each has merits and disavantages and it is important for the reader to recognise that different doctors will use different methods, usually dictated by the facilities and expertise that are available to them.

Laparoscopy and hysteroscopy

Telescopic techniques such as laparoscopy and hysteroscopy are almost always available and in experienced hands can successfully diagnose most of the abnormalities discussed in this chapter. Laparoscopy is a good way of assessing the shape, size and position of the uterus, tubes and ovaries. Many suspected congenital abnormalities will be visualised in this way and, when attached to a video camera, the laparoscope will also provide a pictorial record of the problem. Hysteroscopy is a particularly useful tool, because in addition to diagnosing abnormalities, it can also be used to treat problems such as submucous fibroids, polyps and adhesions, without the need for an additional procedure. Small scissors or a looped cutting wire can be inserted into the uterus alongside the hysteroscope to remove tissues under the telescopic control. However, these techniques usually require a general anaesthetic and a short stay in hospital. They are relatively safe but of course all operative procedures carry with them a small risk of complications. This is one of the reasons why so many alternative methods have been tried, in an attempt to identify non-invasive techniques which are just as accurate.

Hysterosalpingogram

An hysterosalpingogram (HSG) is an X-ray examination of the uterine cavity (hystero-) and the fallopian tubes (salpingo-). The procedure is performed as an outpatient and you will be asked to lie down on a couch in the X-ray department. The doctor will insert a speculum into your vagina and very gently hold the upper lip of the cervix to steady it whilst inserting a tube into the cervical canal. A special radio-opaque dye is then injected into the cervical canal and passes up into the uterine cavity and along the fallopian tubes. The HSG needs to be performed in the X-ray department because your abdomen will be screened with a special low dose X-ray machine whilst the dye is being injected. A television screen will monitor the passage of the dye as it outlines the cavity and the tubes and then several hard copy X-ray films will be taken.

The HSG is usually performed by an experienced radiologist because, in addition to the permanent films taken, useful information can be gathered from watching the passage of the dye during the screening procedure. The HSG is a good method of diagnosing a cervix that is wide (and possibly incompetent), the shape of the uterine cavity and whether adhesions or fibroids are present and distorting its outline. Most congenital abnormalities will be clearly visible using this technique. Since the inside surface of the fallopian tubes is also visualised, HSGs are also used to investigate women who have experienced infertility, to see whether their tubes are open or distorted in some way. The HSG can cause some discomfort but this is not usually more severe than period pain. Some women tell me that they found the HSG very painful but painkillers can be given if you need them. After all the films have been taken, the instruments will be removed from your vagina and you will be able to go straight home.

A few last points need to be mentioned about HSGs. Since the test involves X-rays, it is performed in the first ten days of the menstrual cycle and before ovulation to avoid the risk of irradiating a fertilised ovum or young embryo. Of course, it is possible to perform the test during the second half of the cycle as long as you have used a barrier method of contraception to avoid pregnancy in that cycle. The HSG will be postponed until another date if you are having your period. This is because the pressure of the injected dye is thought to increase the possibilities of pieces of endometrial lining being dislodged backwards into the abdomen and pelvis, where it may cause endometriosis. If you have ever had a uterine or pelvic infection it is very important to tell the doctors this before the HSG is performed. They will probably suggest that you take a course of antibiotics starting before the procedure and continuing for several days afterwards. This is because pelvic infections have a nasty tendency of recurring and the organisms that cause them are often lying quietly in the cervix. This is particularly true for infection caused by chlamydia. If the chlamydia are washed up the cervix and uterus along with the injected dye, a pelvic infection may result and this may have a serious effect on the tubes, possibly causing future infertility. I think there is a lot to be said for giving every woman who has an HSG some prophylactic antibiotics to cover the procedure.

Magnetic resonance imaging and computerised tomography
MRI and CT scans are sophisticated imaging methods which can provide very detailed information about the pelvic organs. They have

not become the 'gold standard' for diagnosing anatomical abnormalities simply because the equipment used is very expensive and not
routinely available at all hospitals. This means that there may be long
waiting lists for these procedures. Furthermore, since the radiologi-
cal expertise required to interpret the images is specialised, very few
gynaecologists have much personal practical experience in interpreting the test results. This is an important point because the only way
to forward research in this area is by comparing results obtained
from a large number of different units and this is just not feasible at
the present time. I should mention here that the new interventional
magnetic resonance imaging technique (see earlier – New treatments
for fibroids) produces really excellent images of the uterus. Since it is
also possible for the operator to stand beside the patient during her
scan in the special new magnet, the possibilities for being able to
instrument the uterus and fallopian tubes to help in the pelvic
assessment are limitless.

Ultrasound

Ultrasound has the enormous advantage of being widely available
and in experienced hands it can be very informative. I consider
myself very lucky to have an excellent ultrasound service, headed by a
radiologist who oversees all the gynaecology scanning. As a result,
the ultrasound reports for all the patients seen at my recurrent
miscarriage clinic are extremely accurate and I am confident that we
diagnose the presence, size and location of any uterine fibroids, the
presence of adhesions and pick up congenital abnormalities in over
95% of cases. Not everyone working in this field has access to such a
good service, but it is worth striving for since ultrasound is non-
invasive, non-painful, cheaper than all other alternatives and has no
complications.

To illustrate (and possibly to justify!) my viewpoint, I think you will
be interested in the results of a study we performed in the miscarriage clinic at St Mary's a few years ago. We reviewed the
ultrasound scans performed on 1000 miscarriage patients and
noted that we had identified 4% of them as having a uterine
abnormality such as a septum, bicornuate or arcuate uterus. A
uterine fibroid (some of them less than 1cm in size) was seen in

10% of the women. We then persuaded nearly 300 of these women to undergo an HSG examination. The HSG identified an abnormality of the uterine cavity in 6% (and uterine fibroids in only 5%) of the women.

Of course, it must be remembered that an HSG can only help to identify submucous fibroids or large intramural fibroids big enough to indent the uterine cavity outline by their pressure. Nonetheless, the only sensible conclusion that we could draw from this research project was that in our department ultrasound is the most efficient method to diagnose anatomical abnormalities. In a single morning or afternoon we can perform 20 ultrasounds or five HSGs. They give us the same and sometimes more information than the HSG and are non-invasive and result in no complications. Furthermore, the introduction of three-dimensional US scanning has truly lived up to its name. It really adds a different dimension to imaging the shape of the uterine cavity. I have only recently had the opportunity of collaborating with a colleague from King's College Hospital, London, on this technique, but I am greatly impressed by the results. As one of my patients said to me recently after her 3-D scan – 'I felt as though I could reach out and touch my uterus, the picture was so clear.' The big difference with 3-D ultrasound is that it is possible to get an impression not just of the outlines of the uterus but also of the volume of the uterus, which is enormously valuable when assessing the potential contribution that a congenital abnormality or a fibroid is making to a woman's recurrent miscarriages.

For women whose anatomical problem requires further investigation, and in particular those women with subfertility, an HSG, laparoscopy and hysteroscopy are important to finalise the diagnosis.

Summary

Having described the various anatomical abnormalities that may be a cause of repeated miscarriages, examined the ways in which we can identify these problems and discussed the methods available to treat them, I think it is important for me to mention again that no one knows the true number of these abnormalities in the general population. All the available evidence points to the fact that a surprisingly large number of women are born with anatomical abnormalities of the uterus and in many cases they cause no problems at all. It is only if the woman experiences problems in getting pregnant (infertility) or staying pregnant (miscarriage) that these structural abnormalities are noticed.

I want to emphasise this point because it is difficult to know whether these structural abnormalities are really an important cause of recurrent miscarriage. The question that is still not answered is whether these congenital abnormalities cause recurrent miscarriages or whether they are casual associations, only identified when the woman experiences problems. If this is the case, then we run the risk of exposing many miscarriage sufferers to needless anxiety and operative procedures to 'correct' a supposed abnormality which, in truth, is just a variant of normal. Hopefully, the introduction of 3-D scans may help to resolve this problem. Doctors in this field need to ask themselves whether they are treating themselves or the patient because they are, understandably, under pressure to do something. Although the newly developed surgical techniques are likely to make a valuable contribution to the management of a few specific cases of uterine abnormality, the message for the future is really 'hands off' and instead of operating, doctors must spend the time examining the other causes of early and late miscarriage, in particular the antiphospholipid syndrome. Finally, I must state again that I believe that true cervical incompetence is a relatively rare problem.

NINE

MATERNAL DISORDERS AND ENVIRONMENTAL FACTORS CAUSING RECURRENT MISCARRIAGES

Maternal disorders

Certain maternal diseases may be the cause of recurrent miscarriages. Women who suffer from chronic kidney (renal) or liver (hepatic) failure are at greater risk of miscarrying repeatedly because the disease causes such severe metabolic and hormonal disturbances that a pregnancy cannot be supported. In the case of women being treated with dialysis, miscarriage is very common, and it is unusual for such women to have successful pregnancies. However, it should also be mentioned that fertility itself is very low in women with kidney or liver failure, and it is unusual for them to fall pregnant in the first place. As a result, the overall number of pregnancies miscarried for this reason is small.

It is interesting to note that if the woman receives a successful organ transplant, her fertility improves dramatically and she is much more likely to fall pregnant. Despite all the drugs that the transplanted woman has to take for the rest of her life, they do not increase her risk of miscarriage.

We now know that these drugs do not increase the risks of a fetal abnormality significantly, although for many years it was generally presumed that the steroids, and other immunosuppressive drugs used in these women, would cause developmental problems in their babies. I mention this point because, over the last 15 years, progress in the field of transplantation has been enormous. As a result, there are more and more young women who have undergone a successful kidney transplant and not surprisingly want to have a baby. With specialised care they can achieve their dream and need to be reassured that their risk of fetal abnormality and miscarriage is not high, although frequently their pregnancies have to be delivered early to prevent blood pressure problems in the mother and growth retardation in the baby.

It is also true that women with congenital heart problems, infection with tuberculosis or various blood disorders have an increased risk of miscarriage. Once again, it is important to remember that maternal disorders are more usually associated with problems in becoming pregnant, rather than staying pregnant. They do not make a significant contribution to the overall numbers of miscarriages. Certainly, relatively rare disorders are correspondingly rarely causes of miscarriage.

Historically, several maternal disorders used to be listed under this section, but our improved understanding of the mechanisms involved in these disorders has demonstrated that they should now be classified differently. For example, diabetes mellitus and thyroid disfunction are now more sensibly considered as potential hormonal causes of miscarriage (see Chapters 4 and 11). Diseases such as lupus and phospholipid antibody problems might once have been considered 'maternal diseases'. They are, of course, but they themselves are caused by more generalised autoimmune disorders in the mothers. Our knowledge of these autoimmune disorders – and the problems they can cause during pregnancy – has mushroomed over the last ten years, which is why, in this book, they warrant a separate chapter (Chapter 12).

Since writing the first edition of this book, we have come to realise that in addition to the phospholipid syndrome there are a lot of other factors (both inherited and acquired) which put the woman at risk of becoming more susceptible to developing blood clots in any of the blood vessels in her body, and particularly in her placental vessels, when she is pregnant. As a result, the search for pro-thrombotic risk factors has become a fast growing and very exciting area of research. Since many of the factors are inherited (genetic), I suspect that we will reclassify some of them in the future and include them in

Chapter 7. Others may find themselves back in this maternal disorders chapter and, of course, some will always remain in the immune section. In the meantime, I think it is quite difficult to know where best to describe them to the reader. I have concluded that for the time being they should stay in the autoimmune section in recognition of the fact that the phospholipid syndrome (an acquired prothrombotic defect) was the first prothrombotic abnormality to be shown to cause pregnancy loss. The potential role that the more recently identified prothrombotic abnormalities may play in miscarriage and later pregnancy problems has only started to be explored as a result of our understanding of the phospholipid syndrome.

Environmental factors

Although many environmental factors have been accused of causing miscarriages and fetal abnormalities, it is often impossible to perform studies that can accurately identify a single agent as the cause of all these reproductive problems. Numerous drugs and environmental chemicals have been shown to cause chromosomal damage in laboratory animals but there are very few data available on the effects of these agents on humans – and I doubt whether we will ever be able to produce them. Much of our human knowledge is based on 'clusters' of miscarriages that occur in a certain geographical area or in a particular workplace. Having noted the miscarriages, a search is then started for a potential cause. In this situation, control groups are often lacking and are even more difficult to recruit. As a result, allegations that a specific factor is to blame may become accepted in the minds of all the individuals involved.

It is impossible, in a single chapter, to cover all the environmental factors that have been implicated as a cause of miscarriage. I think it would be most useful for the reader if I focus on those potential causes that have been the source of the most concern and anxiety to the miscarriage patients attending my clinic. Effectively, this means a brief summary of the questions I am asked most frequently.

Alcohol

Any woman who has a heavy and regular alcohol intake will increase her risks of experiencing both early and late miscarriages. All the research data point towards the fact that the alcohol has both teratogenic (early) and toxic (later) effects on the fetus, and that this is related to the doses of alcohol taken by the mother. During the first few months of pregnancy, large quantities of alcohol can cause severe abnormalities in the development of the baby.

In alcoholic mothers, there is a distinctive pattern to these abnormalities which is known as the 'fetal alcohol abuse syndrome' (FAAS). The syndrome can be difficult to recognise in newborns and the diagnosis is made most accurately around four years of age. The main characteristics are intrauterine growth retardation followed by immediate failure to thrive after delivery and persistently poor postnatal growth below the expected milestones. There is a characterisic facial appearance which includes microcephaly (small head) and thin upper lip, short upturned nose, flattened nasal bridge and general underdevelopment of the middle of the face. There are also severe central nervous system signs seen in the newborn baby, such as irritability, hyperactivity, poor muscle tone, and poor sucking ability. At a later date the neurodevelopmental problems become evident, including attention deficit disorder, language delays and mild to moderate mental retardation.

It is important to realise here that it is the abuse of alcohol rather than any alcohol that is the culprit. It is thought that the fetal alcohol abuse syndrome affects between 0.5 and 1 case per 1000 live births, but this figure is based on studies from the United States where the incidence is very much higher than in Western Europe. Since alcohol consumption in the United States is generally much lower than in Europe, this inverse relationship between background drinking levels and the incidence of FAAS in the US has been called the 'American Paradox'. There are two additional risk factors associated with FAAS. In virtually every instance in which a child has been born with FAAS, his or her mother was noted to be a smoker and of low socioeconomic status, which suggests that poor nutritional status in these women influences the way in which the alcohol intake adversely affects the developing baby.

Some reports have also suggested that moderate regular drinking also increases the risk of miscarriage, milder fetal abnormalities and the possibility of a baby who is growth-retarded when delivered, but these data are much weaker.

It is obviously sensible to reduce your alcohol intake to a minimum during pregnancy, especially during the first three months. However, there are no data to suggest that the occasional drink is harmful in later pregnancy. Studies looking at the effects of alcohol in pregnancy are often difficult to interpret because there are many factors to confuse the result. For example, alcoholics are usually smokers as well – so how do we establish what has caused the miscarriage – smoking or drinking?

Smoking

Women who smoke cigarettes regularly during pregnancy run a greater risk of miscarriage than non-smokers. In a recent review of the effects of nicotine on the function of the ovary, uterus and placenta, cigarette smoking was shown to have a direct effect on the ability of the placenta to invade and proliferate (grow), particularly in the first three months of pregnancy. As I mentioned above, the effects of smoking are often difficult to separate from the effects of alcohol. It is also likely that the increased risk of miscarriage in smokers is in part due to the fact that women who smoke heavily during pregnancy tend to have a poorer diet. Certainly there are many reports that demonstrate that smoking in pregnancy can lead to a reduction in the supply of oxygen and nutrients delivered to the baby. Not only are these babies smaller (or lighter) than average, some of them are actually growth-retarded and suffer from developmental problems. Interestingly, the placenta in smoking mothers is significantly larger compared to non-smokers. This increase in the size and weight of the placenta is an adaptive response to the reduced oxygen available for the baby in smokers. The tree-like projections or villi, which make up the placental lobes, produce many more capillaries (tiny blood vessels) in order to increase the surface area over which oxygen can be extracted and delivered to the baby. For similar reasons, the placentae of pregnant women who live at high altitudes are also larger.

Smoking also has an adverse effect on a woman's ability to become pregnant. Valuable new information has been gained from studies of in vitro fertilisation and other assisted reproduction techniques. Smoking appears to reduce the optimal functioning of the ovary in a dose-dependent manner. It may also affect fertility via effects on the function of the fallopian tubes and uterus. Although the mechanisms are not fully understood, we have known for some time that smoking is associated with a reduced incidence of uterine fibroids, endometriosis and even uterine cancers. This suggests that smoking inhibits the ability of the uterine cells to proliferate (multiply and divide). There is no doubt that men who smoke heavily are at greater risk of having both low sperm counts and producing abnormal sperm. Quitting smoking usually improves the sperm count and motility within about three months. All in all, smoking has a very adverse effect on reproductive outcome.

Coffee

Coffee and other caffeine-containing drinks (such as tea and cola) have also been implicated as a cause of miscarriage. A recent Italian study reported that more than six cups of coffee per day was accompanied by a higher rate of miscarriage. In reality, most pregnant women seem to find coffee unpalatable, particularly in the first few months when the risk of miscarriage is greatest, so I think it is unlikely that they will be consuming large quantities. However, if you have suffered unexplained miscarriages, reducing your coffee intake may be a sensible precaution to take in your next pregnancy.

Cocaine

The use of cocaine and other illegal drugs of addiction is an established risk for early miscarriage and late pregnancy complications, such as preterm labour and placental abruption. There are also studies to suggest that marijuana and some of its derivatives (cannabinoid compounds) cause miscarriage and a slowing of embryo development. Most recently, a study from Rome looked at the enzyme which breaks down the naturally occurring (endogenous) cannabis-like substances that we all have in our bodies. The researchers showed that when the levels of this enzyme are low in our bodies the build up of endogenous cannabinoids is associated with an increased miscarriage rate. The potential power of these observations is that the development of a routine test for this enzyme may, in the future, become a useful test with which we will be able to predict the risk of miscarriage.

X-rays

There is no doubt that ionising radiation can harm the fetus if the doses are high. There have been many sad examples of the damaging effects of radiation. The lessons that we have learnt from the nuclear disasters at Hiroshima, Sellafield and Chernobyl have alerted us to the fact that exposure to radiation has immediate and long-term effects. As a result, every newly qualified doctor is concerned about the potential problems that may result from a pregnant woman undergoing X-ray investigations. I entirely approve of this concern, but it is also important to mention that if you need an X-ray while you are pregnant, it is very unlikely that it will cause any damage to your baby. The doctors looking after you will only advise you to have an X-ray if they feel it is absolutely necessary. I am often asked whether a termination of pregnancy should be offered to a woman who has had an X-ray without knowing that she was pregnant. Let me assure you that the only risk of abnormality to the baby would occur if you had had a large series of X-rays before the eighth week of pregnancy, and even then, this risk is only 0.1% (one in 1,000 cases). A single X-ray will cause no harm.

The long-term effects are a result of the damaging effects that irradiation has upon human gametes – the eggs and sperm cells. We know that men and women exposed to radiation accidents have an increased risk of producing children who develop childhood cancers. Until very recently, we also thought that this risk increased with the dose of radiation that the parent had been exposed to preconceptually (before pregnancy). This was known as the Gardner hypothesis after the scientist who first described the observation. However, in 1999 several important studies were published which cast doubts on the association between the dose of radiation exposure preconceptually and the child's susceptibility to cancer. The highest rates of childhood leukaemia and non-Hodgkins lymphoma were found in the children of men working in the radiation industry who had never been exposed to radiation before their partners became pregnant. It is still not clear what the mechanism is to account for the increase in childhoood cancers in the children of these workers and much effort is currently being put in to trying to find the answer to this important question.

Video Display Units (VDUs)

I receive a lot of anxious enquiries from patients who fear that VDUs may be the cause of miscarriages. Let me reassure you that using a VDU will not cause you to miscarry. Nor is there any association between VDU usage and birth defects in babies. The concerns that have been expressed during the last ten years about VDUs have led to several large research studies being carried out. It is reassuring for everyone that all of these studies have concluded that VDUs do not increase the risk of miscarriage. The studies have also demonstrated that even if your job demands that you work in front of a VDU screen for long periods of time each day, you are not at risk.

Microwaves, electromagnetic fields and radios

Many homes and workplaces now have microwave ovens and I am regularly shown newspaper and magazine articles suggesting that they may cause problems during pregnancy. There is absolutely no scientific data to support these 'scare reports' and the reader can rest assured that the only way to deal with these articles is to treat them with a large pinch of salt. Similarly, there have been one or two articles suggesting that miscarriage and other problems in pregnancy are more common in women who live in the vicinity of electrical substations, electromagnetic fields and radio stations. There is nothing to support these allegations, but they have certainly been the source of considerable anxiety. Ignore them!

Ultrasound

I am often asked whether ultrasound can cause damage to a pregnancy. Following the publication of several large studies which have looked at this issue carefully (see Chapter 7, 'Ultrasound screening') I feel confident in stating firmly that US causes no problems for either mother or baby.Low frequency ultrasound is used in manufacturing watches and fine tools. There are a few reports suggesting that female employees in this field experience more headaches and episodes of vertigo (dizziness). There has never been any suggestion that low frequency ultrasound can cause miscarriage. The ultrasound used to perform obstetric scans is of high frequency.

Over the last few years there have been several 'scare' stories reported in the newspapers suggesting that repeated ultrasound scans during pregnancy may cause damage to the developing baby. Laboratory experiments have suggested that US waves may cause changes in the membranes (covering layers) of cells that potentially could affect the development of the embryo and later growth of the fetus in utero. There are no scientific data to support these assertions and, importantly, a large Swedish study has recently been published which has concluded that there is no association between multiple pregnancy US scans and the later occurrence of childhood leukaemia. Several other large studies looking at the follow-up of babies scanned on many occasions during complicated pregnancies have demonstrated that there are no serious developmental abnormalities in these babies. Indeed, the only difference that I am aware of between pregnancies that are scanned regularly and those that are not, is that a recent Scandinavian study reported an increase in the number of left-handed babies born to the mothers who had received multiple scans. The fear here was that the sound waves had in some way interfered with the development of the baby. Some people may argue that being left-handed is an advantage in life – it is certainly not a disadvantage!

Many women are anxious that vaginal ultrasound probes may cause them to bleed, or aggravate a pregnancy that is threatening to miscarry. This is not true, and avoiding a vaginal scan may obstruct the vital monitoring of your pregnancy.

Hazards in the workplace for women during pregnancy

Over the last few years, I have given several lectures to industrial employers about the potential hazards that pregnant women may encounter at work. This is because the number of women working during pregnancy has increased markedly during the last 30 years. Employers are much more conscious that they must protect women in the workplace from being exposed to physical stresses and toxins that could have an effect on their ability to conceive and the outcome of their pregnancy. I have already mentioned VDUs and X-rays. All radiographers have to wear protective lead jackets when they are in contact with X-rays, whether they are male or female. It is common for female radiographers to be moved to other duties in their department when they are pregnant, although the risks to their baby are negligible because of the strict rules that apply at all times for these workers to protect them from radiation exposure. Other potential hazards for pregnant women at work can be summarised into three broad groups – physical, chemical and biological stresses.

Physical stresses
We know that severe fatigue (tiredness) can be associated with an increase in the risk of miscarriage, premature delivery and low birth weight babies. It can also increase anxiety, stress and the risks of high blood pressure. By fatigue, I mean the physical tiredness of lifting heavy loads, excessively long working hours and long periods of standing.

The reader might be interested, at this point, to learn about the origins of maternity leave. At the end of the last century, a French obstetrician called Adolphe Pinard (the metal ear trumpet used to listen to the baby's heartbeat was named after him) noticed that women who worked in the laundry in his district in Paris had a high risk of premature delivery. He reasoned that this was related to the hard work involved in beating the laundry on the banks of the River Seine.

Dr Pinard persuaded the laundry owners to excuse pregnant woman from the most tiring duties after they reached 32 weeks (I presume that they had to do the ironing rather than the beating and the mangling). As a result, these laundry workers delivered their babies at term. In his treatise, which was published in 1895, he commented that if the laundry workers were excused hard physical work towards the end of their pregnancies the outcome of their pregnancy was as good as the wealthier folk whom he also looked after and who did no work at all. Dr Pinard's observations were the first steps towards the introduction of maternity leave for all pregnant women in the Western world.

Interestingly, one century later, European studies have revisited the association of hard physical work and the risk of preterm delivery and miscarriage in pregnant women. The conclusions are rather different and they suggest that it is not just hard physical effort but the lower socio-economic status of the pregnant woman that determines her being at greater risk of premature birth and pregnancy loss. Presumably this is because of poorer nutrition, the greater likelihood that she smokes, lower take-up of the antenatal services that are offered in our hospitals and other factors that we do not yet fully understand. These studies have fuelled the effort in the UK to encourage employers to provide comprehensive information to their female pregnant workforce about the importance of diet and avoiding smoking. The Tommy's Campaign has actually set up a Pregnancy Accreditation Scheme for UK employers which lays out the optimal requirements for pregnant women in the workplace. As an adviser to this scheme I am happy to report that there are many companies and organisations, both privately and state funded, that have expressed an interest in signing up to this scheme and have, as a result, made significant improvements in the facilities that they provide for pregnant and breast-feeding women in the workplace.

Chemical hazards

There are many toxic chemicals that can affect a woman's reproductive performance. Our knowledge that occupational exposure to lead metal can cause miscarriages, stillbirth and infertility has led to lead levels being carefully regulated in the UK. Mercury is a very toxic organic metal which is widely used in the process of gold extraction. Heavy mercury pollution is found in the air, rivers and fish in the goldfields of Brazil, where many of the pregnancy and childhood studies have been carried out. During pregnancy the mothers absorb the mercury through their gut, which then accumulates in the placenta and can enter the fetal blood circulation, causing growth retardation and brain damage. The mercury is later excreted in breast milk and, since it then accumulates in the newborn's brain, leads to behavioural disorders and mental retardation.

Some types of mercury (inorganic mercury) have been used in dental amalgam (fillings) for 150 years. Concerns have been raised that the mercury vapour, which is released in small quantities during the placement or removal of amalgam, could be harmful to dental workers and their assistants. It is obviously sensible to reduce exposure to any vapour or compound but the reports that dentistry workers are at greater risk of subfertility and menstrual problems have never been confirmed. Theoretically, the removal or placement of fillings in a pregnant woman could allow mercury vapour to cross the placenta and affect the baby's brain, as noted above. However, a recent directive from the Department of Health on the safety of dental amalgam concluded that there was no evidence of any harm being caused to the fetus. Nonetheless, the advice offered was that women should avoid having amalgam fillings during pregnancy. I must add here that they were also advised that there was absolutely no need to have fillings removed before pregnancy. I mention this point because several of my miscarriage and subfertility patients have told me that they have rushed off to have all their amalgam fillings extracted and replaced with ceramic alternatives. This can be a costly procedure so before you consider it do remember that there is no data to implicate amalgam as a real cause of pregnancy loss.

Carbon monoxide gas, produced by coal and gas fires and smoking cigarettes, crosses the placenta and may lead to the baby receiving less oxygen. Ethylene oxide, which is used to ripen fruit, has been shown to increase the risk of miscarriage, so wash your fruit carefully before eating it.

A wide variety of solvents used in manufacturing industries can be the cause of miscarriages if pregnant women are overly exposed to them during their work. Fat-soluble organic solvents can cross the placental barrier and inhaling these compounds may lead to pregnancy problems. Health-care professionals and workers in the clothing and textile industries are the most likely to experience exposure. A recent Canadian study looked at a very large cross-section of women working in factories, laboratories, pharmacies, dry cleaners, garages, funeral parlours, carpentry workshops and artists' studios to name but a few! They found that hydrocarbons, phenols, trichloroethylene, xylene, vinyl chloride, acetone and related compounds were the most common solvent exposures. The study showed that the incidence of congenital abnormalities was increased among the pregnant women exposed to organic solvents during pregnancy but only in those women who described symptoms of exposure. This suggests that the potentially damaging effects of these solvents may be avoided if employers provide well-ventilated working premises and if pregnant women are vigilant about wearing protective clothing and avoiding areas at work where they can smell chemicals. Miscarriages were also more frequent in the women exposed to organic solvents, together with an increase in babies with low birth weight, premature delivery, fetal distress in labour and neonatal complications.

Vinyl chloride can also increase the risk of miscarriage in the wives or partners of male workers (plasterers, for example), if they are exposed to contaminated clothing. The same is true for pesticides used by agricultural workers.

Surgery and anaesthesia

As many as 2% of all pregnant women undergo surgery and anaesthesia during pregnancy and so it is not surprising that many patients ask about the potential risks both of the operation and of the anaesthetic drugs that are used. The safety of surgery in pregnancy is difficult to estimate because there are so many factors that need to be taken into consideration. What is certain is that no doctor is going to suggest that you have an operation whilst you are pregnant unless it is absolutely necessary. However, if you do have the misfortune to need an operation in early pregnancy the chances of you miscarrying will be determined by the type of operation you have to have, your underlying problem, your stress levels, whether you have a fever and possibly by the anaesthetic agent. Abdominal surgery after the pregnancy has reached the second trimester is generally considered to be safer than surgery carried out earlier in pregnancy. However, I suspect this just reflects the fact that the vast majority of miscarriages occur before the end of the first trimester of pregnancy. It is impossible to establish whether a miscarriage occurring to a woman who has to have an operation early in pregnancy was caused by the surgery or whether it would have happened anyway. Abdominal surgery in the third trimester of pregnancy increases the risk of making the uterus irritable, which may lead to threatened preterm labour. If you do have to have an abdominal operation in late pregnancy it is likely that the doctors will give you some tocolytic (uterus quietening) drugs to reduce the chance of this complication occurring.

Doctors and nurses working with anti-cancer drugs have an increased risk of miscarriage if they do not use protective gloves when they are administering the drugs. Anaesthetic gases have also been implicated as a cause of miscarriage and of low birth weight babies amongst anaesthetists and operating department staff. However, these data are not very strong or convincing and, perhaps most importantly, date back to a time when ventilation and scavenger systems in hospitals and dental operating rooms were not nearly as efficient as they are today.

Biological hazards

Many biological agents can affect a baby if the mother is infected during pregnancy. Many of these infectious organisms are mentioned in Chapters 4 and 10. In most cases, the risk of infection for a woman at work is no greater than the general risk of contracting the infection in the community. However, there are some women at greater risk of infections during pregnancy, such as laboratory, health care and nursery workers. I have already discussed the importance of women who are exposed to animals and animal products when they are pregnant (Chapter 4).

Male hazards

It is important to remember that it is not just women who are exposed to environmental hazards that can affect reproduction. Men who work with lead, certain chemicals such as hydrocarbons and steel welders may develop sperm problems leading to subfertility. The declining sperm counts that have been noted in European countries over the last decade are not fully understood. However, it is thought that a variety of pollutants, including a steady increase in the quantities of oestrogen hormone in our water supplies, may be the culprits.

It has also been suggested that there is an increased risk of premature labour in the female partners of men who work in the glass, clay, stone, textile and mining industries. Further studies are needed to confirm these observations. What is certain, is that the children of men who have been exposed to radiation leaks are at risk of developing leukaemia.

Summary

Many maternal disorders and environmental factors have been blamed for causing miscarriages and later problems in pregnancy. The reader will have noticed that many of these factors are difficult to research properly. The mother's age, her social habits, socio-economic status and previous pregnancy history all have a contribution to make and if she is exposed before or during pregnancy to a potential toxin, the dose and the timing of exposure appear to be critically important in determining whether problems result.

The most useful advice I can offer to miscarriage sufferers is to resist the temptation of interpreting scary newspaper and magazine articles as medical fact. The stories that sell newspapers are not necessarily representative of the scientific truth. Take comfort from the fact that pregnant woman are treated as very special people in our society. No employer wants to risk exposing them to agents that could cause them harm. Many of the industrial regulations that are in practice today are over-protective, but it is as well that they remain in force.

TEN

INFECTIOUS CAUSES OF RECURRENT MISCARRIAGE

For many years, doctors have suspected that infections are a major cause of premature labour and miscarriages. I am certain that they are, and some of the latest research into miscarriages suggests that a genetic predisposition to infection (only detectable with the use of sophisticated molecular biological techniques) has a significant part to play in determining whether a baby in utero develops an infection or can fight it off. Until these molecular techniques have been fully explored, we can only try to identify specific infective organisms that could realistically be the cause of recurrent miscarriages.

It is important to remember that a germ capable of causing repeated miscarriages is an unusual beast. It needs to be able to persist for long periods of time, and to produce minimal symptoms in order to escape diagnosis. After being diagnosed, it then has to be resistant to treatment with twenty-first-century drugs or, alternatively, be able to reinfect the woman after the treatment has been stopped. I know of very few germs capable of all these feats.

The medical textbooks still advise doctors to perform a TORCH screen for women who have suffered repeated miscarriages. The problem with TORCH screens is that they provide us with very little useful information with which to help and advise the miscarriage sufferer. When one of the tests in the screen is positive, much distress and anxiety results, although the positive result is usually caused by high levels of antibodies in the woman's blood. This occurs because she has been exposed to an infection in the past and, in most cases, is therefore immune (protected) from future infections. Nevertheless, one of the main aims of this book is to provide you, the reader, with accurate information so that you can make up your own mind as to whether test A, B or C may help you. I therefore feel that a brief discussion about TORCH screening needs to be included.

T stands for toxoplasma – and in Chapter 4 we looked at how this organism can only infect a fetus during the course of the mother's first infection. So, by definition, toxoplasmosis cannot be a cause of recurrent miscarriage. There is one exception to this rule and that is when toxoplasma complicates a pregnancy in a woman whose immune system is suppressed, for example after a kidney or liver transplant.

O does not stand for any bug but conveniently makes up the TORCH acronym. In my reckoning, O ought to stand for 'other', because I hope that in the future we will be able to identify other organisms and other inherited immune problems in both the mother and the father.

R stands for rubella, and as the reader will have realised after reading Chapter 4, a mother infected with German measles produces an antibody response during her first infection which protects her against future infections with the rubella virus.

C stands for cytomegalovirus (CMV) and since CMV can be reactivated in certain situations, it is possible that CMV infection is the cause of some recurrent episodes of miscarriage. (CMV infection is discussed in detail below.)

H stands for herpes and, once again, Chapter 4 showed that maternal herpes virus infections only affect the fetus during the first herpes infection, although the mother may experience repeated episodes herself.

Viral infections which may cause recurrent miscarriages

Some viral infections, such as cytomegalovirus (CMV) can be reactivated. This means that a second episode of CMV infection can be triggered off, under certain circumstances. However, this is very rare and probably only ever occurs in women whose immune system is compromised. For example, those women who are taking immunosuppressive or cytotoxic drugs, such as steroids and anti-cancer drugs. Some viruses persist in the mother's body and remain infective. The classic example of this is the human immunodeficiency virus (HIV). Since both of these viruses are possible causes of recurrent miscarriage, they are discussed here.

Cytomegalovirus infection in pregnancy

CMV is one of the herpes group of viruses and is usually acquired by close physical contact or by infected blood, urine or secretions of saliva and breast milk. In industrialised countries such as the UK, as many as 50% of women have never had an infection with CMV. The maternal infection is usually mild, with fever, sickness, enlarged lymph nodes and an abnormal white blood cell count – it is frequently unrecognised. During pregnancy, 1% of these susceptible women (one in 200) will acquire their first (primary) CMV infection. Among these 200 women, the CMV virus will probably be transmitted to the fetus in 40% of cases, which potentially involves one in 80 of the babies born to affected mothers. Babies born with congenital CMV infection are at risk of mental retardation, but the number of affected babies is very small.

At-risk groups, such as hospital, laboratory staff and nursery workers, need to take simple aseptic precautions such as careful handwashing. At the present time there is no specific treatment available for confirmed cases but this is likely to change in the future with the development of more sophisticated anti-viral agents. If you suffer a CMV infection during your pregnancy, the chance of it causing a severe problem for your baby is very small. In the UK, a proven CMV infection is not considered a valid reason for suggesting a termination of pregnancy.

Human Immunodeficiency Virus (HIV)

We know that HIV can be passed on (transmitted) to the baby in utero. Most of the available data concerns the risk of vertical transmission (the direct passage of the virus from mother to baby during pregnancy and immediately after delivery). The results of several European studies have now been published and have shown that approximately 13% of mothers with HIV infection transmit the virus to their babies during the course of their pregnancy. If the mother is delivered by caesarean section, the transmission rate is much lower, suggesting that an important risk factor is the passage of infected blood from mother to baby at the time of delivery. Perhaps just as important is the exposure of the baby to vaginal secretions during delivery. Certainly, the risk of HIV transmission to the firstborn twin delivered vaginally is greater than the risk to the second twin. In the last few years, antiviral drugs such as zidovudine have been given to pregnant HIV positive women near to the time of delivery. These drugs may be given as single agents or as combinations/cocktails of drugs. Their use has achieved a further dramatic reduction in the risk of vertical transmission of HIV from mother to baby. We also know that HIV positive mothers who breast feed their babies are more likely to transmit the infection than if they bottle feed their babies.

In the Western world, there is now a trend towards delivering HIV positive mothers by caesarean section, after giving them several weeks of antiviral drugs and advising them to avoid breast feeding. Sadly, these measures are not practical or affordable for pregnant women in Third World countries where the prevalence of HIV is much higher. For example, in sub-Saharan Africa, babies who are bottle fed have a much higher risk of dying from gastroenteritis, and since the diarrhoea, vomiting and consequent dehydration claim an enormous number of infant lives, breast milk offers them the best chance of surviving the first few months of their lives.

At the present time there are no good prospective studies which have looked at the passage of the HIV virus at other times during pregnancy. For example, we do not know how many HIV positive mothers transmit their infection to their tiny babies during the first trimester of pregnancy. Without this information, it is impossible to say whether this virus increases the risk of sporadic or recurrent miscarriage. I suspect that this missing information will become available to us quite soon. The new drug therapies available for HIV positive women have significantly improved the lifespan of these women. As the survival intervals increase further, so will the number of women who embark on a pregnancy after their HIV status is known. However, at the present time, all that we can conclude is that since the infection is persistent, the HIV virus is an organism capable of causing recurrent miscarriage.

Bacteria and other micro-organisms

Syphilis

Syphilis is a proven infectious cause of recurrent miscarriage. Fortunately, it is now a rare cause in developed countries because all pregnant women are screened for the infection at their first antenatal clinic visit. Some doctors question whether it should be looked for routinely these days. I would argue that it is very important to do so because the infection is easily diagnosed and successfully treated with penicillin antibiotics. If it is missed, two patients – the mother and the baby – will suffer unnecessary problems. Although relatively few cases are found, I think syphilis deserves a special mention here since the incidence has increased as a result of HIV infection and other sexually transmitted diseases.

In the days when syphilis was common and untreated, this infection caused a lot of miscarriages. Syphilis is referred to in the French literature of the last century as 'la plus grande avorteuse' (the greatest abortionist). The organism is called a spirochaete and its proper name is treponema pallidum. Syphilis is spread by sexual contact. It crosses the placenta and the risk of miscarriage and congenital infection is greatest soon after the mother becomes infected. When the mother is infected shortly before conception, the baby is invariably affected and the likeliest outcome is miscarriage. If she becomes infected during the first trimester of pregnancy, the risk of miscarriage is lower, but congenital infection and abnormalities in the baby are still a big problem. Typical features in the newborn baby are an enlarged liver and spleen, pneumonia, anaemia, jaundice, retarded growth, snuffles, skin ulcers and bone problems.

Many textbooks still state that the syphilis germ cannot cross the placenta until 16 weeks of gestation. This is not true, but the reason for this misunderstanding is interesting. Many years ago it was noted that mothers who were treated for syphilis before 16 weeks delivered babies who appeared not to have the obvious pointers of congenital syphilis. We now realise that a baby's immmune system is not capable of mounting the special inflammatory response – the characteristic skin lesions of syphilis – until about 16 weeks of gestation. However, the organisms can be found in the body of the fetus long before this date.

Streptococcus B

This bug is present in the vagina of one in ten women during pregnancy. Unlike the streptococcus A, the B strain is quite resistant to the acid environment of the vagina and grows well in amniotic fluid. In many women, the streptococcus B bacteria cause no harm, but if the woman experiences a premature rupture of the membranes, this streptococcus can infect the amniotic fluid and the premature baby, causing a severe infection. Respiratory difficulties are the biggest problem in premature babies and male babies are more susceptible to the infection than female babies. The infection of the baby can occur during the vaginal delivery and may result in pneumonia and sometimes meningitis.

The reason why I have included a brief paragraph about this infection in a book concerned with miscarriages is that some women with a history of late miscarriages appear to be chronic carriers of the streptococcus B. I have met several women in my miscarriage clinic who have had repeated problems with streptococcus B and it leads me to wonder whether this organism is actually capable of causing the premature rupture of membranes, as well as infecting the amniotic fluid after the membranes have ruptured. If an infection is suspected at any stage during pregnancy, because of a past history of the problem, or because the pregnant woman has developed a vaginal discharge, it is important that vaginal swabs are taken promptly to look for the streptococci. If the infection is confirmed, it should be treated promptly with penicillin antibiotics. In some obstetric units, all premature babies are given penicillin antibiotics prophylactically.

A new method for detecting streptococcus B has just been identified. It is called the rapid PCR (polymerase chain reaction assay) and takes just a few hours to perform and report the results. It has been shown to provide reliable results in pregnant women in labour both before and after the membranes have ruptured – which is the strength of the technique. The test accurately identifies pregnant women carrying the bacterium at the time of delivery, which means that it will no longer be necessary to screen at risk antenatal women repeatedly before they go into labour and, most importantly, will avoid the use of prophylactic antibiotics for at risk women and will allow us to prescribe treatment for those women who are actually carrying the infection at the time that they labour – which is when their babies are at risk.

Mycoplasma and ureaplasma

If you have already done some reading about the infective causes of recurrent miscarriage, you will have noticed that so far, I have made no mention of mycoplasma or ureaplasma infections. These organisms are very common and are found in the vagina or cervix of as many as 70% of all women who are sexually active. During the first trimester of pregnancy, they can be identified by vaginal and cervical swabs in many women. They are of low virulence and do not usually cause an obvious discharge or infection, although they are an occasional cause of postpartum fevers. Because these organisms are so common and can often be cultured in miscarriage tissues, it has been suggested that they may be a cause of sporadic miscarriage. However, prospective studies have compared the miscarriage rate in women with and without mycoplasma and ureaplasma organisms before conception and during the first few months of pregnancy, and they have not detected any increase in the number of sporadic miscarriages.

Since these organisms are so often found in the vagina and cervix, it has also been suggested that they may be the cause of some recurrent miscarriages because they set up a low grade inflammation in the endometrial lining of the uterus (chronic endometritis). Certainly, chronic endometritis is an important cause of repeated miscarriages in animals. Based on this theory, one study in the late 1970s looked at the effect of treating women sufferers with tetracycline antibiotics before they became pregnant (tetracycline must never be given to pregnant women because this antibiotic causes the teeth and the bones of the baby to turn green). Although the live birth rate was said to increase with antibiotic treatment, no control groups were included and later studies did not confirm any advantage.

This type of treatment was never generally adopted because it did not take long for doctors to realise that using an antibiotic like tetracycline (a 'broad spectrum' antibiotic – meaning that it can be used against a wide variety of infections) meant that other organisms present in the vagina would be prevented from growing too. Many of these organisms are necessary to keep the vaginal environment healthy and if broad spectrum antibiotics are used routinely, they can cause more infective problems than they solve. I am sure that most women reading this book can remember an occasion when they have developed a vaginal thrush infection after taking penicillin antibiotics for an infection somewhere else in their body.

Bacterial vaginosis

More recently, it has been recognised that a vaginal infection called bacterial vaginosis is an important risk factor for premature rupture of the membranes and preterm labour. It is of interest to the readers of this book, since we have noted in previous chapters that the difference between a preterm labour and a late miscarriage is often a grey area. If bacterial vaginosis can be the cause of some premature labours at 26 weeks of gestation, it is logical to consider that the same problem may be the cause of some late miscarriages, say at 22 weeks of gestation.

Bacterial vaginosis (BV) is a condition in which the normal vaginal organisms (which are predominantly lactobacilli) are replaced by anaerobic bacteria, the most common of which are gardnerella vaginalis and mycoplasma hominis. The vaginal secretions become more alkaline or less acidic, as the numbers of lactobacilli decrease and the numbers of anaerobic bacteria increase. The resultant vaginal discharge has a characteristic fishy smell. Bacterial vaginosis is best diagnosed not by culturing swabs but by looking at a smear taken from the top of the vagina at either side of the cervix (in the fornices). The smear of discharge is placed on to a microscope slide and fixed in methyl alcohol. The slides are then stained with Grams stain and examined under the microscope. The smears are graded – I (normal), II (intermediate) and III (bacterial vaginosis) – based on the presence or the absence of the lactobacilli and the numbers of anaerobic bacteria in the smear. The finding of a grade III smear is an indication for offering treatment with antibiotics.

We need to do a lot more research about the triggers that cause bacterial vaginosis. We know that Afro-Caribbean women, smokers and women who use antiseptics when bathing have a greater chance of developing the infection, but this does not explain why bacterial vaginosis develops. Several studies have shown that bacterial vaginosis increases the risk of premature rupture of the membranes and premature delivery. Since prematurity is the most important cause of neonatal mortality and bacterial vaginosis can be successfully treated with antibiotics such as clindamycin or metranidazole, it was obviously important to find out whether antibiotic treatment for bacterial vaginosis can prevent premature delivery.

Two large studies have now been performed to answer this question. They have both come to the same conclusion – namely, that antibiotic treatment for bacterial vaginosis infection during pregnancy is not effective in preventing preterm births. However, the first study, which was carried out in Australia, found that the antibiotic treatment did help a subgroup of pregnant women with bacterial vaginosis who had previously had a premature delivery. This finding raises the possibility that there must be other factors acting together with the infection which result in a woman with bacterial vaginosis going into premature labour. The second study, which has only just been published and was carried out in the United States, did not find this association with previous preterm delivery. So we are still in the dark about how we should manage bacterial vaginosis infections in pregnancy. What we do know now is that the predictive value of a positive test in early pregnancy is poor and it is important that we do not give pregnant women unnecessary drug treatment in the light of the knowledge that it is not going to affect their pregnancy outcome – at least in terms of the risk of premature delivery.

The possibility that bacterial vaginosis is a cause of infertility and early pregnancy loss has also been studied. In infertility patients undergoing IVF treatment it has been shown that bacterial vaginosis present at the time of the treatment cycle does not affect the chances of conception. However, one study has suggested that after achieving a positive pregnancy test the risk of very early miscarriage was increased twofold. In this study, early pregnancies included biochemical pregnancies as well as pregnancies visible on early US scans. The authors suggested that this could be because the bacterial vaginosis causes endometritis (inflammation of the womb lining) which could adversely affect implantation and early embryo development. Of course, these findings could be due to the abnormally high oestrogen levels present in women who are undergoing ovarian stimulation, IVF and embryo transfer. Whichever, since the outcome of IVF treatment is unaffected by the presence of BV it is important to understand that screening and treating women before IVF treatment is not just unnecessary but may also be disadvantageous, since the use of antibiotics will encourage the growth of antibiotic-resistant organisms which may then become introduced into the embryo culture system as a result of the vaginal egg collection procedure. Further studies are needed to see whether the same observations about BV can be made in naturally occurring pregnancies.

Research carried out several years ago at the recurrent miscarriage clinic at St Mary's showed that about 20% of women with a history of late miscarriages have BV infection, compared to only 9% of women with a history of early miscarriages only – a similar figure to the incidence of BV in the general population. What we did not know, and needed to find out, was whether treating the infection at an early stage was useful, or whether bacterial vaginosis can recolonise (redevelop) at a later stage and would therefore require repeated courses of antibiotic treatment. So we went on to follow these women through their next pregnancies to see whether bacterial vaginosis infection in early pregnancy continues throughout the pregnancy. The results were disappointing. Some women went on to develop normal smear tests and others continued to have evidence of BV. An even larger group seemed to chop and change their test results throughout pregnancy. In short, the study demonstrated that recurrent late miscarriage patients, found to be positive for bacterial vaginosis in early pregnancy were unlikely to have the infection present later in pregnancy or at the time of delivery. Faced with all of the above study results it would be difficult to tell a pregnant woman with a history of late recurrent miscarriage that screening for bacterial vaginosis and treating any infection present will be the answer to her problems. The search for infective organisms that are a real cause of late miscarriage continues.

Future developments

In the opening paragraph of this chapter, I mentioned that there is considerable interest in the possibility that inherited immune deficiencies may cause miscarriage. The research is in its very early stages, so it is important that I do not mislead the reader or offer them false hopes for the future. Nonetheless, the concept is an exciting one and a brief summary of the evidence available at the time of writing this chapter may prove useful.

A human being's ability to mount an appropriate defensive action against a foreign invader is very complex. Doubtless, it is designed this way, involving many different mechanisms, in order that we are successful in doing so and do not succumb to life-threatening infections. Recently, it has been found that a mutation (abnormality) in the gene which is in charge of producing a certain protein (mannose binding protein, or MBP) results in low levels of this protein in the blood. A low MBP level in some infants makes them susceptible to severe infections during the first few years of their lives. Interestingly, there is also some evidence to suggest that some couples who experience recurrent miscarriages have low levels of MBP in their blood, when compared to couples with a normal pregnancy history. Although only a theory at the present time, it is possible that these couples pass on to their fetus a double dose of the MBP mutation, which makes their fetus susceptible to overwhelming infection while still in utero.

We have been researching this possibility in the miscarriage clinic at St Mary's by taking blood samples from both parents and, using molecular techniques, looking for the MBP gene mutations. If we can show that a mutation is more common in these couples, we will then be able to extend the research by trying to identify the in utero infections that may be associated with this inherited immune deficiency. Of course, there is a long way to go before this type of research can be translated into a potential treatment. Nevertheless, if you have visited the clinic recently, you will have been asked for a blood sample towards this research project. At the present time, the data do not show that this genetic mutation is more common in recurrent miscarriage couples than in couples with several successful pregnancies. However, there is a suggestion that the MBP mutation is present more frequently in women who have had a previous premature delivery. This may be another piece of evidence to support the hypothesis mentioned earlier in this chapter, that it is not just the presence of a bug that causes preterm labour to start. Instead, several adverse factors have to be working together to allow the bug to get a hold and one likely candidate is the capability of the host (mother's) immune system to deal with the problem.

As I have mentioned on many occasions throughout this book, it is only possible to improve the future outlook for miscarriage sufferers by pushing the research forward. Today's research test may be the new investigation of tomorrow, or more realistically, of next year.

ELEVEN

RECURRENT MISCARRIAGE – HORMONAL CAUSES

An abnormality of the hormones is often the underlying cause of many cases of recurrent miscarriage. In Chapter 4 we discussed the fact that getting pregnant and staying pregnant is dependent upon a complex hormonal jigsaw puzzle and we looked in some detail at the hormonal events which occur during a normal menstrual cycle leading up to a pregnancy. (The reader might find a quick look back to this section of Chapter 4 useful at this point.)

We noted that ovulation, implantation and the early stages of pregnancy require an intricate hormonal (endocrine) environment, which is very finely tuned and has the potential to go wrong at many different stages. Of course, in many cases of sporadic miscarriage, the hormonal imbalance resulting in a miscarriage is a one-off event and is unlikely to be repeated. In this chapter we need to look at those hormonal problems which are likely to be a recurrent cause of pregnancy loss. Strange as it may seem, I think it is fair to say that of all the proposed causes of miscarriage, hormonal factors have been the most studied and yet they remain the most controversial.

Diabetes

Some of this controversy is historical. Not unreasonably, any long-standing (chronic) hormonal problem was considered to be a potential cause of miscarriage. Since women who are diabetic continue to be diabetic, they were thought to be at risk of repeated miscarriages because the problem was present in each of their pregnancies. We now know that well-controlled diabetes is not an important cause of miscarriage. But if you are diabetic and your diabetes is poorly controlled, then you do have a higher risk of miscarriage. You will also be at risk of developing a serious fetal abnormality, which is why it is very important that your sugar levels are well controlled at the time you become pregnant and during the pregnancy. Fortunately there is a very good blood test called glycosylated haemoglobin A1c that assesses how well the glucose levels in your body have been controlled over the last few months. When the HbA1c levels are high they reflect the fact that your sugars have been out of control many weeks before and this test therefore gives us some idea as to whether the tiny embryo has been exposed to a potential danger. On the other hand, if the HbA1c levels are normal this is reassuring and also helps to give the diabetic mother confidence that she is controlling her sugar levels well despite the added complication of being pregnant.

Women with poorly controlled diabetes may also experience problems in becoming pregnant and this is probably because the high glucose levels cause a break-up (fragmentation) and hence a reduction in the cells that make up the tiny embryo, which occurs before the embryo has even had a chance to try to implant in the uterine lining. The newest molecular biology techniques have also allowed us to see that high glucose levels encourage the normal process of programmed cell death to become unbalanced. Instead of there being a careful balance between cells that are being protected and cells that are being allowed to die, the cell-death-promoting pathways go into overdrive in the tiny embryo. I am conscious of the fact that all this scientific detail sounds a bit frightening. However, I have included it in this edition because so many of my patients have asked me about the mechanisms involved over the last couple of years.

Once again I want to emphasise that if your diabetes is well controlled, you are no more likely to miscarry than a non-diabetic, and it is very unlikely that you will need any help in becoming pregnant.

We recently performed an audit of all the patients attending our recurrent miscarriage clinic over the last five years, looking specifically at whether they had any history of diabetes or gestational diabetes. Gestational diabetes is a type of diabetes which is induced by pregnancy, but which usually disappears when the baby is delivered. We found that the incidence of diabetes in this large group of several thousand recurrent miscarriage sufferers is significantly less than the incidence in the general population. This study confirmed my belief – based on practical experience – that diabetes is never first diagnosed when a woman presents herself at a recurrent miscarriage clinic. In my view, screening for previously undiagnosed (occult) diabetes in women with recurrent miscarriage, by performing glucose tolerance tests, is invariably unhelpful and can no longer be justified financially.

Thyroid problems

For similar reasons, screening recurrent miscarriage sufferers for previously undiagnosed thyroid disease is not a helpful exercise. Although abnormalities of the thyroid gland may be a cause of infertility (both overactive and underactive thyroids may result in difficulties for a woman who is trying to become pregnant), I have rarely met a recurrent miscarrier in whom I have diagnosed thyroid disease which was unrecognised before then. The clinic audit that I mentioned in the previous paragraph also included a search for thyroid abnormalities. The results showed that thyroid abnormalities were no more common among recurrent miscarriers than in the normal female population, of whom about 3% have established thyroid disorders.

Recurrent miscarriage patients do seem to have a greater tendency for the presence of thyroid auto-antibodies in their blood. For some time now, it has been suggested that the finding of these antibodies may be a way to identify women who have undiagnosed thyroid disease, may be at risk of developing a future problem with their thyroid gland, or alternatively may be at greater risk of miscarriage.

None of these suggestions, however, has stood up to research testing. Having screened several thousand women visiting our miscarriage clinic for the presence or absence of thyroid antibodies, I am now in a position to say that their risk of future miscarriage is not dependent on their thyroid antibodies. It is true that they do have an increased incidence of thyroid antibodies (both the thyroid microsmal and thyroglobulin types) but this does not correlate with abnormal thyroid function testing. We did find a few women with very high levels of antibodies who theoretically may be at risk of developing an underactive thyroid in the future. We advised these women to have their thyroid function checked on a regular basis in the future and to watch out for any symptoms of an underactive thyroid. However, the number of women that fell into this category was so small that I certainly could not suggest that thyroid antibody tests should be used as a routine investigation in the clinic.

We also used to think that the presence, or the development, of these thyroid auto-antibodies was an indication that the woman was more likely to also have the antiphospholipid syndrome (see Chapter 12). Indeed, we used to use the thyroid antibody result as a prompt to look carefully (and repeatedly) for the presence of antiphospholipid antibodies, either the LA (lupus anticoagulant) or ACA (anticardiolipin antibodies). As we will see in the next chapter, making a diagnosis of antiphospholipid syndrome is one of the most useful ways of improving a woman's chances of a successful pregnancy.

Certainly, antiphospholipid antibodies are more prevalent among women with recurrent miscarriage compared to the normal pregnant population and are thought to arise because of abnormal autoimmune activation. However, we now know that there is no direct correlation or link between thyroid antibodies and antiphospholipid antibodies. The recent studies at the St Mary's clinic identified that the percentage of thyroid antibodies was the same among phospholipid antibody negative and phospholipid positive recurrent miscarriers. It seems therefore that different autoimmune abnormalities are responsible for the development of thyroid and phospholipid antibodies.

In summary, being thyroid antibody positive does not increase the risk of miscarrying in a future pregnancy for women with a history of recurrent pregnancy loss. Our clinic has now abandoned routine screening for thyroid antibodies since it offers our patients no practical benefits.

Progesterone deficiency

We have known for over 40 years that progesterone hormone is essential for the maintenance of early pregnancy. Progesterone is produced by the ovary in the corpus luteum – this is the follicle which still contains cells and is left behind in the ovary after the egg has been released (see Chapter 4 for details). In the 1970s a scientist called Csapo performed some very delicate animal experiments and showed that if the corpus luteum was removed surgically from the ovary before seven weeks of pregnancy, then miscarriage inevitably resulted. After this date, removing the corpus luteum does not cause a miscarriage, because the placenta has implanted successfully and taken over the production of progesterone which is necessary to support the pregnancy. Further evidence that progesterone deficiency can determine the outcome of an early pregnancy comes from our recent discovery that anti-progesterone hormones can be used to terminate a pregnancy before nine weeks of gestation. After this date, this method of termination is not very effective.

It is important for the reader to understand how this works. The ovary produces progesterone until the placenta has implanted properly and can manufacture its own supply for the baby. If the corpus luteum is not functioning properly, for example, because the ovulation was poor (suboptimal), the production of progesterone will be low and the pregnancy may not implant successfully. After the placenta has taken over the production of progesterone and the corpus luteum has withered away, low progesterone levels demonstrate that the placenta is not functioning properly, so effectively the pregnancy has already failed.

An inadequate corpus luteum is quite common in women with a history of recurrent miscarriage. It is sometimes referred to as luteal phase defect, or corpus luteum deficiency. There have been many studies looking at the incidence of this problem among miscarriage sufferers and the figures quoted have varied from 20 to 60%. However, low progesterone levels in the luteal phase of the cycle and an endometrial lining which is retarded (behind) in its development are the characteristic findings. Much research has been carried out as to which are the most useful investigations and tests to make the diagnosis of corpus luteum or luteal phase defect. The problem with many of these investigations is that they can only be carried out in cycles where it is known that a pregnancy has not occurred. For example, taking a biopsy of the endometrial lining can only be done in a non-conception cycle, since the biopsy may interfere with the implantation of a tiny embryo. Some of the more recent research suggests that luteal phase defects may be due to the endometrial lining failing to respond adequately to normal circulating progesterone levels. This may well be one of the reasons why attempts at treating corpus luteum and luteal phase defects with progesterone have been so disappointing.

Progesterone and HCG treatment in early pregnancy

As I have mentioned in Chapter 4, many women and their doctors hope that injections of progesterone hormone will salvage their pregnancy and prevent a miscarriage. Armed with the facts above I think that most readers will realise that no amount of injected progesterone can make the placenta implant more successfully at this stage of pregnancy and come alive again. Furthermore, the amount of hormone contained in an injection is very small – a drop in the ocean compared to the quantities that a healthy corpus luteum and a healthy placenta are producing in a successful pregnancy. Injections of hormone in the early weeks of a pregnancy at risk may prolong the miscarriage but they cannot reverse it. The die is cast. This is the reason why all those clinical trials of treatment with progesterone in early pregnancy have repeatedly failed to show any benefit. Low progesterone levels in early pregnancy are the result rather than the cause of miscarriage.

If you have had assisted fertility treatment, such as in vitro fertilisation (IVF), you will probably have been treated with regular progesterone or HCG injections from soon after the embryos were replaced in your uterus. Many IVF units believe that this is an important aid to the successful implantation of the embryos, particularly when drugs have been used to desensitise the pituitary gland before inducing the ovaries to produce multiple eggs (see Chapter 13). Although there are no research data to specifically confirm this hypothesis, the concept is a sensible one, in my opinion. If progester-one treatment is to be of any benefit, it should probably be started before implantation takes place. There are a few recent studies which suggest that giving patients progesterone in the luteal phase of their menstrual cycle (after ovulation and at the time of implantation) may be helpful in improving the implantation rate, but there is certainly no benefit in giving this hormone in early pregnancy.

In theory, treatment with HCG in the luteal phase (second half of the menstrual cycle) should stimulate the corpus luteum to produce progesterone. However, abnormal HCG production is often a reflection of the fact that the embryo is abnormal. In this situation, treatment of any sort is probably inappropriate. It is interesting to note the results of a large multicentre trial of the use of HCG injections in women with a history of recurrent miscarriages, which was published in the 1980s. The study failed to show any benefit in pregnancy outcome, when compared to the placebo group who received dummy injections.

More recently, a small study of women with unexplained recurrent miscarriages has suggested that HCG is only useful in a subgroup of miscarriage sufferers who also have irregular menstrual cycles (oligomenorrhoea) – in those women with regular cycles, no improvement was achieved. It is possible that the earlier HCG trial missed this beneficial effect because all recurrent miscarriers were included in the study group. These results have prompted a proposal to perform a multicentre trial of HCG for women with recurrent miscarriages and irregular cycles. When the final results of this trial are ready to be analysed, I think it will be important for us to remember that pregnancies recruited to a study between six and eight weeks of gestation are likely to be successful anyway. As we have seen earlier in this book, the majority of early miscarriages will already have been determined by this date.

More recent hormonal theories for miscarriage

We now need to move away from the historical viewpoint that miscarriages occur solely because of hormonal problems in early pregnancy. The more modern view is that the hormonal events before ovulation dictate the quality of the luteal phase of the cycle and, as a result, determine whether a fertilised egg will implant successfully in the womb lining. It is interesting to remember at this point that as many as one third of all recurrent miscarriage sufferers have also had problems in becoming pregnant. When this subfertility is looked at more closely, it becomes evident that recurrent miscarriers usually suffer from ovulatory problems, rather than sperm problems or tubal disease.

These findings all point to the likelihood that subfertility and early miscarriage are two different types of the same reproductive disorder, both of which start with an abnormality in the follicular phase (first half) of the menstrual cycle, before ovulation has occurred. The consequent luteal phase is then unable to support implantation of the embryo (subfertility) or the implantation process is faulty and continuation of an early pregnancy is impossible (miscarriage).

We now need to turn to the problems that can develop in the follicular phase, before ovulation has occurred. Undoubtedly there are many, but during the last 15 years it has become increasingly clear that high levels of luteinising hormone have an unfavourable effect on a woman's ability to get pregnant. You may remember from Chapter 4 that luteinising hormone (LH) is one of two gonadotrophin hormones secreted by the pituitary gland in response to another hormonal signal from the hypothalamus in the brain – gonadotrophin hormone releasing hormone (GnRH).

Early in a normal menstrual cycle, follicle stimulating hormone (FSH) is secreted and makes the ovarian follicles start to grow. As the follicles enlarge in size, they produce oestrogen. The rising levels of oestrogen 'feed back' to the brain, telling the hypothalamus that the egg is nearly ready to be released from the follicle and the production of FSH is slowed. The levels of LH are quite low during the early phase, but around the middle of the cycle, in response to the message from the hypothalamus triggered by the higher oestrogen levels, the pituitary gland releases a short sharp burst of LH, known as the LH surge. This LH surge releases the egg from its follicle (see Chapter 4).

High LH levels

Several problems may occur if the levels of LH are too high during the follicular phase of the cycle. Perhaps the most important is that ovulation may not occur at all (known as 'anovulation'), despite the high levels of LH which have been present during the follicular phase, because the LH surge needed to release the egg does not occur. This is a common and important cause of infertility. In fact, it was the dramatic effect that high LH levels have upon a woman's ability to become pregnant which first brought doctors' attention to this problem.

In 1985 a research paper was published from an assisted fertility unit, which showed that when LH levels were high at the time that the eggs were harvested in women undergoing IVF treatment, the fertilisation of these eggs was poor. During the next few years, numerous studies were conducted, all showing that high LH had a very detrimental effect upon fertility. Not only was fertilisation compromised, but those eggs that did fertilise were less likely to divide into embryos, the embryos were less likely to implant in the womb lining and, of most interest to the readers of this book, the embryos were more likely to miscarry. Of course, it was possible that these high LH problems were a complication of IVF treatment, but when women undergoing fertility treatment that did not include IVF were also studied, the same correlation of poor implantation and high miscarriage rates was noted if they had high LH levels before ovulation.

The reader who remembers me talking about the Cambridge pregnancy loss study in Chapter 5 will recall that we were fortunate enough to have a captive population of women with no infertility history, who had volunteered to join the research programme before they became pregnant. They provided us with an opportunity to see whether the LH and miscarriage story held up for women who were not undergoing infertility treatment. We took blood samples from them on day 8 of their menstrual cycle and then watched what happened in their next pregnancy. The results were quite dramatic. We found that high LH levels in the follicular phase of the cycle were a risk factor for a future miscarriage. Whatever the past obstetric history, the finding of elevated LH levels before pregnancy resulted in a higher miscarriage rate. These women also took longer to fall pregnant. Women with a history of successful pregnancies and women with a history of miscarriages ran a higher risk of miscarrying if they had high LH levels before conception, when compared to women with the same past obstetric histories who had normal LH levels before conception.

Of course, this study can be criticised because we did not measure the LH levels in the cycle in which the woman became pregnant and we know that LH secretion can vary from cycle to cycle. Nonetheless, at the time it was performed in the late 1980s, the results of this research project offered us the potential of a simple test with which we might be able to predict those women who were at risk of miscarriage in future pregnancies. As we will see later in this chapter, this LH test became a part of the routine investigations carried out in the recurrent miscarriage clinic at St Mary's. However, our most recent studies have led us to realise that the test is not nearly as useful as we had originally hoped it would be.

High LH – how it causes problems

Having identified that high LH levels may be a cause of miscarriage, the next question is why. During the last 15 years a host of theories have been suggested, some more plausible than others. There are three potential places that may be adversely affected by high LH levels – the ovary, the egg and the endometrial lining. The ovary may respond to high circulating LH levels by producing inappropriate amounts of hormones at the wrong time. There are certainly some research data to suggest that testosterone levels are higher in women who miscarry repeatedly. Then there are the reports to suggest that progesterone production is switched on too early in women with high LH levels, and other reports which assert that it is too much oestrogen production which is the cause of the miscarriages. Certainly, it appears that the balance is wrong for successful implantation and the development of the early pregnancy. Much more research is needed to sort out the answers to this fundamental question.

Then there is the theory that high LH levels cause the egg to mature too early in the follicle and that when the egg is released, it is old, less fertilisable and less capable of implanting sucessfully, or if it implants, it is not able to progress into a viable pregnancy. Certainly there are data from animal studies to support this hypothesis, but in humans it is virtually impossible to perform the experiments necessary to address this question directly. Nonetheless, this theory remains an attractive one, since we know that it is the LH surge in a normal menstrual cycle that makes the egg come out of the dormant stage it has been in ever since it was in the fetal ovary. When the LH levels are high during the follicular phase, it enters the follicles and restarts the second division in the egg, which is needed before ovulation can proceed. Normally, this is timed carefully to occur in the middle of the cycle, which ensures that the egg is of optimal maturity and quality when it comes into contact with the sperm and the endometrium is at its most receptive.

The other possibility is that the high LH levels cause problems in the endometrial lining, making it less receptive for a tiny embryo to implant. Certainly, if implantation is adversely affected, this might explain why miscarriages are sometimes the consequence for women with abnormally high LH levels. However, at the present time it is too early to say whether abnormally high levels of LH hormone contribute directly to an unreceptive endometrium, or whether they are just a downstream marker of some other hormonal problem that we have yet to discover.

Polycystic ovaries

Having noted that high LH levels have such an adverse effect on fertility and miscarriage, we then needed to look at what causes a woman to have persistently high LH levels. Although most women have high levels during the LH surge just before ovulation, it is only women with polycystic ovaries who produce high levels of LH at other times in their menstrual cycle.

The term polycystic literally means 'many cysts'. This description is a bit misleading and, for many women, it is worrying, because the use of the word 'cyst' may conjure up the vision of diseased ovaries and can even raise the suspicion that the cyst on the ovary is cancerous. So it is important for me to start this section by emphasising strongly that polycystic ovaries are not cancerous or even pre-cancerous.

Furthermore, all normally functioning ovaries contain cysts, which should be referred to as follicles. As we have seen earlier in this chapter and in Chapter 4, an ovary without follicles would mean an ovary without eggs and in that situation there would be no chance of a successful pregnancy.

When doctors talk about polycystic ovaries (in contrast to polycystic ovary syndrome – see later) what they are referring to is the appearance of the ovary on an ultrasound scan. Compared to normal ovaries, polycystic ovaries are usually slightly larger in size and contain more follicles. The characteristic scan picture shows that the follicles are positioned around the outside of the ovary and that the central tissue of the ovary (the stroma) is increased. Perhaps the best way to picture a polycystic ovary is to imagine a string of pearls. The pearls are the follicles arranged around the ovary in the same way that a necklace sits around the wearer's neck.

Polycystic ovaries are very common. About one in five women in the general population have them and they do not cause any problems. Indeed, most women with polycystic ovaries do not realise this unless they have an ultrasound scan. These women have regular periods, normal fertility and no hormonal problems. We also know that polycystic ovaries run in families, so it is likely that they are inherited.

Polycystic ovary syndrome

Some women with polycystic ovaries (PCO) also have polycystic ovary syndrome, which means that they develop certain symptoms because the polycystic ovaries are the cause of a hormonal imbalance. Their periods are irregular, light and may disappear altogether. This is because the follicles in their ovaries do not develop to the right size and so ovulation does not occur. Since the hormones produced after ovulation are missing, the endometrial lining is not shed regularly. These women usually present to their doctor because of difficulties in becoming pregnant. Others are troubled because they develop unwanted facial and body hair, which is called hirsutism. When the syndrome is present, the woman usually has raised LH levels and may also have abnormally high testosterone levels. Testosterone is the male hormone which all women produce in small amounts from the ovaries. However, it should be mentioned here that some unfortunate women are extremely sensitive to the effects of testosterone and although the levels in their blood may not be raised, they still experience the unwanted facial and body hair growth. Approximately one third of women with polycystic ovaries are overweight and there is some evidence to suggest that women with polycystic ovaries are more prone to gaining weight. If you have symptoms from your polycystic ovaries and you are overweight, the first step in your treatment will be to encourage you to lose some of this weight. Weight loss will help to improve the hormonal imbalance and if additional treatment with drugs is necessary to help you ovulate or get rid of unwanted hair, it will be much more effective.

Polycystic ovaries and recurrent miscarriage

It must be evident to the reader that polycystic ovaries can cause a wide spectrum of problems. At one end of the spectrum you may have no symptoms at all. At the other end of the spectrum, you may suffer from infertility, absent periods and hirsutism. Of course, like most other spectrums in life, the majority of people are in the middle and they do not have all the problems, just one or possibly two of them.

This is the point at which we must return to the subject of recurrent miscarriage. Polycystic ovaries are very common in miscarriage sufferers. So common that we perform an ultrasound scan on every woman who attends the recurrent miscarriage clinic at St Mary's just before their first consultation. We find that nearly half of our patients have the pearl necklace sign on the US scan. It is more than just a coincidence that they are present in 50% of patients that we see in this clinic, when the incidence in the general population is only 20%.

As we noted earlier in this chapter, high LH is a risk factor for miscarriage and high LH levels are only found in women with polycystic ovaries. So the finding of polycystic ovaries alerts us to the possibility that this recurrent miscarrier may have high LH levels, even though she may have no obvious symptoms of the polycystic syndrome.

We also perform a blood test for LH in the early follicular phase of the cycle (between days 2–8) and when this is raised, there is little need for further tests. However, since the LH hormone is secreted in pulses from the pituitary gland every 90 minutes, a single blood test early in the cycle can fail to identify high LH levels. We found that taking daily samples of urine throughout a complete menstrual cycle was a more sensitive method of identifying LH abnormalities. Interestingly, we also found that the abnormalities in LH secretion were not just confined to the follicular phase of the cycle. They were also present in the luteal phase and in the majority of miscarriers that we investigated with urine testing, abnormal secretion in both phases of the cycle was present.

I think it is important to remind the reader at this point that not every woman with a history of recurrent miscarriage and polycystic ovaries has high LH. Polycystic ovaries are found in 50% of recurrent miscarriers. Two thirds of these recurrent miscarriers who have polycystic ovaries can be shown to have an abnormality of LH secretion in either blood or urine tests. Simple mathematics allows us to calculate that this means that only 35% of all recurrent miscarriers show any evidence of abnormal LH secretion.

One further point needs mentioning here. Any woman who has visited our miscarriage clinic will tell you that, along with the LH test, she also had her FSH levels measured. In the vast majority of patients, the FSH is normal but in a small and very significant group of older women, the FSH levels are raised. Sadly, this is an early indication that the woman is starting to become menopausal. The results of a single test do not clinch the diagnosis and may be a reflection that the blood test was taken on the wrong day of the cycle.

However, when the FSH levels are raised repeatedly over several cycles, the chances of becoming pregnant and staying pregnant start to dwindle. This is because when the ovary has no more viable follicles, the oestrogen levels are so low that the pituitary gland responds by pumping out more and more FSH in a vain attempt to get the ovary to respond. If it is unable to do so, the FSH levels remain raised. I think it is important to continue to perform this test routinely in our clinic, since the finding of a persistently raised FSH, although bad news, has an important role in the future management of the patient. If there are no eggs left in the ovary, then no amount of ovulation induction and miscarriage treatment will achieve a successful pregnancy. The only option available in this situation is IVF treatment using donor eggs. It is better to appreciate this situation earlier rather than later.

Possible treatments

If high LH levels are an important factor in determining whether a woman with polycystic ovaries can become pregnant and stay pregnant, suppressing the LH levels would be expected to improve fertility and lower the miscarriage rate. Since we now have drugs (the gonadotrophin releasing hormone analogues) that are capable of preventing the pituitary gland from producing LH and FSH, we can effectively suppress the high LH being produced by the polycystic ovaries to very low levels. Of course, this treatment also shuts down the normal cyclical activity in the ovary. In order for the woman to become pregnant, we therefore need to give her drugs to produce eggs and help her to ovulate these eggs.

This type of treatment was first tried in women with infertility. There have been several large studies of women attending fertility units which have demonstrated that about 50% of these women have polycystic ovaries. Although not all of them have high LH levels, it has been shown that the fertility treatment is less successful when the LH levels are high. Some fertility units have claimed that suppressing the high LH before the woman starts her ovulation induction treatment improves the chances of getting pregnant and reduces the number of pregnancies that end in an early miscarriage, although no study to date has included proper control groups.

The possibility that this treatment would help recurrent miscarriers prompted us to set up a controlled research trial to see if there was a real benefit offered by this method of treatment. We recruited over 100 women with a history of recurrent miscarriages, polycystic ovaries and high LH levels, and divided them into three groups. If there was any suspicion that the woman had another cause for her recurrent miscarriages, such as antiphospholipid syndrome or a genetic problem, or if she had experienced any subfertility in the past, she was excluded from the trial. It took three years to complete and I would like to mention here my appreciation of the research fellows and patients who participated.

The first group were given the LH suppressing drug for several weeks until we could show that their LH levels were very low. This drug is often called the 'sniffing' drug because one of the ways of giving it is by sniffing it up your nostrils several times a day. It can also be given by injections in the skin. When we were sure that the ovaries were completely shut down, low doses of the follicle-inducing drug were given and when the follicle had reached the correct size, an injection of HCG was given to make the egg ovulate. After ovulation, these women were all given progesterone pessaries twice daily. The second group were allowed to get pregnant naturally with no drugs, but they were monitored by scans and blood tests so that we knew when ovulation occurred. After ovulation they too were given progesterone pessaries. The third group were treated in exactly the same way as group 2, but instead of progesterone pessaries, they received dummy pessaries.

I think it is helpful for the reader to understand why the trial was designed in this way. The best treatment trials are 'double blinded', which means that both the patient and the doctor are unaware of which drugs the patient has been given. This is the only way to eliminate bias. The problem for us was that it is impossible to 'blind' the effects of the LH suppressing drug, since it gives the woman menopausal symptoms, such as hot flushes, which are immediately recognisable to both the patient and her doctor. Even if we had given one of the groups of patients a 'dummy' suppressant drug, we would have known who was taking what. So we did not try to 'blind' this arm of the trial. However, we were able to 'blind' the treatment received by the women in groups two and three. Only the pharmacist who sealed the envelopes of pessaries knew whether the women received real progesterone or dummy pessaries. Groups two and three were an essential part of the trial because we needed to know whether the progesterone pessaries were having an effect of their own. Without these arms to the trial we would have been unable to assess the treatment given to group 1 accurately.

The results of this trial came as quite a surprise to us. We found that the live birth rate in the women who were given pessaries only was slightly higher than the live birth rate in the women who were given LH suppressant and ovulation induction. Furthermore, there was no difference in the number of miscarriages experienced by the women who received progesterone or dummy progesterone pessaries. All of the treatment groups enjoyed a live birth rate in the region of 70%. These findings convinced us that the use of a complicated, labour intensive, expensive and emotionally stressful treatment with the LH suppressant and ovulation induction drugs cannot be justified for women with recurrent miscarriages and high LH levels. 'Cannot be justified' may seem a harsh statement, but it is important to remember that pituitary desensitisation and ovulation induction treatment take a toll on the patient and her doctor. This treatment involves numerous visits to the clinic for ultrasound scans and blood tests. The menopausal symptoms from the LH suppressant drug can be very troublesome and the risk of multiple pregnancy should never be underestimated. We had 3 sets of twins in group 1, and luckily none of them had any severe complications of prematurity.

Above all, the results of this controlled trial demonstrated that even if women do have high LH levels, polycystic ovaries and a history of recurrent miscarriage, they can still look forward to a 70% chance of a healthy baby if they are prepared to spend time visiting a dedicated clinic. I take my hat off to all the women who participated in this trial since it cost them a lot of physical and emotional effort. Their efforts were rewarded, since they all did so well in their future pregnancies. Their willing participation in a 'new venture' has ensured that we have uncovered the answer to an important clinical question. This treatment does not improve the miscarriage rate and so we no longer subject recurrent miscarriers to this stressful treatment in our clinic. I am unable to finish this section without telling the reader that the results of this trial have confirmed my belief that all miscarriage sufferers do much better if they join research programmes and are looked after by staff who have a special interest and expertise in their particular problem (see Chapter 21).

Androgens and recurrent miscarriage

During the time period that we were carrying out the LH studies described above, several other units were exploring the possibility that high androgen levels – specifically testosterone and androstenedione – were predictive in identifying women with polycystic ovaries who were likely to have miscarriage problems. The results have been variable. Some of the data have suggested that recurrent miscarriers have higher androgen levels and that these increased concentrations lead to the endometrium being retarded in its development during the luteal phase. As a result, implantation into the suboptimal endometrium or decidua is suboptimal and both failure to conceive and future miscarriages are more likely.

We recently reanalysed our database with an even larger population of recurrent miscarriers than the one we used for the LH studies and treatment trial detailed earlier. This time we decided not to use the more sophisticated urinary LH testing and to rely on the blood levels of LH and testosterone alone. In the earlier studies we had noted that both serum LH and testosterone levels were raised in a minority of the miscarriage patients. In this larger study, the LH and testosterone levels among our PCO recurrent miscarriers were in the normal range for the laboratory assay that we are currently using. However, it may well be relevant that the LH and testosterone levels were significantly higher in our PCO patients when compared to non PCO miscarriage sufferers, even though the average levels of these hormones remained within the normal range.

We are urgently in need of further studies to explore the effect of androgens, produced by the ovary and by the adrenal glands, on the endometrium in much greater detail. Once again we find ourselves hampered by the fact that we do not really understand the effects of androgen on the endometrium in the normal luteal phase and in the decidua of normal early pregnancies, which makes interpreting results gained from failed pregnancies even more difficult. Nonetheless, I think there are sufficient pointers to suggest that the action of androgens on the endometrium in the latter half of the luteal phase may well prove to be a key to understanding the causes of adverse pregnancy outcome.

Prolactin and recurrent miscarriage

Women with hyperprolactinaemia (raised prolactin levels) usually visit gynaecologists because of irregular or absent periods or because they cannot become pregnant. The symptoms are all interrelated and secondary to the fact that the secretion of high levels of prolactin from the pituitary gland invariably stops the woman from ovulating and hence the period and conception problems follow. When I first became interested in the field of pregnancy loss, I remember researching into the miscarriage rates that were experienced by women who had become pregnant as a result of fertility treatment. What I recall vividly was that several eminent fertility experts at that time stated categorically that when women with hyperprolactinaemia were treated with bromocryptine (the drug that suppresses prolactin secretion) and became pregnant, their miscarriage rates were no different from the sporadic miscarriage rate in the general population.

I was unaware of other work carried out in this area until recently, when a Japanese group reported that 18% of women with recurrent miscarriage have a marginally elevated prolactin level. Moreover, they felt that these slightly elevated levels could not be explained by other ovarian or endocrine abnormalities. This seems a very high prevalence of hyperprolactinaemia (nearly one in five women tested) and it is possible that the study is flawed because of the laboratory assay that was used. However, I don't think we can dismiss the results that easily since these workers went on to correct the prolactin levels with bromocryptine treatment. They found that the subsequent live birth rate was significantly higher among the recurrent miscarriers with high prolactin who received treatment compared with those who were left untreated. We need to perform more studies on the association of prolactin with recurrent miscarriage.

New research into endometrial function and recurrent miscarriage

During the luteal phase of every normal menstrual cycle, the endometrial lining is transformed into 'decidua'. This change is essential to prepare the endometrium for the implantation of an embryo. The cells of the womb lining become swollen with nutrients, which are secreted into the cavity to support any developing embryo. The supporting tissue around the cells (called the stroma) also undergoes complex changes. We have known that this transformation is under hormonal control for many years.

What has not been appreciated until relatively recently is that successful implantation also requires the presence of specialised immune cells in the decidua, which produce cytokines (special chemicals) that help to control and modify this structural change. These cells are called 'endometrial lymphocytes' and they increase in number dramatically during the luteal phase of the cycle. If a pregnancy occurs, they remain in the decidua until the end of the first trimester of pregnancy. If no pregnancy occurs, their numbers start to dwindle just before the menstrual period starts. These cyclical changes suggest that the lymphocytes are also under hormonal control. The lymphocytes have special properties to ensure that the embryo and its placenta are able to burrow into the decidua and gain a foothold, but at the same time they prevent the process of invasion from going too deep into the uterus. How they manage to do this is a burning research question and much work is currently under way trying to sort out the exact mechanisms.

All we can definitely say, at the present time, is that implantation involves a complex interplay of hormonal and immune factors in the decidua. A fine balance is needed for the invasion process to proceed to the right depth and no further. Many cases of infertility and miscarriage result when the invasion is too shallow or faulty in some other way. Indeed, we also know that some late pregnancy problems, such as pre-eclampsia, stem from events dictated by the quality of implantation at a very early stage in pregnancy. At the other end of the scale, when invasion is too deep, the placenta becomes so deeply embedded that it can actually grow through the deeper levels of the uterine wall. This situation is called placenta accreta. In the most extreme case, which is fortunately very rare in this country, the placenta actually behaves like a tumour and grows out of control – a choriocarcinoma or hydatidiform mole, as described in Chapter 3. In the future, when we have worked out the controlling mechanisms, we hope to be able to prevent abnormal cases of implantation. It is likely we will find that hormonal imbalances have an important part to play, but it is too early to say whether abnormally high levels of LH or testosterone or prolactin hormone contribute directly to an unreceptive endometrium, or whether they are just downstream markers of other hormonal abnormalities that we have yet to discover.

Summary

We still do not understand why polycystic ovaries are so prevalent among recurrent miscarriage sufferers. Although previous research suggested that high LH and testosterone levels could be used as markers of risk for future miscarriage, these data are now under question. We now know that suppressing high LH levels in recurrent miscarriers before they become pregnant does not improve the live birth rate over and above that of women with PCO who undergo careful monitoring before and during the early stages of their next pregnancy. It may be that the drugs available to us at the present time to suppress LH levels have an adverse effect on the ovary, the egg, or the endometrium. Whichever, this treatment cannot be justified and we must now change the direction of our research and start to focus on other factors controlling the receptivity of the endometrium at the time of implantation.

To this end, we have recently embarked on a large endometrial study in the recurrent miscarriage clinic at St Mary's. By recruiting women with unexplained miscarriages and performing hormonal tests to pinpoint the day of ovulation we are then able to sample the endometrium at the time in the luteal phase when implantation should occur. These endometrial biopsies are then carefully processed and stored for a wide variety of experiments. Using this method we hope to be able to better understand the differences in the special lymphocytes of the decidua (together with the hormones, other chemicals and the receptors that control them) in women with recurrent miscarriage, infertility and normal pregnancy histories.

I feel sure that if we continue to carry out carefully controlled research studies we will eventually find hormonal explanations for many cases of pregnancy loss.

TWELVE

RECURRENT MISCARRIAGE – IMMUNE AND PROTHROMBOTIC CAUSES

The human immune system plays several very important roles in reproduction. A woman's ability to become pregnant, remain pregnant and go on to deliver a healthy baby are all affected by a complicated jigsaw of immune factors. Many of these immune factors are still not clearly understood and much medical research is still needed to find the missing pieces to this puzzle.

During the last fifteen years, our understanding of reproductive immunology has increased enormously. As a result, we now recognise that abnormalities in the different types of immune response may cause a pregnancy to miscarry. The two which have received most attention are alloimmune and autoimmune abnormalities and these are discussed in detail below. However, we now know that the alloimmune and autoimmune factors we can measure in the mother's general blood stream are only part of the story. There is also a local and highly specialised immune system that develops during pregnancy at the materno-fetal interface. This interface or contact point is in the decidual bed – the part of the endometrial lining into which the placenta implants. Hence, the study of decidual immunity is now an active area of research. Hopefully a better understanding of the immune mechanisms that occur at the materno-fetal interface will help us to appreciate how a successful pregnancy is achieved and lead us on to find out what goes wrong in pregnancies that miscarry.

The reader may be wondering why this chapter is called 'immune and prothrombotic causes' of recurrent miscarriage. When we first recognised that women with SLE and other autoimmune diseases were at risk of pregnancy complications, they were classified as maternal disorders (see below and Chapter 9). Further studies identified that it was the women who carried antiphospholipid antibodies that were at greatest risk of miscarriage and as we will see later in this chapter a significant number of recurrent miscarriage sufferers have this problem. As a result it was felt that they merited their own section and moved into this chapter on immune causes.

More recently, we have come to realise that the antiphospholipid antibody syndrome, as well as being an autoimmune abnormality, is also an acquired type of prothrombotic disorder. This means that having developed or acquired the antibodies the woman becomes more susceptible to miscarriage because she is at greater risk of developing a blood clot (thrombosis) in the narrow blood vessels of her placenta. There are many different types of prothrombotic abnormality. Some are acquired and others are inherited (genetically determined) and have only been discovered in the last few years. They may also prove to be an important cause of miscarriage, but much further work is needed before we can definitely conclude that this is the case.

It is difficult to decide whether we should classify these newly identified defects in the genetic or immune sections, or alternatively set up a completely new category called prothrombotic abnormalities. Whichever, the reader needs to understand that this area of medical research is changing so fast that by the time this edition of *Miscarriage* is in print, another handful of genetically determined prothrombotic disorders will have been discovered.

The Immune System in Pregnancy

I have received many requests from readers of the first edition of *Miscarriage* for more details about the immunology of pregnancy, which is why I have included this next section. However, I need to emphasise that the theories I have tried to summarise below are exactly that – theories. At the present time there are no investigative tests that can reliably identify whether a pregnant woman has the correct immune response to protect her pregnancy. Nor are there any established tests available with which we can identify potential miscarriage sufferers, and no miracle treatments, either. There is much research being carried out in this field and I hope that everyone who reads this book will feel encouraged by this fact and seek out opportunities to contribute to these research projects.

The immune system is designed to protect our bodies from foreign invaders. There are two levels of immune response – innate and acquired. Innate immunity is present from birth. It is non-specific and forms a first line of defence against foreign invaders. The main cell types involved are white blood cells and natural killer cells. The second line of defence is provided by our acquired or adaptive immunity. This is a specific response and it takes time to develop. The acquired immune response involves a variety of cells that are capable of a) attacking foreign material entering the body (cell mediated or cytotoxic responses) and b) producing antibodies and developing a memory to the specific invaders in the body (humoral immunity).

Human pregnancy is a unique immune challenge to the mother and her baby. The baby develops in a specialised organ within the woman's body – the uterus. It is protected by a special barrier called the decidua – the name given to the endometrial lining which undergoes an extraordinary sequence of changes when the woman becomes pregnant. As the pregnancy increases in size it also exerts progressively more and more influence on the mother's body. For example, it produces many products, such as hormones and chemicals called cytokines, which are capable of altering the way that many of the mother's body systems work. Furthermore, cells from the baby and placenta float off into the mother's blood stream on a daily basis. She has to deal with these cells which, as we will see below, is no small feat, since they are genetically different from her own and we should expect that the mother's immune system would recognise them as foreign and try to get rid of them.

Many theories have been suggested to explain the enigma of the mother's immune relationship with her baby. We know that both the innate and acquired systems are involved but we are still ignorant of the exact mechanisms. Eminent scientists have worked on this puzzle for many years. Some believe that in order for pregnancy to continue successfully, the mother's immune response must be suppressed during her pregnancy. But this cannot be the whole story since pregnant women do not become obviously susceptible to infections and other illnesses during pregnancy. The alternative hypothesis is that pregnancy requires the mother's immune system to be activated in a very specific way. Again, the details are not fully understood but it appears that there is an alteration in the balance between her innate and adaptive immune responses that allows her to tolerate the baby, but at the same time preserves her capacity to fight off any infection she meets during her pregnancy. In brief, it appears that the innate (non-specific) immune system becomes relatively active and the adaptive (specific) immune system shifts to a less aggressive type of immune response during pregnancy. The reader may have heard this alteration in balance described as a shift from Th-1 (T helper-1) immune responses to the less damaging Th-2 (T helper-2) immune responses.

I mentioned in the introduction to this chapter that it is probably too simplistic to consider the mother's systemic (blood stream) immune response to pregnancy in isolation. Certainly, our experience in trying to pinpoint reliable and consistent alterations in her blood during pregnancy have been unsuccessful. As a result, much attention is now being directed towards the specific localised immune responses that occur at the materno-fetal interface (in the decidual bed) during pregnancy. A short section on decidual immunity is included later in this chapter for the interested reader.

Alloimmune miscarriage

Alloimmunity is the immune reaction which occurs between the tissues of different human beings. When a tissue is taken from one human being and placed into another human being, for example, during a kidney transplant, the transplanted tissue is called an allograft. Although the transplant has occurred between two humans, the genetic makeup of the donated kidney and the genetic makeup of the body into which it has been transplanted are different.

In order to reduce the chances of rejection, the transplanted kidney and the person receiving it are carefully matched so that they are as genetically similar as possible. But they are not exactly the same (only identical twins have exactly the same genetic makeup) and so drugs to suppress the alloimmune reaction are necessary.

The amazing thing about pregnancy is that the developing baby (or fetus) is genetically different from the mother in which it develops. The fetus carries genetic material inherited from the mother and the father. As such, it has a unique genetic 'code' and is effectively a foreign transplant in the mother's uterus. The question that no one has been able to answer is: why is the baby not rejected immediately by the mother's immune system? We know that the baby is in close contact with the mother's blood supply. We also know that the uterus is not protected from immune attack. If skin from another person is placed in the uterus, it is rejected like any other foreign tissue. For many years, it was supposed that the fetus had not developed an immune system of its own, but we now know that even tiny embryos have a complex genetic structure. Furthermore, although the mother's immune system may be altered during pregnancy, it is not dampened down sufficiently to explain why she does not reject her foreign transplant – the baby.

The possibility that some cases of recurrent miscarriage are due to an abnormality in the immune relationship between mother and fetus is an attractive one. If we understood how the baby avoids rejection, we might be able to develop treatments which prevented some miscarriages. The most popular explanation that has been suggested is that successful pregnancy depends upon the mother's ability to develop a special protective response towards her baby.

This theory has undergone numerous alterations over the years as researchers have tried, in vain, to identify the exact nature of this 'protective response'. Since some women seem to miscarry repeatedly with one partner, but are able to carry a pregnancy successfully with a different partner, the genetic makeup of these couples was studied. Surprisingly, some researchers reported that miscarriage occurred more frequently in couples who shared more genetic similarities (not dissimilarities) than would be expected by chance.

As a result of these findings, it was suggested that in order for the mother's body to form the appropriate protective response towards her baby, her immune system needed to recognise the 'foreign' nature of her baby. Furthermore, if the mother shared many genetic similarities with her partner, then there was a likelihood that her body would not make an adequate response, and miscarriage might result. However, more recent research has cast doubt upon whether genetic sharing really does increase the risk of miscarriage.

Immunotherapy

Despite the lack of specific data to support the hypothesis, some centres have recommended a type of immunisation (or vaccination) for women who miscarry repeatedly. The woman is immunised with a transfusion of white blood cells taken from her partner. The idea is that this infusion of foreign white blood cells will prime her immune system to make a protective response in a future pregnancy. When she becomes pregnant again, her immune system will recognise the same foreign genetic material (contributed by the father) in her baby. As a result, the correct immune response will be 'remembered' and reinforced and the baby will be protected from rejection.

The drawback to this simple and apparently magical cure is that there is considerable doubt that it actually works. Since the first exciting reports of its use were published, a lot of doctors have tried immunotherapy, but the results have been very variable. Fifteen years after its introduction, only one controlled trial of immunisation treatment has demonstrated a significant benefit to miscarriage patients. Several similar controlled trials have concluded that the treatment is of no benefit at all.

This is a very important point because, as you will read in a later chapter of this book, unless a treatment trial is controlled (by including patients who receive the new treatment and patients who are given placebo, or dummy, treatment) it is impossible to know whether the successful outcome is due to the treatment itself or the 'special care' that every patient involved in a trial receives. Another important issue that can no longer be ignored is that doctors who support the use of immunisation treatment are still unable to explain exactly why it should work.

For the sake of completeness, I should also mention that immunisation treatment using infusions of placental tissue, white blood cells from unrelated (third party) donors and purified immunoglobulin preparations have also been tried. None of them has been shown to improve the live birth rate.

By now you will have gathered that I feel very sceptical about immunisation treatment for recurrent miscarriage, and it is interesting that most doctors feel very strongly either for or against it. Such divided opinion usually reflects the fact that those involved have developed a prejudice due to their research or clinical interests. I want, now, to give you a brief explanation of why I believe this treatment should not be used. You will then be in a position to make up your own mind, should it be offered to you in the future.

When I first became interested in the reasons why women miscarry repeatedly I felt very excited about immunisation treatment. The women I treated with white cell infusions did very well – 65% had a live baby following treatment. But when I reviewed the outcome of pregnancy in the patients who did not receive any treatment, I found that 70% of this group had a successful pregnancy. Effectively, both groups had identical pregnancy outcomes – the difference between 65 and 70% is not different statistically. So I then turned my attention to the possible differences that there may have been between these two groups of patients. I could not find any. All of the women had attended the same clinic, been offered the same investigative tests, and received the same specialised care before and during their pregnancies.

APCA testing

Next I had to consider whether the test that we used to decide who was suitable for this treatment was right. At that time, all miscarriage sufferers who were interested in having immunisation treatment had their blood tested for the presence of antipaternal cytotoxic antibody (APCA). The APCA test examines the response of the mother's blood to her partner's white blood cells. A positive APCA test result suggested that the mother was not suitable for immunisation because the presence of APCA in her blood showed that her immune system had already recognised the foreign nature of her partner's contribution to the pregnancies, and responded to it. A negative APCA test result suggested that she was suitable for immunisation because she had not mounted the protective immune response to her partner's genetic material.

Helped by medical colleagues in Cambridge, I set up a prospective study to examine the natural history of APC antibodies in normal pregnancies. We recruited women before they became pregnant and measured their APCA levels every month throughout their next pregnancy. The results forced me to reconsider the value of using APCA tests.

The study, which involved over 400 women in the general population, showed that it is rare for any pregnant woman to develop APCA in her blood before the 28th week of pregnancy. If the antibodies developed in later pregnancy, they usually disappeared in the interval between pregnancies. So what value is a negative result in a woman who has miscarried frequently in the past, and is not pregnant at the time of the APCA test? The absence of APCA in a non-pregnant woman is to be expected, so I had to conclude that the APCA test should not be used to identify women as suitable for immunisation treatment.

I have met many miscarriage patients who have told me that they have had a negative APCA test result and that immunisation treatment was presented to them as the answer to their problem. I used to think that although this was not correct, at least the negative result suggested that these women would not suffer side-effects if treated with white cell infusions. With the passage of time, however, I find it harder and harder not to interfere and try to dissuade patients from undergoing this treatment because the evidence is accumulating that the side-effects may be very serious.

Problems with Immunotherapy

Transfusion reactions, anaphylactic shock (a potentially life-threatening allergic reaction to foreign blood cells) and viral infections such as hepatitis were all reported at early stages after the introduction of this treatment. But now there are other long-term problems: some of my colleagues working in infertility centres have patients who appear to have become infertile as a result of the treatment – they have changed from miscarrying repeatedly to being unable to conceive at all. This is particularly noticeable in older women who have had the treatment. I am married to a liver specialist, who has regularly shown me case reports from medical journals, in which miscarriage sufferers given white cell immunotherapy in the past have suffered from chronic hepatitis at a later date.

Supporters of immunisation have often argued that as a result of small patient numbers in trials, the true benefit of immunisation treatment may have been missed. As a result, many centres offering immunisation treatment decided to pool their results. The results of this wide-scale analysis were eagerly awaited, and were published in 1995. Disappointingly, they showed that the benefit of immunisation is very small, if it exists at all. However, this was not the end of the story. Despite the lack of concrete data to support this treatment it continued to be offered in some centres, many of them located in the United States. I suspect that one of the reasons that immunotherapy has remained an option for so long is because of the extensive publicity it has received on the Internet. If I was a recurrent miscarriage sufferer I would be impressed by the adverts, too. I just hope that someone would have explained to me that the data published on the worldwide web are not subjected to peer review and that the majority of immunotherapy results reported did not offer comparisons of the pregnancy outcome among control groups – because they were never performed. A colleague of mine in the US published a frank account of immunotherapy for recurrent miscarriage a few years ago entitled 'Standard of care or buyer beware'. He was brave to do so and I think the title of his article sums up the problem for the readers of this book.

The uncontrolled treatment studies continued and, meanwhile, a group of American and Canadian doctors performed a randomised controlled treatment trial. The results were published in a paper in the *Lancet* medical journal in July 1999. Their conclusions were important – namely that immunotherapy has no place in the management of women with recurrent miscarriage. No ifs or buts were added – the concluding statement was very definite. It is time to firmly close the door on white cell immunotherapy and ensure that future research effort into alloimmune miscarriage is focused on theories for which objective evidence is available. I believe that miscarriage sufferers deserve better than to be offered 'treatment' which no one can explain or monitor effectively, and which comes without guarantee that no serious side-effects will result.

Intravenous immunoglobulin (IVIG)

The reader will have noted how much space I have given to the description of the story of white cell immunotherapy. I must now add that the intravenous immunoglobulin (IVIG) story promises to be a mirror image of the white cell story. The theory with IVIG was that the immunoglobulin infusions helped the mother's immune system to mop up any foreign antigen material in her body, presumably produced as a reaction to her developing baby. As a result, the immune rejection of her genetically different fetus was prevented. Once again the theory was interesting but the data to support the actual events going on in her immune system was difficult to pinpoint. There are no specific tests to identify those women who may be most suitable for this treatment and no accepted methods for monitoring the progress of the treatment.

The initial reports of IVIG, which were uncontrolled, suggested that regular infusions of immunoglobulin during pregnancy were of benefit to some women with a history of unexplained recurrent miscarriage. The details of the treatment differed between different centres. Some used multiple doses in early pregnancy only; others advised that the infusions should continue at variable doses and intervals throughout pregnancy. Next came a couple of controlled studies of IVIG therapy which cast doubt on the benefits of this treatment.

At this point several clinicians started to query whether it was possible to justify such a high expenditure on a treatment without any proven benefit. Several financial analyses have been performed and it was estimated that this treatment could cost up to forty thousand pounds per pregnancy, but there was no guarantee of success. Just like with white cell immunisation, it was then decided that a meta-analysis of all the treatment studies available be performed. This proved disappointing – no definite benefit could be identified. But this was not the end of the story and a further multi-centred controlled treatment trial of IVIG was commenced. At the time of writing this edition of *Miscarriage* the results are not freely available but it does not seem that this further treatment trial is going to come up with any new findings. So we have to ask ourselves why it was necessary to perform another trial when the previous trials and the meta-analysis demonstrated that IVIG does not significantly increase the number of live take home babies for recurrent miscarriage sufferers.

Nonetheless, several centres have developed increasingly more complex sets of pre-treatment investigations, most of them blood tests measuring the number and type of special white blood cells (called large granular lymphocytes) in the woman's blood. The purpose appears to be to identify those recurrent miscarriage sufferers with 'abnormal' results who might benefit from IVIG therapy to modify their immune responses. As we will see in the next section, the cells that we can analyse in the woman's circulating blood stream may not have any bearing on the cells that are active at the materno-fetal interface, so the reader needs to be careful when undergoing these investigations. Of course, blood tests are not dangerous but they can cost a lot of money and, more importantly, they can raise expectations that may be difficult to fulfil and lead to bitter disappointments.

Decidual immunity

In Chapter 11 we looked at the factors which transform the endometrial lining into 'decidua' during the luteal phase of every normal menstrual cycle. This change is essential to prepare the endometrium for the implantation of an embryo. The cells of the womb lining become swollen with nutrients, which are secreted into the cavity to support any developing embryo. The supporting tissues around the cells (called the stroma) also undergo complex changes. We have known that this transformation is under hormonal control for many years. What has not been appreciated until relatively recently is that successful implantation also requires the presence of specialised immune cells in the decidua, which produce cytokines (special chemicals) that help to control and modify this structural change. These cells are called endometrial leucocytes (white cells) or large granular lymphocytes (because they contain granules visible under the microscope giving them a distinctive appearance). These LGLs increase in number dramatically during the luteal phase of the cycle. If a pregnancy occurs, they remain in the decidua until the end of the first trimester of pregnancy. If no pregnancy occurs, their numbers start to dwindle just before the menstrual period starts and these cyclical changes suggest that the lymphocytes are also under hormonal control. The lymphocytes (LGLs) have special properties to ensure that the embryo and its placenta are able to burrow into the decidua and gain a foothold, but at the same time they prevent the process of invasion from going too deep into the uterus. How they manage to do this is a burning research question and much work is currently under way trying to sort out the exact mechanisms.

What we do know is that the LGLs found in the endometrium at the time of implantation have highly specialised surface markers that are only occasionally seen on the surface of the lymphocytes which are circulating in the rest of our body. Once again, this points to the possibility that they have developed in order to facilitate implantation and, of course, this function is not needed anywhere else in our bodies. This is why I mentioned earlier in this chapter that we need to move away from measuring the immune responses found in the systemic blood and concentrate more on the events that occur at the materno-fetal interface. This is easy to say but very difficult to do. I am sure the reader will recognise that it is extremely difficult to obtain tissue samples from this site except when we know that the woman is not pregnant.

However, a few studies have been performed and the results are very exciting. Two studies performed in women with a history of recurrent miscarriage who had endometrial samples (biopsies) taken in the luteal phase of their menstrual cycles reported that there were too many LGLs with a particular surface marker called CD56 when compared with normal control samples from women with successful pregnancy histories. One study then went on to show that the women with higher numbers of CD56-positive cells were more likely to miscarry again in their next pregnancy. Interestingly, in women with infertility there appears to be too few of these same cells. Taken together, these results all point to the possibility that the numbers of LGLs with the CD56 surface marker play a role in deciding whether implantation of the tiny embryo is successful or unsuccessful. I am sure that there are many more surface markers that are also important and we need to develop these endometrial biopsy studies in order to try and work out the exact mechanisms.

If you have visited the miscarriage clinic at St Mary's recently, you will have been asked if you would like to participate in this research. I hope that you decide to join, since these studies are the only way that we are going to be able to unravel this particular part of the jigsaw puzzle and develop new treatments to combat recurrent miscarriage. As you will read in a later chapter of this book, joining an active research project is one of the best ways to receive the best help for your problem. Firstly, because all the clinic staff involved are really up to date with all the new discoveries and secondly, because you will feel much more positive about your miscarriage problems if you do something positive to help yourself.

The scientific mystery which has earned the fetus the name of 'nature's successful allograft' remains unsolved. The team of people who eventually unravel this code will have good reason to feel proud. Not only will they unlock the doors to our understanding of how a normal pregnancy is allowed to continue in a foreign host body, they will also allow us to understand the immune mechanisms responsible for some pregnancy failures, and to deal with them.

Autoimmune miscarriage

Autoimmunity is the term used to describe immune reactions in the body, caused by the production of antibodies which act against our own tissues (anti-'self' antibodies). Our bodies are capable of producing autoantibodies which work against many different tissues and organs. In general, these autoantibodies are destructive and cause a variety of diseases. Why these immune reactions develop in some people is not fully understood, although they are often passed on from generation to generation. They are more common in women and tend to develop in middle age, although they can also occur at earlier ages. Common examples are rheumatoid arthritis and certain types of diabetes and thyroid disease.

Systemic lupus erythematosis (SLE)

It has been known for many years that women with the auto-immune disorder called systemic lupus erythematosus (SLE), often referred to as 'lupus', experience a variety of complications in pregnancy. SLE is the most common autoimmune disorder in women of reproductive age. Although SLE sufferers appear to have no trouble falling pregnant, they have a high rate of miscarriage, which can occur at any stage during the pregnancy. They are at greater risk of developing pre-eclampsia (toxaemia), growth retardation in the baby and placental abruption – severe bleeding behind the placenta causing the placenta to shear away from the wall of the womb, cutting off the blood supply to the baby. However, not every woman with SLE develops pregnancy complications. Many of them have completely normal pregnancies. We now recognise that it is only the women with SLE who have antiphospholipid antibodies (or APA) who experience the miscarriages and later pregnancy problems.

Primary antiphospholipid syndrome (PAPS)

These antibodies may also be found in women who do not have obvious symptoms or signs of SLE, but consult their doctor for the first time complaining of recurrent episodes of miscarriage. This realisation has led to the identification of a distinct clinical condition – the Primary Antiphospholipid Syndrome – the association between APA and recurrent miscarriage in women who do not have full-blown SLE. Effectively, this means that we can use APA as a marker to look for pregnancies at risk of miscarriage and later obstetric problems. Indeed, a recent international medical conference concluded that in addition to women with three or more miscarriages, the antiphospholipid syndrome should be expanded to include those women who had suffered a single unexplained preterm delivery or who had developed severe pre-eclampsia in a previous pregnancy.

Antiphospholipid antibodies (APA)

Antiphospholipid antibody is the collective name used to describe a large family of autoantibodies. They are strongly associated with recurrent miscarriage and the development of thrombosis (blood clots). Historically, the most popular explanation as to how these antibodies exert their damaging effect on a pregnancy has been that they cause clotting in the blood vessels of the placenta. The steady accumulation of tiny clots results in parts of the placenta being unable to function (placental infarction), which eventually leads to the death of the baby.

Recent research suggests that these antibodies can also attack the cells of the placenta directly. By causing inflammation and turbulence of the blood flow, they disturb the normal pattern of invasion of the placenta into the maternal tissues, which is essential for successful 'implantation' and a continuing pregnancy. This explains how APA can cause miscarriage at all stages of pregnancy. It also explains why early miscarriages which have developed a fetal heart suddenly fail, why late miscarriages are often associated with small, gritty placentas, blood clots behind the placenta and an undernourished baby, and why pre-eclampsia and premature labour are more common in these women. All these pregnancy complications may result from the effects of APA on the blood flow to the placenta.

In all fields of medicine, making the correct diagnosis rests largely upon knowing the right questions to ask. Recurrent miscarriage patients may have other symptoms to suggest that the antiphospholipid syndrome is the cause of their pregnancy losses. I find that the miscarriage and obstetric problems which these women have experienced are frequently accompanied by evidence of thrombosis, arthritis, skin rashes, migraine headaches and occasionally epilepsy. Furthermore, there is often a history of thrombosis, heart attack or stroke occurring before the age of 50 years in a member of their close family. These are all useful pointers suggesting that the diagnosis may be antiphospholipid syndrome. As one doctor who recently visited the clinic commented to me: 'The more you look, the more you find these APA!'

This is certainly the case. In the recurrent miscarriage clinic at St Mary's hospital we screen every patient we see on several occasions (see below) for the main types of APA, which are known as lupus anticoagulant (LA) and anticardiolipin antibodies (ACA). We have established that one in every six recurrent miscarriers we see has the antiphospholipid syndrome. This incidence of 15% may not seem very impressive at first glance, but when you consider that only 2% of women with no previous history of miscarriage have APA, it becomes clearer that these antibodies make a significant contribution to the problem of recurrent miscarriage. Lupus anticoagulant is found more commonly than ACA and very few women are positive for both tests. This is why it is important that both tests are routinely used and is a point that needs to be emphasised. Many women I see in the clinic tell me that they have already been tested for the 'lupus factor' but frequently the records show that only one of the tests has been performed (usually the ACA, which is more readily available). Testing for only one of these antibodies will mean that as many as half of those women with APA will escape diagnosis.

I need to mention here that the lupus anticoagulant and anticardiolipin antibodies are only two of the many APA and other autoantibodies that can be tested for. Extensive research has shown that it is only the lupus anticoagulant and the two subclasses of anticardiolipin (IgG and IgM) that are associated with recurrent pregnancy loss. This is an important point for the reader to understand since there are several clinics which advertise their services on the Internet and suggest that women with recurrent miscarriage will benefit from undergoing many more autoantibody tests. These tests are costly and I feel confident in stating here that they do not help in the diagnosis or identification of women at risk of recurrent miscarriage.

The medical textbooks used to suggest that APA were only the cause of late miscarriages. Certainly they can be found in a larger percentage of women whose pregnancies miscarry after 13 weeks and in whom complications such as pre-eclampsia and growth retardation have occurred. However, it is important to remember that the vast majority (75%) of women with recurrent miscarriages have only experienced early losses (see Chapter 6). Our research studies have demonstrated that antiphospholipid syndrome is also an important cause of early miscarriages. If only late miscarriage sufferers are screened for APA, then the majority of patients with the syndrome will remain undetected.

The next issue is the accuracy of the laboratory tests used to detect these antibodies. This is an important point, and often a source of confusion to both patients and doctors alike. There is a wide variation in the performance of these tests, and international guidelines have recently been drawn up in an attempt to reduce this laboratory variation.

Several tests are available for the detection of lupus anticoagulant. The curiously named 'dilute Russell's Viper Venom Time' test is the most accurate for women with recurrent miscarriage. When testing for lupus anticoagulant, it is particularly important that (a) the blood sample is taken without using a cuff, (b) it is a free flowing sample, and (c) it is processed in the laboratory within one hour of being taken. If these guidelines are not strictly adhered to, the test for LA will often be reported as negative. There are similar problems with anticardiolipin tests.

I am often asked by patients how they can have a negative test for either LA or ACA at one hospital and then be told they tested positive at another hospital. The problem is that, as with many other antibodies, the levels of APA fluctuate over time. This has been shown both in women with recurrent miscarriage and with SLE. It is therefore important that, before making the decision as to whether a woman has APA or not, she is tested on several occasions, as a single test cannot determine her APA status – either positive or negative.

The final point to remember about APA tests is that, apart from false negative results – due to incorrectly performed laboratory tests – a number of women will have temporarily positive tests. These test results are not thought to be of significance and are most commonly caused by viral or other infections (such as the common cold). Before a woman can be said to have the antiphospholipid syndrome, she should test positive for either LA and/or ACA on at least two occasions more than six to eight weeks apart.

As you can see, testing for APA and the interpretation of results is not straightforward. The best way to achieve accurate results is to have the tests performed in laboratories with particular expertise in the detection of these antibodies. Most importantly, the doctor who orders the test needs to know what methods the laboratory uses. This requires regular liaison between the doctor in the clinic and the haematologist in the laboratory.

Pregnancy outcome in untreated phospholipid patients

I have put much emphasis on the importance of performing the right tests for APA on all miscarriage patients. The reason why I am so 'picky' is simple. Undetected recurrent miscarriers with APA syndrome can be expected to have a dismal outcome in future pregnancies. When we started to look for APA in the miscarriage clinic, we followed a group of women with APA during their next pregnancy and compared their outcome with another group of women who were APA negative. In the APA positive group, only 10% had a live birth, whereas 65% of the APA negative women had a successful pregnancy. A cynical person might argue that any treatment must be better than nothing for this unfortunate group of women!

Steroid treatment

Not surprisingly, this high miscarriage rate in women with APA has led to a variety of treatments being used in an attempt to improve the outcome of future pregnancies. Since steroids have long been used to treat women with active SLE, this was the first line of therapy tried for APA syndrome. The results were disappointing, not just in terms of live births achieved, but also because the steroids had side-effects for both the mother and baby. In a recent study carried out in Canada it was clearly shown that women found to have auto-antibodies who were given steroids during pregnancy have a significantly higher incidence of pre-eclampsia, gestational diabetes and of delivering prematurely, with all the attendant risks to the baby associated with these problems. Most doctors have now abandoned the use of steroids in women with APA syndrome. Having said all this I want to add that that there are some medical problems which necessitate treatment with steroids even when the woman is pregnant. If you are one of these women, please do not worry. Your doctors will know that you are at risk of later pregnancy complications and will ensure that you and your baby are carefully monitored. You may have to be delivered early but as long as the delivery is planned and carried out in a centre with the experience and facilities to look after you, both you and your baby will be safe.

How do phospholipid antibodies cause pregnancy complications?

This is an important question and at the present time there is no simple answer. As mentioned earlier in this chapter, it has been thought for some years that miscarriage in women with APA is due to thrombosis (or the development of blood clots) in the placenta and in the blood vessels leading to the placenta. This certainly explains many cases of late miscarriage but it does not explain the many miscarriages that occur early in pregnancy before the placenta has grown to a significant size. More recently, evidence has been accumulating to suggest that these APA also have a direct effect on the cells of the placenta, resulting in inflammation and turbulent blood flow, probably because they disrupt the normal anticoagulant mechanisms that the placenta uses to combat the formation of clots on the surface of its cells.

If this seems a strange explanation, then just think about what the placenta has to do. The placenta has to invade the maternal decidual bed in order to implant in the womb. It must secure a position that allows the development of the pregnancy but the invasion process has to be carefully controlled. It cannot be too aggressive because this would result in the placenta behaving like a tumour or cancer behaves – taking over the host body and destroying it. No, the placenta has to invade up to a point that allows the baby access to all the blood and nutrients that it needs from the mother. But it must not invade past that point because this would endanger her ability to control the situation. Most of the time the invasion is not too aggressive since, as we noted in an earlier chapter in this book, placental tumours, or hydatidiform moles as they are called, are quite rare.

The mechanisms that control this fine tuning are complex and many researchers are trying to work out the many pieces of this jigsaw puzzle. Recent studies carried out in our unit at St Mary's point to the possibility that APA also have an effect on the decidual bed cells and lead to the placenta invading too shallowly to support the optimal development of the placenta during the later stages of pregnancy. Importantly, this does not seem to be an all or nothing mechanism. If the APA are present they do not necessarily lead to an early miscarriage or end of the pregnancy, they can also store up problems leading to later miscarriages or pregnancy complications such as pre-eclampsia in the mother and growth retardation in the baby.

Treatment with aspirin and heparin

The most effective treatment for women with APA is the use of low-dose aspirin in combination with the anticoagulant drug heparin. When we first started using this treatment for miscarriage sufferers I used to explain to my patients that these two drugs improved the outcome of pregnancy for women with APA because aspirin and heparin are both capable of thinning the blood and improving the blood flow through the placenta, albeit using different mechanisms. With more experience we now know that this is far from being the whole story. Our most recent studies suggest that aspirin and heparin also have an effect on the way in which the young placenta manages to invade the maternal uterine blood vessels.

In 1997 our team at St Mary's published the results of the first large randomised controlled trial comparing the use of aspirin with aspirin in combination with heparin. The results from this trial were very exciting. They showed that the miscarriage rate in women with APA can be reduced dramatically with low dose aspirin and heparin treatment. The trial took three years to complete, but I think that the results justify all the hard work and dedication required from everyone involved. We found that in the women taking aspirin alone, the miscarriage rate fell from 90% (see earlier results in untreated women with APA) to 60%, meaning that 40% of these women had a successful pregnancy. For the women who were taking heparin as well, the live birth rate rose to over 70%. Several other clinics have published similar excellent results and we can now definitely conclude that low-dose aspirin in combination with heparin has very beneficial effects in treating recurrent miscarriage in women with APA syndrome. We introduced this treatment into our routine clinical practice several years ago and, since completing the original trial, many hundreds of women have undergone this treatment at our centre. Happily I can report to you that the high live birth rate has been maintained.

I am repeatedly asked by both patients and doctors about this treatment, so I want to include details here for the interested reader. Only those women with a definite diagnosis of antiphospholipid syndrome (two positive APA tests more than eight weeks apart) identified in the non-pregnant state are suitable for this treatment. As soon as the next home pregnancy test is positive we ask the women to start taking low-dose aspirin tablets, 75mg daily, and contact us immediately. We then give them an appointment to attend the very next week's early pregnancy clinic. At this clinic we perform an ultrasound scan and as soon as we can see a pregnancy sac in the uterine cavity we teach the woman how to start the low-dose heparin injections. We used to use unfractionated heparin which has to be injected twice daily, but over the last couple of years we have switched to low molecular weight heparin preparations. These offer the great advantage of only requiring a once daily injection and are just as beneficial as the twice daily unfractionated alternative. I should mention here that there are several different types of low molecular weight heparin on the market and they are all as good as each other. The only down side to the low molecular weight heparins is that they are more expensive and some hospitals and GPs are reluctant to prescribe them. If you find yourself in this situation, do not worry. The twice daily heparin injections are just as good as the once daily treatment in terms of the pregnancy success rate.

Although many women coming to our clinic are worried about whether they will be able to cope with learning how to inject themselves with heparin, I can tell you that I have never known a miscarriage sufferer with APA who has not been able to conquer the technique quickly and satisfactorily. Indeed, in the original treatment trial it was notable to all of us involved that no woman dropped out of the trial even though they were injecting twice daily at that time. It is true that some women suffer bruising at the injection sites, but they invariably weather this side-effect with very little complaint and soon become expert at avoiding sites on their tummy which make them more prone to bruising.

Most women attending our early pregnancy clinic like to return weekly or fortnightly to see us until they reach 12 weeks when we make arrangements for them to attend the antenatal clinic either at St Mary's or at their local hospital. We call the 12 week visit to the miscarriage clinic the graduation visit and use it as an opportunity to make sure that all the medical records for that woman are summarised and sent to the doctors who will look after them for the remainder of the pregnancy. Many of my patients look very amused when they hear me dictate a letter to myself summarising the care that she has received to date and making suggestions about what monitoring tests are appropriate over the next six months. But I think that is important to continue to do so since most pregnant women carry their own antenatal notes with them (a practice that I fully support). They do not always include copies of all the pre-pregnancy investigations and sometimes important facts about their particular case are forgotten unless a summary letter is written and included in these notes. We also give the women a pregnancy questionnaire at their 12 week visit and ask them to fill in all the details and return it to us after their baby has been delivered along with a photograph for our 'Rogue's Gallery'!

We usually advise ultrasound monitoring of the babies' growth and the blood flow through the placenta – called Doppler scans. These scans can be very helpful in predicting which women are likely to develop problems such as pre-eclampsia or fetal growth retardation later in pregnancy. For those women who have previously suffered a blood clot or thrombosis in pregnancy we continue the treatment until at least six weeks after the delivery of the baby. But for the vast majority of women we stop the aspirin and heparin treatment at the end of the 34th week of pregnancy. I am frequently asked why we stop the treatment at this stage and the answer is quite simple. When we first introduced this treatment our ethics committee were worried about the potential risks of heparin in pregnancy and requested that we limit the duration of the treatment to the shortest possible time. We felt that after 34 weeks most babies would not require specialist neonatal care if it became necessary to deliver them and that they could be safely delivered at the woman's local hospital. We now know that heparin is quite safe to use for long periods of time in pregnancy which is very reassuring (see safety issues below).

However, we are still not sure whether continuing the heparin until the time of delivery can further improve the outcome of pregnancy. Every woman in the original trial who reached 34 weeks of gestation went on to have a live take home baby and obviously we cannot improve on this! However, some women went on to suffer pre-eclampsia, a growth retarded baby or had a preterm birth (defined as delivery before 37 completed weeks). So when I talk about a further improvement in outcome I am only referring to the possibility that some of these later pregnancy complications may be reduced by continuing the treatment. We are trying to answer this important question by performing another trial comparing the incidence of late pregnancy complications among women who stop treatment at 34 weeks and those who continue treatment until delivery. If you have visited us in the miscarriage clinic at St Mary's recently and been found to have APA you will have been invited to join this randomised trial – and thanks to all your help and enthusiasm we will soon have enough pregnancy outcomes to be able to analyse the data and provide you with the answer. Why bother to perform this trial? This is a question I have been asked by many women and their doctors. Well of course it would be easier just to insist that every woman continues the heparin injections until delivery, but this means another possible six weeks of daily injections, another lot of bruises and further expense which I feel should not be imposed upon our patients unless we can be certain that they are really improving the situation.

Safety of aspirin and heparin in pregnancy

If aspirin and heparin are capable of changing the outcome of pregnancy for women with APA syndrome, we must understand how these drugs work and ensure that they have no serious side-effects for either the mother or her baby. Aspirin is a drug which combats inflammation and also prevents blood from clotting. It has been tried and tested in pregnancy and found to have no side-effects upon the baby, although it does cross (i.e. enter) the placenta. A large European study (called the CLASP study), which looked at whether aspirin treatment could reduce the risk of pre-eclampsia, was published some years ago and fortunately the investigators went on to follow up all the babies who were exposed to aspirin during their time in the womb. Happily I can report to you that the physical and neurological development of these babies is entirely normal – some of the children have been followed to the age of seven years and no problems have been identified.

Heparin is an anticoagulant drug which thins the blood at high doses, which is why it is used to treat patients who have already developed a thrombosis. In low doses (such as those used in our treatment), heparin does not affect the clotting of blood directly, although we have known for a long time that small doses of heparin can prevent thrombosis. This is why many hospital patients are given heparin injections before and after major surgery. It is not entirely clear how low-dose heparin prevents the development of blood clots in the body. However, recent research work on placental tissue suggests that heparin may actually bind to the surface of the placental cells and also to some of the cells lining the maternal blood vessels in close contact with the placenta. Possibly the heparin prevents antiphospholipid antibodies from damaging the placenta or causing inflammation of the blood vessel walls, by blocking their access to these cells.

The reader will be interested to hear that when we analysed the original trial data it became apparent that the beneficial effect of heparin was greatest during the first 14 weeks of pregnancy. After that time it was rare for a pregnancy to miscarry. This finding raised two important questions which are closely linked. The first was whether we could stop the heparin and aspirin much earlier, at about 15 weeks. We did try to answer this question by stopping the heparin earlier but the results were alarming. Several women who had managed to get through the first 12 to 16 weeks of pregnancy went on to suffer a late miscarriage, and although the results of a few pregnancies should not dictate future protocols, I confess that I stopped this treatment trial before we had randomised more than a handful of women to it. I felt that we could not continue with this trial knowing that the 34 week treatment protocol resulted in such a high live birth rate and so few late miscarriages. The second question was: how is the heparin working? We know that until 10 to 12 weeks of pregnancy the blood flow through the young placenta is very small and hence it is difficult to conclude that the heparin is preventing the formation of blood clots if there is no significant blood flow going on at this stage. This question is a lot more difficult to answer but brings us back to the points made in the previous paragraph – namely that heparin must have additional effects on the cells of the placenta and the decidual lining of the womb. At the present time we do not really understand the mechanisms involved, but I can assure you that there is much ongoing research which is trying to understand them. My personal view is that heparin probably works in two different ways. In the early weeks of pregnancy it must act on the placental and decidual cells to prevent the adverse effects of APA, and after the blood flow to the placenta becomes fully established, it then helps to prevent the formation of blood clots in the placental vessels – which may be why we found that those few women who stopped the heparin at 15 weeks went on to suffer later miscarriages.

Heparin has no side-effects on the baby, because it cannot cross the placental barrier and therefore never reaches the baby. However, heparin can occasionally cause complications in the mother and must always be used with caution and closely monitored. I have already mentioned that bruising at the injection sites can occur and may be troublesome. Rarely, heparin has been reported to cause a devastating fall in the mother's blood platelet count, resulting in generalised bleeding. Although we have never encountered this problem in our miscarriage patients, we take the precaution of checking the mother's platelet count on several occasions after starting heparin treatment.

When we first started using heparin for the treatment of APA-positive miscarriage sufferers the most serious potential complication to consider were reports that women taking heparin during pregnancy may develop thinning of their bones, similar to that seen in osteoporosis. A few very frightening accounts of young, healthy women developing fractures of their spine after long term heparin use in pregnancy needed to be considered before we could freely recommend this treatment for all APA-positive miscarriage patients. So we set up another large research study in which we measured the bone density of all our patients taking heparin on several occasions during their pregnancy. The results were fascinating and also very reassuring. We showed that women do lose about 3 to 4% of their bone density when taking heparin throughout their pregnancy. However, our study also included pregnant women who were not taking heparin and their bone density losses were almost identical. In summary, we can now confidently tell you that being pregnant means that your bone density will decrease by a factor of about 4%, but that taking low-dose heparin for the APA syndrome does not put you at greater risk of osteoporosis over and above the normal risk for any pregnant woman. Interestingly, our study also showed that there are a few women who start their pregnancies with borderline osteoporosis and I suspect that it is these few women when treated with heparin who developed the fracture complications. These results make a good case for women at risk of osteoporosis (thin women, smokers, those with a family history of oesteoporosis or a medical history of steroid drug use) to be offered bone density scans before pregnancy. If they are found to have low densities they should be offered calcium and vitamin D treatment during pregnancy.

Prothrombotic disorders – future research

The discovery of APA syndrome as a cause of recurrent miscarriage and the knowledge that aspirin and heparin treatment is an effective remedy have opened exciting new doors for future research. Indeed, it could be argued that these findings have produced more questions than have been answered. Why is it, for instance, that some women still miscarry after treatment with heparin? They may experience a sporadic miscarriage due to a fetal chromosomal abnormality that is entirely unrelated to their APA syndrome. Alternatively, it may be because they have another type of clotting or prothrombotic disorder that at the present time we do not have a specific name for, but that in the future we will be able to diagnose and offer different treatment.

In several chapters of this book I have referred to the molecular biology revolution that is changing our understanding of many different areas of medicine. The prothrombotic disorders are one of those fields and the discoveries are happening so quickly that before this edition of *Miscarriage* is in print what I am going to say in the following paragraphs will probably be out of date. If this sounds a bit over the top then let me share with the reader a brief summary of the prothrombotic disorders that have been discovered over the last few years. In 1993 we knew about a couple of very rare disorders that placed individuals, both male and female, at greater risk of developing thrombosis, usually a blood clot in their legs or lungs, during their lifetime. We had also recently come to understand that the APA syndrome was a particular problem for pregnant women because they were at greater risk of miscarriage and other later pregnancy complications. What happened in 1993 was a real milestone in our understanding of prothrombotic abnormalities. It was discovered that resistance to the effects of activated protein C is a powerful cause of blood clotting. Protein C is a natural anticoagulant that is produced by the lining of our blood cells when they realise that a blood clot is being deposited on their surface. This protein C needs to be activated by other factors in the blood stream in order to be able to start the fibrinolytic (or clot dissolving blood pathway) and prevent the formation of damaging blood clots or thrombosis. Tests for activated protein C resistance became available which relied on special laboratory assays of coagulation.

The very next year a clever scientist who worked in Leiden, Belgium, discovered that 90% of all cases of activated protein C resistance are due to an abnormality in the gene that produces factor V – an essential component in the blood clot dissolving process. This genetic mutation (inherited abnormality) at one point in the vast factor V gene was capable of making the whole of our body resistant to the effects of our natural defence against this part of our blood clotting system. In honour of its discoverer, the mutation was called the Factor V Leiden mutation. It did not take much longer for the experts to find that this mutation is very common – it is present in 5% of all Caucasians although the mutation is much less frequent in African and Asian peoples. There is no doubt that carrying this mutation increases an individual's lifetime risk of having a thrombosis, since some 40% of patients attending a thrombosis clinic have the mutation. But if being Factor V Leiden positive meant that the individual was definitely going to suffer a thrombosis then the incidence of thrombosis should be 5% (occurring in one in 20 people) and this is not the case. The overall incidence of thrombosis is much, much lower.

So why do some people develop thrombosis and many others escape this problem? The answer must be that it is only when there are additional prothrombotic risk factors present that a thrombosis results. The search for these other factors has become a major medical quest. We do not have all the answers yet but the concept that 'multiple hits' are necessary before a man or woman develops a thrombosis is a very important one. The search for other genetic mutations that predispose to thrombosis has been productive. Since the discovery of Factor V Leiden in 1994, several other genetic mutations have been identified, such as the prothrombin gene mutation (present in approximately 2% of the general population) and the hyperhomocystenaemia gene mutation (known as the MTHFR mutation) which is found in as many as 33% of the general population. A further factor V mutation discovered in Cambridge has now been reported and many other candidate mutations are being investigated.

Whether or not these genetic prothrombotic mutations contribute to the problem of recurrent miscarriage and later pregnancy complications has not been established, and indeed they could not be definitely implicated, since the mutations are so new that it would be impossible to have performed the necessary prospective prevalence studies that would allow us to come to this conclusion. I want to emphasise this point strongly, since there have been a large number of recent research papers published in the medical literature, based on retrospective groups of obstetric patients, which have claimed that these gene mutations account for almost every obstetric complication known. The reader needs to understand that if we perform genetic tests on a group of women who have already had a serious pregnancy complication and recorded that the incidence is high, that this does not mean that these gene mutations always lead to that particular problem. The only way that we can reach this conclusion is if we screen every pregnant woman for all of the mutations, observe what happens to them during the rest of their pregnancy and can then demonstrate that the mutation carriers all suffer the complications.

This appears to be far from the truth. An important Israeli study published in 1999 suggested that 65% of women with serious pregnancy complications such as miscarriage, pre-eclampsia, growth retardation and stillbirth had one or more inherited or acquired prothrombotic abnormality. However, in the control group who suffered none of these problems some 17% of the pregnant women carried the same inherited or acquired abnormalities. Here we need to remember some basic mathematics. Only 5% of all pregnant women are affected by these serious pregnancy complications and the Israeli study reported that 65% of them carried a prothrombotic abnormality. Two thirds of 5% comes to just over 3%. In contrast, 95% of pregnant women enjoy normal uncomplicated pregnancies and if 17% of these women carry the same prothrombotic defects we should expect that a much larger percentage of pregnant women should suffer the same complications – and we know that they do not. There must be other factors that determine whether a pregnant woman with a known prothrombotic abnormality is at risk of developing pregnancy complications. Let me share with you a few examples.

Activated protein C resistance

When APC resistance was first described in 1993, we looked at a large number of our recurrent miscarriage patients and found that late miscarriage sufferers were more likely to have APC resistance when compared to early miscarriers and control women with normal obstetric histories. This data was exciting and suggested that there are a group of women with recurrent pregnancy loss who develop APC resistance during pregnancy which may place their baby at risk of miscarriage and later pregnancy complications. Soon after, we learnt that APC resistance develops progressively in normal pregnancy and is one of the reasons that pregnant women are at greater risk of thrombosis. Next came the discovery of the Factor V Leiden mutation and the medical journals were soon full of confusing reports. Some said that the prevalence of Factor V Leiden was increased in women with a history of miscarriage and late pregnancy complications. Other studies reported that the prevalence was no different from the general population. The problem here is that most of the available studies have included insufficient numbers to allow us to draw meaningful conclusions. Furthermore, many of the studies have been performed in high risk groups of women who have been tested because they have suffered a previous thrombosis in pregnancy. The results from these women are unlikely to be representative of women presenting to doctors because they have suffered recurrent miscarriages.

So we set out to screen one thousand consecutive women attending our clinic. The results showed that just over 4% of them carried the Factor V Leiden mutation, which is no different from the general population prevalence. The next step was to follow some of these Factor V Leiden positive women through their next pregnancy and compare their outcome to recurrent miscarriers without the gene mutation. No woman in this study was taking any treatment apart from folic acid in pregnancy. The results demonstrated that the Factor V Leiden positive women do appear to have a lower live birth rate and a higher incidence of late pregnancy complications. However, since some of them had entirely uncomplicated pregnancies, we now have to find ways of identifying those women who are at greater risk of pregnancy complications and protect those women who are not at risk from unnecessary drug treatment.

Here, again, we return to the important concept that it is 'multiple hits' and not a single prothrombotic or abnormal blood clotting test that results in a woman suffering pregnancy problems. How are we going to identify the additional 'hits' or risk factors? I think the first thing we need to do is reflect on the fact that prothrombotic disorders are a new field and that there must be many abnormalities that we do not yet understand. In time, we will find many other specific gene defects that contribute to the overall problem, but this is no comfort to the woman who is suffering pregnancy complications now.

Future tests for prothrombotic abnormalities

What we need at the present time is a general test that can identify recurrent miscarriers who may be at risk of developing a prothrombotic problem during pregnancy. This is why our research group at St Mary's has been exploring the potential of using thromboelastography (TEG for short) to identify these women. Conventional prothrombotic tests measure specific abnormalities but the TEG test provides us with a general assessment of the woman's prothrombotic state which includes all those hidden or yet to be discovered factors. The TEG test measures the speed and the strength of the blood clot produced when a small sample of blood is placed into a special machine which mimics the physical conditions found in blood vessels in the body. The great advantage of this test is that it is quick – results are obtained in just over one hour. It is also cheap and reproducible – which means that the test can be performed repeatedly and the same answers obtained.

Our TEG results are very exciting. We have been able to show that there are some women who present to our miscarriage clinic who are in a prothrombotic state even when they are not pregnant. They may not have phospholipid antibodies, or any of the recognised genetic mutations that we are able to test for, but they produce blood clots more quickly and these clots are stronger than those produced by women with normal pregnancy histories. We have also demonstrated that women with a history of late miscarriages have more TEG abnormalities than women with early miscarriage. More importantly, we have been able to show that pre-pregnancy TEG abnormalities are predictive of miscarriage and other pregnancy complications in the next pregnancy, which raises the possibility that we can identify recurrent miscarriers who may benefit from treatment which allows them to continue their pregnancies.

If this sounds a bit far fetched then let me also tell you that our TEG testing has also shown that some women only develop prothrombotic abnormalities when they are pregnant. We have followed a group of women during the first three months of pregnancy and been able to see that the TEG test becomes progressively more abnormal in those women who go on to suffer a further miscarriage. Further, the sequential TEG tests in women destined to have a successful pregnancy seem to be normal. These findings suggest that there are opportunities to identify pregnant women who have prothrombotic abnormalities in the first few crucial weeks of their pregnancy, and by looking at the TEG results decide whether they may benefit from taking aspirin treatment. I mention aspirin because we have conducted some studies which show that aspirin in gradually increasing doses can return the TEG test abnormalities to normal, but these results need to be investigated much further before we can advise that aspirin in early pregnancy is the answer to all miscarriage problems.

I need to emphasise this point because a recent study in our clinic has shown that in women with unexplained early recurrent miscarriage, empirical aspirin treatment in the next pregnancy does NOT improve the live take home baby rate although, for the much smaller number of women with recurrent late miscarriages, there appears to be a benefit from aspirin treatment. These data suggest to me that the late miscarriage sufferers may have prothrombotic abnormalities for which, at the present time, we do not have labels or names. At the risk of repeating myself, there will be some new discoveries that further reduce the pool of unexplained prothrombotic risk factors that pregnant women are exposed to before this edition of *Miscarriage* is published. Having said this, I also believe that at the present time our ability to identify inherited prothrombotic abnormalities has outstripped our understanding of the natural history of thrombosis, and pregnancy complications. Multiple hits or risk factors determine who develops a systemic thrombosis, and I suspect that we will conclude in the next few years that there are multiple hits and risk factors that decide whether a woman with a history of recurrent miscarriage is more likely to develop a pregnancy complication, such as further miscarriage or pre-eclampsia and growth retardation in later pregnancy.

Long-term health issues for women with prothrombotic abnormalities

A major advance has been made by our identifying that some women with recurrent miscarriage have an increased clotting tendency even when not pregnant. This finding has important implications for the long-term health of these young women who first come to the notice of doctors when they report recurrent miscarriages. For example, concerns about the third generation contraceptive pills that may increase the risk of thrombosis in women who are not pregnant has led to the suggestion that all young women should be screened for inherited APC resistance before they commence the contraceptive pill. The reality is that these same women are at greater risk of thrombosis if they become pregnant and we do not know at the present time whether their lifetime risk of thrombosis or other general medical problems justifies the screening of all women, pregnant or not.

We need to establish whether women with any of the problems discussed in this chapter should be offered long-term follow-up in an attempt to try and prevent other medical problems in later life, after the reproductive years have ended. My personal view is that it is very important that we set up long-term surveillance studies that can answer these questions. And that is exactly what we have done. Every woman who comes to our miscarriage clinic and is found to have a prothrombotic abnormality is asked to attend our follow-up clinics. We are hoping that it will not be too long before we can determine the answers to important questions such as 'Is it safe to take the contraceptive pill?' and 'Is it safe to take hormone replacement therapy?' if I have been found to have the antiphospholipid syndrome or another prothrombotic abnormality. These studies will take a very long time to reach conclusions and considerable funding will be needed to ensure that we can establish clear answers.

Other types of immune miscarriage

Blood group incompatibilities

Blood group incompatibilities between mother and father may cause miscarriage, but this is a rare occurrence. Evidence that parental incompatibility in the ABO and the P blood group systems, reported in the 1960s as an occasional cause of miscarriage, is weak. Detailed testing of blood groups in couples with a history of miscarriage is of no practical help.

The classic example of blood group incompatibility is severe rhesus disease, which occurs when a rhesus D negative mother and rhesus D positive father have a rhesus D positive fetus. If blood cells from the baby enter the mother's blood stream, she recognises the rhesus positive fetal blood cells and produces antibodies which travel back across the placenta and destroy the baby's blood cells. Since fetal red blood cells usually only enter the mother's circulation after haemorrhage from the placenta, most cases occur at the time of delivery, which is why rhesus disease usually affects second or later pregnancies with greater severity.

This problem can be avoided if rhesus negative mothers are all given an injection of anti-D at the time of delivery of their rhesus positive baby. The anti-D then 'mops up' any rhesus positive cells from the baby and prevents the mother's immune system from recognising these foreign cells and developing antibodies to them, which will cause problems in a future pregnancy. Fortunately, rhesus disease is now very rare in this country, thanks to the introduction of routine treatment for rhesus negative mothers after delivery and miscarriage. Although the risk to a rhesus negative mother is low at the time of an early complete miscarriage, most doctors still advise a dose of anti-D when the miscarriage has to be dealt with surgically, whatever the age of the pregnancy, to ensure that no antibodies are produced in the future.

Anti-D is also given after ectopic pregnancies, pre-natal diagnostic procedures such as amniocentesis and chorion villus biopsy and all cases of antepartum haemorrhage (bleeding in pregnancy after 28 weeks). Furthermore, many hospitals have now introduced routine injections of anti-D at 28 and 36 weeks of pregnancy for all rhesus negative women, in the hope that we will be able to eradicate rhesus disease in the new born baby completely.

Anti-sperm antibodies

There have been a few studies suggesting that men and women who develop antibodies to sperm in their blood, or in the case of some men on the sperms, have an increased risk of miscarriage. I am not very convinced by these reports. They are usually based on small numbers of patients undergoing infertility investigations and treatments and normal control groups are lacking. The apparent increase in the miscarriage rate is just as likely to be due to the infertility problems and their treatment, as to the sperm antibodies. We do not recommend testing for anti-sperm antibodies in couples with recurrent miscarriage.

PART THREE

PRACTICAL ISSUES AND ANSWERS TO QUESTIONS

THIRTEEN

IS MISCARRIAGE MORE COMMON IN WOMEN WITH INFERTILITY PROBLEMS?

To miscarry after a prolonged period of infertility is devastating. Many women tell me that losing this long-awaited baby is even more distressing than not being able to conceive. I believe them – and I am sure that most individuals who have desperately wanted something in life can understand the pain of glimpsing the winning post before it is snatched away from them.

The theory that the risk of miscarriage is higher than normal in patients with infertility is not a new one. It was first suggested some 40 years ago and certainly predates our modern methods of treating infertility. The causes of infertility are many and diverse, but with the development of assisted conception techniques, it is now possible to overcome or at least circumvent the majority of problems presented by the subfertile couple.

As infertility treatment improves, it becomes increasingly important to ascertain how many miscarriages occur in women who have been successfully treated for infertility. If miscarriage is more common in women with infertility problems, is it related to all cases of infertility, or only certain types of infertility? Do the various therapies now available increase the rate of miscarriage or fetal abnormality? It may be that associated factors are responsible for the increased miscarriage rate, for example, increasing maternal age or the past pregnancy outcome. Alternatively, it may be that the early pregnancy monitoring and surveillance that women with infertility usually undergo, means that we are diagnosing more pregnancies which might have been missed in a woman with no infertility history.

Before we can attempt to answer these questions, we need to compare the miscarriage rate after a period of infertility to the miscarriage rate in women of proven fertility. In Chapter 2 we noted that the fate of a fertilised egg is an unhappy one – one in three conceptions miscarry before pregnancy is declared. Although we know that one in four women will suffer a sporadic miscarriage, the exact incidence depends upon whether we are looking at the clinical or subclinical miscarriage rate. So when we consider miscarriage in women with a history of infertility, we must specify whether we are looking at subclinical losses or clinical losses. Of all clinically recognised pregnancies, one in six will end in miscarriage. We also know that one in six couples seek treatment for infertility. Even worse, one in three recurrent miscarriers also has subfertility.

The next task is to remind ourselves of the recognised causes of miscarriage – genetic, anatomical, infection, maternal, endocrine (hormonal), immune and prothrombotic factors – in order to focus on factors which may be particularly important in subfertile women. For example, in the genetic category, we need to establish whether chromosomal abnormalities in the baby are increased by the use of fertility drugs, or by the laboratory techniques used to manipulate the eggs and the sperm in treatments such as *in vitro* fertilisation (IVF) and intracytoplasmic sperm injection (ICSI).

The presence of a fibroid near the cavity of the uterus may hinder implantation of a fertilised egg. A previous infection may have resulted in damage to the fallopian tubes or an infection of the womb lining, increasing the chance of an ectopic pregnancy. We know that women who suffer from thyroid disease experience difficulties in falling pregnant and many other hormonal disorders may prevent a potential pregnancy from implanting successfully. Disorders of the immune system are also a cause of fertility problems (see Chapter 12).

Maternal age and infertility

Infertility patients tend to be older, and chromosomal abnormalities in the baby increase with advancing maternal age. At least 50% of all sporadic miscarriages are due to chromosomal abnormalities, but a recent study performed in Italy showed that in women aged 40 years and older, genetic abnormalities were present in 83% of the miscarriages.

Delaying the age at which the first pregnancy is conceived also increases the risks of ovulatory disorders, endometriosis and the possibility that a woman may have undergone previous gynaecological or abdominal surgery, causing damage to the uterus and/or the fallopian tubes. Perhaps most importantly, increasing maternal age is accompanied by a natural decline in fertility. The number and quality of the eggs available for fertilisation falls dramatically after the age of 40 years (earlier for some unfortunate women). The womb lining becomes progressively less suitable for the implantation of an embryo and thus places the pregnancy at greater risk.

Past obstetric history

In Chapter 5, we noted that a woman's past obstetric history is very important in determining the likelihood of miscarriage. Primiparous women (who have never been pregnant before) have a very low risk of miscarriage, as do women who have enjoyed successful pregnancies. However, women who have miscarried in the past have an increased risk of future miscarriage. If we now look at women who have suffered infertility, we can see a similar pattern emerging. In the Cambridge population study described in Chapter 5, we were able to include a group of 90 women who were being treated for infertility. By following these women carefully, we discovered that women with primary infertility (a first pregnancy achieved following fertility treatment) have the same low risk of miscarriage as first pregnancies in women with no infertility problems. This was not the case for multiparous women (women who have had a previous pregnancy) who had suffered a miscarriage or an ectopic pregnancy after fertility treatment. For these sufferers of secondary infertility, the risk of miscarriage was much higher if they had difficulty becoming pregnant again. Secondary infertility is therefore strongly associated with a poor obstetric history – 75% of these women have had previous pregnancy losses.

Recurrent miscarriage and infertility

Fortunately, women who suffer from recurrent miscarriages are relatively uncommon. However, they deserve a special mention in this chapter, since they undoubtedly share some important characteristics with infertility patients. When I first became interested in the field of recurrent miscarriage, I was puzzled that so many of the women I talked to appeared to have difficulties in becoming pregnant, as well as staying pregnant. It occurred to me that there must be some important thread linking infertility and subsequent recurrent early miscarriage. The only difference betweeen the infertile women and the sufferers of miscarriage, in short, was the result of the pregnancy test.

Years later, with more experience and a large recurrent miscarriage database to draw upon, I think my gut feeling was right. Infertility and very early miscarriage represent two points on the same spectrum of reproductive disease. At one end of this spectrum sits the infertility patient whose fertilised egg tries to implant in the womb lining but does not gain a strong enough foothold to allow it to produce enough HCG (pregnancy) hormone to turn the pregnancy test positive. At the other end of the spectrum sits the early miscarriage patient, whose embryo manages to implant sufficiently to start manufacturing HCG, but because the implantation process is faulty, cannot continue to develop. These explanations are no longer just ideas from an interested young doctor. There are now some research data to support these views.

By taking a careful history from all women attending the miscarriage clinic at St Mary's Hospital, we now know that one in three women with recurrent miscarriage have also experienced a degree of subfertility. The most useful question to ask them is how long it has taken them to get pregnant before each miscarriage. A delay of 12 months or more is an abnormally long period of time. Many of these women have undergone a variety of 'infertility' investigations in the past. Further questioning often reveals that these women have irregular periods, ovulation difficulties and have, in the past, been given drugs to help them ovulate. In Chapter 11 the links between recurrent miscarriage and ovulatory problems (in particular poly-cystic ovaries) are described in detail for the interested reader.

In summary, I think it is very important to identify recurrent miscarriage sufferers who also have difficulty getting pregnant, at the first clinic visit. If this association (which is present in one-third of miscarriage patients) is overlooked, the opportunity of identifying the root cause of the problem may be lost. As a result, the chances of achieving a successful pregnancy may be delayed or greatly reduced.

Early pregnancy surveillance

One of the main differences between pregnancies achieved sponta-neously and after infertility treatment, is the intensity of the early pregnancy monitoring that occurs. It is customary to perform a pregnancy test at the end of the cycle on approximately day 27/28 for those undergoing assisted fertility treatment such as IVF. In this way many women will know that they are pregnant before the time of the expected start of the next period. By contrast, it is usual for the woman who conceives spontaneously to wait until the expected menstrual period is delayed and then perform a pregnancy test on day 35 of the cycle or later. As a result, biochemical pregnancies which do not continue into clinically recognisable pregnancies are identified more frequently in women undergoing assisted fertility treatment. Infertility patients are also more likely to have an ultrasound scan performed at the end of a cycle of treatment. Using vaginal ultrasound, an intrauterine sac will be visible between four and five weeks after the last missed menstrual period.

Types of infertility

It is beyond the scope of this chapter to provide a detailed classification of the causes of infertility. However, we need a simple checklist to work with. I find the most useful aide-memoire when talking to patients is to divide the causes of infertility very roughly into four groups; ovulatory problems, tubal problems, male factor (sperm) problems and unexplained infertility. Conveniently, these four groups each account for approximately 25% of all cases of infertility.

Lots of studies have looked at the incidence of miscarriage after infertility treatments. Overall the miscarriage rate ranges from 10% to 45% and this wide variation undoubtedly reflects the fact that the risk of miscarriage depends on the underlying cause of the infertility. For example, if the woman has high prolactin levels (hyperprolactinae-mia), simple treatment with a drug called bromocryptine usually resolves the difficulty in conceiving very quickly and simply. Inter-estingly, the miscarriage rate after this treatment is very low, about 12%, which is similar to the incidence of sporadic miscarriage in the general population (but see Chapter 11, Prolactin and recurrent miscarriage).

Similar results can be expected when a severe male factor problem is the only cause of infertility and the couple choose artificial insemination from a donor (AID). Donor sperm does not increase the miscarriage rate, but if other infertility factors are also present, the miscarriage rate rises. For example, when artificial insemination by the husband/partner is the chosen treatment method, the mis-carriage rate can be much higher, because the root of the problem in this situation is often more complex than a low sperm count alone. There may be problems with ovulation as well, requiring treatment to induce the growth and release of an egg. For exactly the same reasons the risk of miscarriage following surgery to unblock fallopian tubes is very variable. If the problem is purely mechanical, the miscarriage rate is low, but when drugs are required to ensure that ovulation is regular, the miscarriage rate goes up.

Sperm abnormalities

Judging by the large number of anxious enquiries that we receive at the miscarriage clinic, it is important to make a few comments about sperm abnormalities and the risk of miscarriage. The use of donor sperm does not increase the miscarriage rate *per se*. As noted earlier in this chapter, it is only when there are additional fertility problems requiring treatment that the miscarriage rate increases.

There has been much discussion about the role of abnormal sperm and whether they affect the rate of miscarriage. Sperm may be classified as abnormal on the basis of their structure (morphology) as seen under the microscope, or they may be chromosomally (genetically) abnormal. A good example of the latter situation is found in couples with recurrent miscarriage, when the male partner is known to carry a certain abnormality called a 'balanced translocation' (see Chapter 7). Of all the sperm that this man produces, 50% will carry the translocation. If one of these genetically abnormal sperms manages to fertilise an egg, then a chromosomally abnormal fetus will result and the vast majority of these pregnancies are miscarried.

The situation is less certain when there is an abnormality in the numbers, mobility or physical structure of the sperms. Some doctors have suggested that there is an increase in the miscarriage rate in these situations, but I must emphasise to the reader that evidence to support this viewpoint is sparse. Sperm counts which are exceptionally high or low may result in delays in conceiving but we usually consider that they do not increase the risk of miscarriage. However, there are some reports that men aged 45 years or older have higher rates of structural sperm chromosomal abnormalities. Further, that advancing paternal age is linked to an increased rate of autosomal dominant disorders and congenital malformations.

Similarly, fertility may be reduced when there are abnormalities in the shape, structure or motility of the sperm, but these problems are not thought to be accompanied by an increased miscarriage rate. Most of the currently available evidence suggests that sperm work to an 'all or none' rule. If they are capable of fertilising an egg, then the resultant embryo is not abnormal. However, many abnormal sperm are incapable of successful fertilisation, in which case no pregnancy occurs. For eggs, this is not the case. An abnormal egg may be fertilised by a normal sperm and in this situation a miscarriage may well be the result. Having said all this, I think it is important to remember that our understanding of subchromosomal mechanisms that may be the cause of miscarriages is still in its infancy. Abnormal sperm morphology may be reflecting that there are mutations present at the molecular level that we are ignorant of at present. Small deletions or duplications are not detectable by conventional chromosomal analysis or even by the newer FISH (fluorescent in situ hybridisation) techniques (see Chapter 7 for further details).

One last point needs to be mentioned here. There has been much concern expressed about the possibility that the newest high-tech assisted fertility treatments may cause an increase in the numbers of miscarriages or abormalities in the babies born. For example, intracytoplasmic sperm injection (ICSI) involves injecting sperm from men with very low abnormal sperm counts into the woman's eggs using a microscopic technique. This procedure could potentially allow a grossly abnormal sperm to fertilise an egg, but fortunately, this has never occurred. Several thousands of pregnancies have now been achieved as a result of this ground-breaking technique, and to date there have been no reports of an increase in the miscarriage rate. The number of major congenital abnormalities in babies born after ICSI treatment does not appear to be higher when allowance is made for the increased numbers of multiple pregnancies and premature births that occur, both of which are independent risk factors for abnormalities. However, there is an increase in the incidence of hypospadias (when the urethral opening or urine hole does not reach the end of the penis) in male infants but since this is easily correctible by surgery, it is considered a minor abnormality. Overall, ICSI treatment has proved to be the most important breakthrough in assisted fertility therapy since the technique of IVF was first described in 1974.

Influence of fertility drugs on the miscarriage rate

There is no doubt that drugs which improve ovulation carry with them a penalty of an increased miscarriage rate. What is not so clearly understood is whether it is the drugs themselves or the underlying ovulation problem which determines this increase in the miscarriage rate.

We noted earlier that ovulatory failure (anovulation) accounts for at least 25% of infertility. In about three quarters of all cases of anovulatory infertility, the problem is due to the presence of polycystic ovaries. Furthermore, we know that polycystic ovaries are associated with a higher rate of miscarriage when compared to the miscarriage rate in women with normal ovaries (see Chapter 11). So any increase in the number of miscarriages experienced by women with polycystic ovaries and infertility could be due to the effect of the drugs used or it may reflect that the drugs are making an egg ovulate which, if fertilised, is already at greater risk of miscarrying.

Over the last 30 years, a variety of drug treatments have been used to induce ovulation. Regular ovulation can be achieved in about 80% of women with polycystic ovaries using modern drug therapy. However, ovulation does not guarantee a pregnancy or a successful birth. Broadly speaking, there are three groups of drugs that can be used singly or in combination, depending on the type of fertility treatment undertaken. These are the anti-oestrogens (clomiphene citrate or tamoxifen), the gonadotrophins (human menopausal gonadotrophin or pure follicle stimulating hormone) and the gonadotrophin releasing hormone (GnRH) agonists (buserelin).

Ovulation induction with clomiphene citrate

This was the first drug used to induce ovulation and is still the most widely prescribed. It is cheap and has fewer side effects than HMG, hence it has an important place in first line therapy for anovulation. Clomiphene has anti-oestrogen effects and it is thought to promote ovulation by stimulating the release of natural follicle stimulating hormone (FSH) from the pituitary. FSH acts upon the ovaries to produce follicles. There have been many studies undertaken to examine the effect of this drug and very variable miscarriage rates have been reported ranging from 9 to 50%! Before ultrasound was routinely used to watch the growth of the ovarian follicles, it was often very difficult to monitor the individual's response to the clomiphene. The diagnosis of pregnancy was usually not made until the period had been delayed, and so the true rate of miscarriage for these patients was never really determined.

If we look at the results from recent studies, most doctors would agree that when clomiphene is used, the miscarriage rate is in the region of 20 to 30%. Many patients I meet have been alarmed (unnecessarily) by suggestions that the miscarriage rate increases even further when pregnancy occurs during the first cycle of clomiphene treatment or after seven cycles of treatment. There is no truth in these rather wild assertions.

One of the concerns about the use of Clomiphene has been whether it increases the incidence of chromosomal abnormalities and congenital abnormalities. There have been several reports suggesting an association between the use of clomiphene and neural tube defects, such as spina bifida. However, recent studies have been very reassuring and suggest that there is no evidence for concern on this issue. Indeed, it is now generally agreed that babies born after the mother's treatment with clomiphene are no more at risk of being malformed than if they were conceived spontaneously.

Many doctors believe that the increased risk of miscarriage after clomiphene treatment is because the drug causes an abnormal hormonal environment, which in turn has an adverse effect on the developing egg. Clomiphene increases the secretion of FSH and LH in the early part of the menstrual cycle before ovulation. The effect of these high levels of LH during the time at which the egg is under-going maturation may result in the ovulation of an egg which is 'over-ripe' and which, if fertilised, is less likely to be able to implant successfully and miscarries early.

The most common cause of persistently high LH levels is polycystic ovary syndrome (see Chapter 11) and in such cases, clomiphene probably exaggerates the already high LH levels, leading in turn to miscarriage problems. The best approach to ovulation induction in women with PCOS is aimed at preventing the high LH levels from occurring. To this end, some doctors use tamoxifen as an alternative to clomiphene citrate because this drug has been shown to induce ovulation without increasing LH concentrations.

I frequently meet patients in the miscarriage clinic who, despite the fact that they ovulate spontaneously, have been given clomiphene (or want it prescribed) in the mistaken belief that this drug will 'improve their fertility'. It is important for me to emphasise that this use of clomiphene is unhelpful and frequently leads to problems. Because clomiphene has an anti-oestrogen effect, it can thicken the cervical mucus and prevent sperm from penetrating. It can also interfere with the uterine lining, preventing the embryo from implanting. The ovaries may produce cysts and interfere with the normal ovulatory pattern.

Lastly, clomiphene is invariably unsuccessful in treating women over the age of 40 years when there is no evidence to suggest that they are not ovulating. Indeed, in this situation it is likely that the only result will be the occasional release of an abnormal egg, which if it does get fertilised, will not implant or will miscarry soon after. These are all good reasons why clomiphene should only be taken when there is a genuine problem with ovulation and only when its use is supervised and carefully monitored to prevent complications.

Ovulation induction with gonadotrophins

For those women who do not respond to clomiphene citrate, gonadotrophin treatment may be needed to induce ovulation. There are a variety of preparations available, either human menopausal gonadotrophin (HMG, marketed as Pergonal or Humegon) which contains equal quantities of both FSH and LH, or purified FSH (Metrodin or Puregon), which is very expensive to produce. Although it was previously thought that preparations containing low levels of LH would benefit women with polycystic ovaries, by minimising circulating LH levels, experience has shown that the use of purified FSH offers no advantage.

Whatever preparation is used, the main problems with gonadotrophin treatment are the multiple pregnancy and miscarriage rate, two problems which are often related to each other. The miscarriage rate after gonadotrophin-induced ovulation ranges from 10 to 48%. There is no difference in the miscarriage rate if the conception occurs in the first or the subsequent treatment cycle. However, in a very large study of HMG pregnancies reported quite recently, it was noted that the miscarriage rate following HMG therapy was dependent on the outcome of previous pregnancies. This is in keeping with the miscarriage pattern seen in natural conceptions (see Chapter 5). For example, although the miscarriage rate in the first treatment cycle was 24%, the miscarriage rate rose to 48% in the women whose first HMG pregnancy had ended in miscarriage. By contrast, if the first HMG-induced pregnancy was successful, the incidence of miscarriage in the second HMG pregnancy was only 7%.

It is very important that HMG treatment is carefully controlled. Some women overreact to the gonadotrophins and develop 'ovarian hyperstimulation syndrome'. Their ovaries become grossly enlarged and cystic and large quantities of fluid are produced, which leak into the peritoneal cavity (the space surrounding all the organs in the abdomen). Not only is this complication extremely painful, it is also potentially life-threatening. There is also a serious risk that HMG treatment will result in the production of many follicles, each containing an egg, all of which may be released if careful monitoring is not performed. By watching the growth of the follicles using ultrasound scans and performing regular hormone measurements, this problem can be limited. Where necessary, the doses of the drugs given can be adjusted and injection of HCG (human chorionic gonadotrophin), which triggers ovulation, can be withheld in cases when too many follicles have been produced.

Several theories have been proposed to explain why the miscarriage rate is high after gonadotrophin therapy. We know that the miscarriage rate increases with maternal age and also when the mother is very overweight (obese). Approximately one third of patients with polycystic ovaries suffer from moderate obesity and it is important to advise women who are overweight that their chances of a successful pregnancy will be better if they lose weight before undergoing treatment. High levels of LH, as we know, have a definite contribution: studies show that women with infertility, polycystic ovaries and high LH have a far poorer outcome of pregnancy after gonadotrophin treatment than women with infertility, polycystic ovaries and normal LH levels.

Recent studies that have included several thousand newborn infants have shown that the babies conceived following treatment with gonadotrophins do not suffer from any increased risk of abnormality. They have the same incidence of congenital abnormalities as the general population.

Controlling the ovaries

In recent years, there has been a definite move towards using gonadotrophin-releasing hormone (GnRH) agonists in order to control the number of eggs produced. The agonists effectively shut down (desensitise) the pituitary gland and impose a kind of menopausal state upon the woman. This may seem a strange way to improve the chances of becoming pregnant, but this treatment allows us to take over the control of egg development. Having suppressed the pituitary gland, the ovaries are also suppressed and they are then very receptive to gonadotrophins such as HMG, and not affected by any spontaneous hormonal changes. Using this method to down-regulate the ovary has improved pregnancy rates in IVF programmes and has been adopted widely. This type of treatment is particularly useful for women with polycystic ovary syndrome, since it allows the doctors to actually suppress the high levels of LH. Eggs produced in this way appear to fertilise better than those from other treatment cycles. However, it is important to mention that the use of this treatment for women with recurrent miscarriage and high LH levels does not improve the miscarriage rate. (See Chapter 11 for more details.)

The influence of IVF and related procedures on the miscarriage rate

The number of pregnancies that miscarry after IVF and related procedures varies widely. Overall, the miscarriage rate is in the region of 25%, but in older women the figure is certainly higher. Many patients are concerned that the laboratory techniques involved in IVF treatments may increase the risk of miscarriage, but this does not seem to be true. Nor is there any increase in the numbers of congenital malformations in the babies born as a result of IVF (see earlier in this chapter).

Multiple pregnancy

For every 80 pregnancies that are conceived naturally, one will result in the delivery of twins. The delivery of triplets is much rarer, only occurring once in 6000 spontaneous pregnancies. When fertility drugs are used, the number of multiple pregnancies is much higher. After clomiphene treatment, more than one in ten pregnancies are multiple, and when gonadotrophin treatment is used, the figure rises to one in five pregnancies, even when the treatment has been carefully controlled.

Now that early ultrasound scans are so widely used in pregnancy, we know that many pregnancies start with more than one pregnancy 'sac' in the uterus and that many potential twins and triplets are miscarried very early. Indeed, some doctors think that as many as two-thirds of twin sacs seen on the scan during the first eight weeks of pregnancy 'vanish' and result in a single baby being delivered at the end of the pregnancy. It is reassuring to note that when one of the sacs vanishes very early, the pregnancy usually continues without complications.

Multiple pregnancies involving more than two embryos are often associated with disastrous outcomes. There is a much higher risk of early and late miscarriage, stillbirth and an inevitable risk of premature delivery, not to mention the long-term complications of being born too early in babies who survive the neonatal period. If this sounds frightening, then I have succeeded in making my point. I cannot overstate the importance of ensuring that fertility treatment does not result in a multiple pregnancy of triplets or more.

Happily the UK regulatory body for assisted fertility treatment – the Human Fertilisation and Embryo Authority (HFEA) – has done much to help reduce the multiple pregnancy rates in women undergoing IVF and other related procedures, by enforcing their recommendations that no more than two embryos be transferred into the uterine cavity. As a result, most of the multiple pregnancies that are now conceived in the UK are secondary to the use of clomiphene and other ovulation induction agents. However, many clinicians who have had to deal with the complications associated with multiple pregnancies now argue that the best way to safeguard against these disasters is to allow the transfer of only one embryo at a time. In a memorable sound bite one fertility specialist that I know was recently quoted as saying: 'Transfer as many embryos as you like – as long as you do it one at a time.' Now that the facilities for embryo freezing are more freely available, I hope that this advice becomes routine good practice in the foreseeable future.

Antiphospholipid antibodies

I mentioned in Chapter 12 that antiphospholipid antibodies (APA) have been associated with previously unexplained infertility. In particular, they are reported to be more common in women who have had repeated IVF treatment failures. Not surprisingly, an increasing number of doctors and their patients have explored the possibility that treatment with aspirin and heparin may have the same beneficial effect in infertility patients that it offers women with recurrent miscarriage. However, the results have been disappointing and they warrant a brief description here, since many couples that I meet appear to believe that the aspirin and heparin treatment is the answer to their infertility problems. At the present time it is important that I state quite firmly that this is not the case.

There have been several studies published, mostly centred in private fertility units in the United States, that have shown a high prevalence of phospholipid antibodies in their patients. The figures quoted have varied enormously but some units have reported prevalence rates of over 50%. I hope these variable figures raise as many queries in the reader's head as they do in mine. I think the only reasonable explanation can be that the assays used to detect the phospholipid antibodies have not been standardised and must therefore be regarded with suspicion.

In an attempt to answer this question we recently performed a large study in collaboration with fertility colleagues at the Hammersmith Hospital in London. By ensuring that all the tests were performed in the same specialist haemostasis laboratory and that they adhered strictly with international laboratory guidelines, we were able to demonstrate that APA are present in 23% of women embarking on an IVF treatment cycle. However, the most important finding from our study was that the presence of APA did not affect the outcome of IVF treatment. The success rates in terms of pregnancies achieved and the ongoing pregnancy rates and live births were identical in women with and without phospholipid antibodies. These results convinced me that the use of aspirin and heparin in these women is quite simply unethical. If this sounds strong language then I think the reader needs to reflect on the fact that no drug treatment is ever completely without side-effects and complications. Since our pregnancy outcome study has shown that the success of IVF treatment is unchanged by the presence of the APA, I would find it enormously difficult to have to look a couple straight in the eye who had experienced complications or side-effects (with not just one but two drugs) and try to argue that I had used the treatment in their best interests. There is no evidence to justify the treatment.

My views are not shared by all fertility units and many IVF doctors are prescribing aspirin and heparin treatment for their patients. At best it is an expensive intervention which raises false hopes and expectations in couples who feel desperate, but at worst it could be the source of future clinical side-effects and litigation procedures. If and when a properly randomised controlled treatment trial of aspirin and heparin demonstrates that this therapy significantly improves the chances of conceiving and achieving a live take home baby in women undergoing fertility treatment then I will happily and humbly retract my comments and applaud the study. But at the present time this is not the case and the empirical use of this treatment only serves to muddy the already murky waters still further.

Conclusions

There are specific factors that increase the risk of miscarriage in women who have had infertility. These are advancing maternal age, poor obstetric history, multiple pregnancy and obesity. I would argue that miscarriage is more common in women with infertility because of these associations. However, it is important to note that the treatments used to improve fertility do not in themselves increase the risk of miscarriage. Nor do they increase the risk of abnormalities in the babies that they help to produce.

FOURTEEN

How will I recognise a threatened miscarriage?

Miscarriage is a process, not a single event. A detailed account of the ways in which the woman and her doctor can diagnose the various types and stages of miscarriage was given in Chapter 3. In this chapter, I will mention some of these points again. However, the aim of this chapter is to talk about the questions that I am most frequently asked by women when they are threatening to miscarry or have just suffered a definite miscarriage.

One of the first signs of threatened miscarriage is vaginal bleeding. It can occur at any time after a missed period. The bleeding usually starts lightly and is much less heavy than a menstrual period. Often the bleeding is first noticed when going to the toilet. You may see a smear of pink, brown or red blood on the tissue paper. Bright red blood indicates that the bleeding is fresh, whereas brown blood suggests that the bleeding has occurred some time ago and that the blood is old. Sometimes the blood comes in a gush and can be very heavy with large clots. As a general rule, the older the pregnancy, the heavier the bleeding may be. But whatever the stage of pregnancy, it is sensible to report it to your doctor without delay.

Whatever the quantity or the colour of the blood, it is always very frightening and upsetting. I meet many couples who are quite simply devastated when they experience some bleeding in pregnancy. I think much of the distress is because we feel so helpless in this situation. Certainly, this was the feeling uppermost in my mind when I suddenly had an episode of heavy bleeding six weeks into my own pregnancy. I found it difficult to believe that it was happening to me and since I was sitting quietly in a meeting with about 20 other gynaecologists, I can remember thinking that all the expert help in the world could do nothing to help. Happily, my twins did not bat an eyelid (so to speak), and the only casualty was the chair I was sitting on!

It is important for you to realise that bleeding in early pregnancy is extremely common. Most importantly, you need to remember that in most cases, the pregnancy continues safely. Every doctor who has cared for women with bleeding in early pregnancy will tell you that even when the bleeding is quite heavy, this does not necessarily mean that the pregnancy has been lost. There is still a good chance that the pregnancy will progress normally. This is one of the reasons that an ultrasound scan is usually performed before we assume that the pregnancy has ended. I never cease to be amazed by the amount of blood that can be lost and yet when I turn on the ultrasound machine, there is the beating fetal heart clearly visible in the tiny pregnancy.

Many women I see are worried that bleeding in early pregnancy may cause some damage to the baby. This is not true. Even if you bleed quite heavily, the baby will come to no harm if the pregnancy continues. In later pregnancy, bleeding may also occur and be a source of great anxiety. Once again, if the pregnancy does not miscarry, the baby will not be deprived of its oxygen and nutrient supplies, and you can feel reassured as long as the episode of bleeding has been carefully investigated by your doctor.

When lower abdominal pain occurs with or after the bleeding, the situation is more worrying. This is because cramping pain may be a sign that the pregnancy is about to miscarry. Sometimes women describe pain in the lower back or at the top of the vagina. Having said this, I must emphasise strongly to you that lower abdominal pain is common during early pregnancy and does not necessarily mean that anything is seriously wrong. If the pain becomes severe, resembling labour pains, and the bleeding becomes heavier, then it is important to see your doctor.

When lower abdominal pain occurs before any bleeding is noticed, it is possible that the pregnancy is ectopic. This is a potentially serious complication and the whereabouts of the pregnancy needs to be confirmed straight away (see Chapter 3).

Some women are extremely sensitive to the general symptoms of pregnancy such as nausea, breast tenderness and tiredness. Such women may actually be able to tell that their pregnancy has miscarried before they experience any physical signs such as bleeding or pain. It is true that the complete disappearance of these symptoms in early pregnancy is unusual, and that when they fade away, this might be a signal that the pregnancy is not continuing. It is also true, however, that some women do not experience the symptoms in the first place. It is important to understand that a lessening of these symptoms does not necessarily mean that a miscarriage has occurred. It is to be expected that these symptoms will pass away after 14 weeks, and in some women, even earlier.

So please do not panic if you do not feel as pregnant today as you did yesterday. Remember that for every woman who recounts her personal story of how she knew exactly when she lost her pregnancy, there are many more women who have also had this sensation, but have not turned this into a story – because everything turned out well. It is much more likely that your pregnancy is progressing normally. If you are worried that something is 'not quite right', then go and see your doctor. He or she will probably suggest that you have an ultrasound scan to assess the situation and hopefully provide you with the reassurance you need.

One further point needs mentioning here. I know that some women who experience a missed miscarriage (see Chapter 3) feel very distressed that they did not realise that their pregnancy had died until some time after the event. I make a special point of telling women that this in no way suggests that they have been negligent or insensitive, and assuring them that they will be every bit as capable a mother when their successful pregnancy does come about.

Perhaps the most painful question that I have to try and answer when I am talking to a woman who is threatening to miscarry is, 'What can I do to prevent it?' I am sorry to say that there is nothing you can do in very early pregnancy. The outcome of the pregnancy has already been determined and you cannot change this outcome whatever you do. Of course in later pregnancy, there are some treatments that may stop the uterus from contracting or the cervix from dilating, such as bed rest and the use of some drugs. But in early pregnancy these remedies do not help. I mention this here, not to fill you with gloom but to make sure that you realise that retiring to your bed and wrapping yourself in cotton wool is unlikely to prevent a miscarriage. Although many women believe that the bleeding restarts only when they stop lying down, this is because the blood collects at the top of the vagina and only drains away when they get up to walk around or go to the toilet. If you feel that going to bed may reassure you, then go to bed. If, on the other hand, lying in bed thinking about the problem non-stop makes you feel even worse, then don't go to bed and get on with your everyday life.

FIFTEEN

WHAT TESTS ARE AVAILABLE TO DIAGNOSE MY MISCARRIAGE?

There are several methods which may help you and your doctors to diagnose that you have miscarried. We have already discussed the importance of a physical vaginal examination (Chapter 3). When the cervix is closed and the uterus is firm and of normal size, it is likely that the uterus is empty and the miscarriage is described as complete. When the cervix is still open and the uterus feels soft and bulky, it is possible that there are still products of conception (usually pieces of placental tissue) in the cavity. The diagnosis of an incomplete miscarriage can be confirmed with an ultrasound scan, although this is not always necessary.

If you have had a missed miscarriage, the physical examination will reveal that the uterus is smaller in size than would be expected for your pregnancy dates and the cervix is usually closed. An ultrasound scan will show that the baby has died and has started to be reabsorbed. In this type of miscarriage, the woman is often aware that her pregnancy symptoms have faded, because the hormones of pregnancy have stopped being produced.

Pregnancy tests

Although the pregnancy test is very useful to diagnose that you are pregnant, it is not always helpful in deciding that you have miscarried. This is because the human chorionic gonadotrophin (HCG) hormone that is being measured in the pregnancy test takes time to completely clear from your body after the pregnancy is ended. This time delay is referred to as the 'half life' of the hormone and in the case of HCG the half life is about 36 hours. This means that the levels of HCG will fall by half every 36 hours that pass after the pregnancy dies.

If the miscarriage occurs very early and the HCG levels have never been high, the pregnancy test will become negative very quickly. A good example of this is a biochemical pregnancy (see Chapter 2), in which the woman may have no physical symptoms or signs of pregnancy. On the other hand, if the levels of HCG have reached a high level by the time the miscarriage occurs, it may take many days for the HCG to clear completely and for the pregnancy test to read negative. This applies to both blood and urine tests and explains why your pregnancy test may still be positive when the ultrasound scan shows that the pregnancy has miscarried. This can be a cause of great confusion and distress for women who have just miscarried.

Nowadays, the HCG pregnancy tests that are performed on blood samples can be 'quantified' very accurately. Instead of a yes or no result, the actual levels of HCG may be reported. Knowing the number of units of HCG present in the blood may be useful in certain situations. If the levels are increasing very slowly in the early weeks of pregnancy, this is often a sign that the pregnancy is not developing properly, but this is not a hard and fast rule. I do not use HCG tests very often for miscarriage patients because I find that they rarely influence how I manage my patient.

The exception to this is when I suspect that a woman has an ectopic pregnancy (see Chapter 3). In this situation it may be possible to avoid an operation if the levels of HCG start to fall. Some ectopic pregnancies do stop growing before they reach a size which endangers the woman (due to the risk of rupturing through the wall of her fallopian tube). The ectopic may just shrivel up and be absorbed within the tube or it may miscarry out of the end of the tube into the abdominal cavity. If the woman is not experiencing abdominal pain and the HCG levels are starting to fall, it may be possible to keep a close eye on her, repeating the HCG test every couple of days until the levels reach zero.

Sometimes it may be possible to perform a laparoscopy (telescope procedure through the navel) and inject an ectopic pregnancy that is still growing with a substance to stop it progressing. After the injection the HCG levels are monitored carefully to ensure that this 'conservative' treatment has been successful. However, this should only be carried out by doctors experienced in this method of treatment for an ectopic pregnancy.

Progesterone tests

It is true that your blood levels of progesterone hormone will usually be lower than normal if you are miscarrying, but this is not a helpful test. I always advise doctors not to perform it and explain to my patients why it is not useful for them to request this test. Very low progesterone levels reflect the fact that the ovary and/or the early placenta are not working properly. The production of hormone falls because the pregnancy has failed and is destined to miscarry. Since injections of progesterone (or HCG) cannot make the pregnancy come alive again (see Chapter 4), the information gained from a progesterone test is of no practical use.

I know that many women who have had fertility treatment are offered regular progesterone tests in early pregnancy. The reason for this is that high levels can be interpreted as showing that the pregnancy is off to a good start. While this may be comforting for some women, I think it is important to remember that progesterone levels may vary widely from individual to individual. A lower than average level does not necessarily mean that the pregnancy is in trouble, but the low result almost always causes anxiety and distress. I think progesterone tests in early pregnancy should be avoided. In later pregnancy they are of no help at all.

Development of future blood tests

The medical journals and the lay press are always very quick to report potential new tests which may help us to predict pregnancies that are at risk of miscarrying. The problem is that many of the new wonder tests do not stand up to long term detailed examination. Some of them are very sensitive, which means that they pick up a lot of possible abnormalities – but frequently they are then found to be poor in specificity, which means that they identify too many false positive results. Of course, the reverse can also be the case – good in specificity but not sensitive enough to pick up all the potential abnormalities.

So the best advice I can give you is by all means investigate the possibility that the latest test described in your daily newspaper or favourite magazine is helpful, but make sure that you also find out how many false positive and false negative results this test is likely to produce. Trying to tease out the most useful test results has always been a difficult task, but now that most individuals have access to the Internet, I think the problems have escalated. The information that is placed on the world wide web does not have to be peer reviewed or scrutinised and criticised by experts in the field in the same way that information published in reputable journals has undergone scrutiny. So be wary and try to ensure that you don't rush off and undergo new tests that lead to untried treatments until you feel confident that there is enough sound evidence to justify your participating in potentially disappointing and possibly harmful procedures.

I am going to resist the temptation of including all of the potential new tests that have been reported in the last few months because I believe that the readers of this book need to receive information that is evidence based and tried and tested. However, I am already anticipating that I will be posed numerous questions in the near future about several avenues of investigation that have received a lot of press coverage recently. So I will mention one of them briefly here – the importance of vitamins C and E in combating the damage that free radicals (the waste products produced by all of our cells as they metabolise oxygen) lead to. Although oxygen is essential for life, we now understand that as we use the oxygen it gives rise to very toxic waste products, which cause all sorts of damage to our cells. The papers are full of information, some useful, some not, about dietary methods of tackling free radicals – which are called antioxidants. Red wine, vegetables, fruit – particularly tomatoes (lots of them) are great natural sources of antioxidants.

A recent study has found that women with pre-eclampsia have an increased risk from this problem, which is called 'oxidative stress', and that they can reduce their risk of pre-eclampsia by taking vitamin C and E supplements during pregnancy. Not surprisingly, this information has fuelled interest in the possibility that women who have suffered recurrent miscarriages may also be victims of oxidative stress. This may well prove to be the case but at the present time there are no data to support this hypothesis. More worrying to me is that several newspapers have suggested that recurrrent miscarriers might benefit from taking vitamin supplements in early pregnancy. As I said earlier, we do not know whether these will be helpful and, perhaps more importantly, we do not know the effect that extra vitamins may have on the development of the tiny embryo. Every woman and every obstetric doctor I work with knows about the fetal abnormalities and tragic problems that the use of thalidomide caused. But when thalidomide was first offered as a treatment for early pregnancy it was heralded as a wonder drug. We need to make a conscious effort not to fall into the same trap again. I promise you that studies are already planned to establish whether these vitamin supplements are beneficial in reducing the problem of miscarriage.

Ultrasound scans

Without doubt the most useful method to find out what is happening to your early pregnancy is the ultrasound scan. I often wonder to myself how we used to manage when ultrasounds were not so freely available. Of course, the answer is that many women experienced long periods of worry and uncertainty about whether their pregnancy was safe or at risk.

A wide range of early pregnancy US signs and appearances have been studied in the hope that they will provide us with information as to whether the pregnancy is going to continue successfully or fail to progress. Several studies have suggested that an irregular shape to the gestation sac or yolk sac, a slow fetal heartbeat, slow growth of the early embryo and the presence of blood clots behind the placenta are indicative of a poor outcome or prognosis. I need to emphasise here that none of these signs are conclusive.

The first questions you will want answered if you experience pain or bleeding in early pregnancy are, 'Am I still pregnant?' and, 'Is my baby all right?' An ultrasound scan will be able to see whether the pregnancy sac is intact and whether there is an embryo present in the sac. It will also be able to tell you whether the pregnancy is in the right place. If there is no sac visible in the cavity of the uterus, it is important to find out whether you have had a complete miscarriage or whether the pregnancy is in an ectopic site, most usually the fallopian tubes. Ectopics are notoriously difficult to visualise on the scan, but there may be tell-tale signs suggesting that you are pregnant, even though no pregnancy sac can be seen. These are thickening of the uterine lining in the absence of a small round early pregnancy sac, and fluid in the space behind the body of the uterus – known as the pouch of douglas. This fluid which collects in the pouch is usually blood which has escaped from the fallopian tubes. These scan findings will alert your doctor to the fact that you may have an ectopic pregnancy.

If you have a vaginal ultrasound scan, it is usually possible to see whether there is a tiny embryo with a fetal heartbeat by six weeks into the pregnancy. If there is a heart beat, this is a very encouraging sign because many miscarriages happen before the baby has grown to a size that requires a proper circulation of blood with a heartbeat.

If there is no heartbeat, but a tiny fetal pole is visible, it is still possible that a heartbeat will develop by the seventh week. It is important to remember that sometimes your pregnancy dates will be wrong or you may have a particularly long menstrual cycle which means that you became pregnant later than you thought! By seven weeks, if there is a fetal pole within a healthy looking sac, you should be able to see a heartbeat.

For women who have not had miscarriages, the likelihood of the pregnancy being successful after a fetal heart has been seen is over 95%. For women who have experienced several miscarriages, the prognostic value of a fetal heart is not so good. Some cases of auto-immune recurrent miscarriage due to phospholipid antibodies (see Chapter 12) are notorious for miscarrying after fetal heart activity has been seen, but this problem affects no more than 15% of all recurrent miscarriage sufferers.

If you have experienced some bleeding, you will want to know where it is coming from. The US scan may be able to see an area of blood clot behind the placenta (haematoma). It may also demonstrate that there is another sac in the uterus which is not developing and is starting to break up, which is the cause of the bleeding you are experiencing. Second sacs (twin conceptions) are actually very common. We did not realise this until US scans became so routine a procedure in early pregnancy. A further scan in a week or two will probably be able to show you that the blood clot is smaller in size or the second sac is being reabsorbed.

I think you will be comforted to hear about the results of a recent study we performed at St Mary's Hospital. We looked back into the miscarriage clinic database over a period of several years and collected together all the women who had attended our dedicated early pregnancy scanning clinic during their next pregnancy. When we analysed their early pregnancy scan reports we found that the presence of intrauterine haematomas was really quite common. 12% of our patients with a history of recurrent miscarriage developed a haematoma in their next pregnancy. We then looked at the final pregnancy outcomes of these women and happily we were able to identify that the presence of an intrauterine haematoma in early pregnancy did not predict a further miscarriage or later pregnancy complication such as fetal growth retardation, pre-eclampsia or premature delivery. Yes, it is true that the haematoma patients did experience more episodes of vaginal bleeding and they were also more likely to have the phospholipid syndrome (see Chapter 12) but this did not affect the final pregnancy outcome. I think this a very reassuring finding and I hope that it will give you some comfort if you are told that you have a haematoma on the US scan in your next pregnancy.

Try not to worry if the scan does not identify any obvious cause for the bleeding. This situation is very common and in most cases the bleeding will stop and the pregnancy will continue safely. As mentioned earlier in this book, red bleeding is fresh or recent, but when the blood is brown, this means that it is old. There is only one place for the blood to drain out of the uterus and that is through the cervix and into the vagina. It may continue draining for some time, so try not to worry about brown discharge if the pregnancy is continuing to grow on the scan.

I think one of the greatest uses of early pregnancy US scans is to show you that the pregnancy is developing. At five weeks the pregnancy sac is small, but it will probably contain a small yolk sac, which looks like a thick-rimmed circle or balloon near the edge of the sac. One week later the sac will have doubled in size and the fetal pole will be visible. By seven weeks the sac will again have grown, the fetal pole will be longer and the heartbeat will be visible. By eight weeks the baby is starting to lose its comma-like shape and by nine weeks it will have a recognisable head and body. It may also be possible to see the baby's legs and the umbilical cord which attaches the baby to the placenta.

Week by week, the scan will be able to show you whether the baby is growing. Of course, if you find that the baby has not grown over a period of two weeks, this is a cause for concern. If the fetal heart is still visible there is still hope, but if the fetal heart disappears, then sadly, your doctor will have to make the diagnosis that the baby has died. This is always very distressing and some women will not be able to believe it at first. You may feel that you want to wait for a few more days and have another scan. Although the result will almost always be the same, this need for proof is very understandable. I never try to persuade any woman I see in this situation to have an evacuation (ERPC) until she is absolutely sure in her own mind that the pregnancy is truly over.

Having said this, I think the scan is enormously helpful in this situation, because it can avoid delays in making the diagnosis. For many women I meet, the most upsetting problem is being unsure of what is happening. If you have only had a scan at eight weeks and the result suggests that the baby is smaller than it should be, it is difficult for the doctor to know whether there is a problem with the pregnancy or whether it is simply that your dates are wrong and that the pregnancy is younger than you thought. In this situation, it is likely that your doctor will suggest that you wait for another week or two and then have a repeat scan to confirm what is going on. But if you have had an earlier scan, the doctor will be able to compare the two reports and will be able to make a much more accurate assessment of the situation.

In addition to the emotional trauma that delays in the diagnosis of a miscarriage may cause, the delay can also mean that the opportunity of obtaining fresh tissue for genetic analysis is lost. This is one of the reasons that I try and persuade my patients to undergo an ERPC as soon as they are confident in their own minds that the pregnancy has died. Although this is unlikely to be at the top of your priority list when you have just received the sad news. I promise you that when the initial shock wears off, you will want as much information as possible about your pregnancy and why it miscarried.

Knowing the genetic makeup of the baby is of great value, as I have mentioned in several chapters of this book. If the baby was chromosomally abnormal, I think you will be surprised how much comfort this information will provide you with in the future. Of course, it does not bring back the baby you have lost, but it does allow you to understand why the miscarriage occurred. For so many women who have no knowledge of why they lost their pregnancy, this is a piece of information that they would dearly love to have.

Examination of the placental tissues can also prove to be very useful, as I discussed in detail in Chapter 3. In the short term the pathologist can tell us whether the placental tissues were developing normally, whether there was evidence of infection or possibly a prothrombotic abnormality (see Chapter 12). However, the microscope slides can be stored for many years if required and this is potentially very valuable. As we improve our understanding of the causes of miscarriage it may be possible to go back to these slides and carry out newly discovered tests on the stored tissues. If this sounds fanciful, then let me give you an example. Many of the latest medical advances rely on extracting the DNA (genetic code) from tissues and it is now becoming possible to do this from tissues even when they have been fixed in formalin, embedded in paraffin and stored for some years. As new genetic disorders are identified we will be able to go back and literally 'probe' the miscarriage tissues to find these molecular abnormalities. I believe that this is one of the most exciting avenues for future research into the causes of pregnancy loss.

I frequently talk to anxious couples in the miscarriage clinic who are concerned that their pregnancy is not the 'right' size for dates. What matters in this situation is not the actual size of the pregnancy, but whether the pregnancy is growing. For example if the scan at seven weeks shows a small sac only, but two weeks later it shows that the pregnancy has increased in size by two weeks' worth of growth, then it really does not matter that the size of the baby is still smaller than the original dates would suggest.

Another source of concern is whether the repeated scans may cause any harm to the baby. About this issue I feel very confident in telling you: no, the scans will not harm your baby in any way. Several large studies have shown that repeated ultrasound scans have no adverse effects on the development of the baby (for further details see Chapter 9).

Doppler ultrasound

Some hospitals now have US machines which are also capable of looking at the blood flow through the blood vessels in the uterus and the placenta. This is called Doppler ultrasound and the patterns of blood flow can be translated into different colours on the scan picture. This technique has taught us a lot about the development of blood circulation in the uterus and placenta. We hope in the future that reading the pattern of blood flow in the uterus and the early placenta will help us to identify pregnancies that are at risk of miscarrying.

If this technique can be developed successfully, a Doppler scan would also be a very helpful way for us to reassure women who have experienced problems of bleeding or pain in early pregnancy. However, at the present time, Doppler scans are not able to offer us clear information about what is happening or just about to happen to your early pregnancy. I think it is very important to encourage research into this area, but it is too early to make clinical decisions on the basis of the results of Doppler scans in early pregnancy.

Later pregnancy – investigations available

If you have suffered a late miscarriage, you will have noticed that this chapter has not offered you much information about the tests available in later pregnancy to diagnose a miscarriage or a pregnancy that is in trouble. There are no useful blood tests, but the ultrasound scan can provide useful information. Slow growth of the baby, a placenta which appears small and gritty and a reduced level of amniotic fluid (liquor) around the baby are all signs that the baby is in trouble.

The problem (or rather the limitation) with these US findings in later pregnancy is that even when they diagnose that the baby is at risk, there is nothing that can be done about it. It is only after 26 weeks when the baby has a chance of surviving, if it is delivered, that the results of these US scans can influence how we manage the pregnancy. Before this date the only thing we can do is cross our fingers and hope that the pregnancy will continue until the baby has reached a size that is potentially viable in the outside world.

At the present time Doppler blood flow scans in later pregnancy are much more useful than in early pregnancy. For example, they can identify that the blood flow to the baby is reduced before the baby's growth starts to fall off. This is an enormously important development and means that we can 'rescue' some babies before serious trouble develops, by making a decision to deliver them early. But this is only feasible after 26 weeks and exciting as it is, I recognise that further details are beyond the scope of this book.

SIXTEEN

THE PHYSICAL PROCESS OF MISCARRIAGE – WHAT TO EXPECT

It is difficult to make generalisations about the physical events that may occur at the time of your miscarriage. They usually depend upon the stage in pregnancy at which the miscarriage occurs. And of course they will vary from woman to woman and pregnancy to pregnancy. What usually happens in early pregnancy is that you will experience some bleeding and will be seen by your GP or by one of the doctors at the local hospital. They will examine you and may suggest that you have an ultrasound scan if it is not clear what is going on.

You may actually see the miscarried pregnancy if the bleeding is heavy or occurs suddenly. If you pass a creamy coloured sac of membranes, with or without a tiny embryo inside it, then you will immediately recognise it. More often, you will be aware of passing large clots of blood but not be sure whether there is tissue in the clots. If the miscarriage starts at home, you may have tried to save the tissue you have passed so that the doctor can look at it. Many women I see worry about what happens to these tissues. If you have suffered several miscarriages, the doctors will probably arrange for them to be sent to the genetics laboratory for analysis. Alternatively, they may be sent to the routine pathology laboratory where they will be fixed in formalin (see Chapter 4) and examined under the microscope. This type of analysis may show that the embryo or the placental tissues are malformed in some way, but it will not establish the genetic makeup of the baby. This can only be done in the genetics laboratory.

If the miscarriage occurs before eight weeks and is complete (see Chapter 3) it may not be necessary for you to be admitted to hospital.

If you are, and the physical examination or ultrasound scan shows that the uterus is empty, you will be able to go home without any treatment. Indeed, you may not even have to visit the hospital if your GP has been looking after you and has made the diagnosis of a complete miscarriage.

If you have experienced a lot of bleeding, which is continuing, and the physical examination or ultrasound scan suggests that there are still tissues present in the uterine cavity, then you will be advised to go into hospital and undergo a short operation to clear out the uterus. This is called an ERPC (evacuation of retained products of conception). You will be admitted to hospital and you will be asked to sign a form in which you give your consent to the operation. It is important that you do not have anything to eat or drink for at least four hours before the operation so that you will not have any complications with the anaesthetic. You will probably be taken into the anaesthetic room (which is just outside the operating room) lying on a trolley bed. Here you will meet the anaesthetist who will explain that you are going to have an injection in your arm to put you to sleep. The general anaesthetic is light and you will recover quickly from it.

During the operation your cervix will be gently dilated (opened) so that small instruments can be inserted into the uterine cavity to clear out any tissues that remain there. When the pregnancy is less than 12 weeks, the tissues are usually sucked out of the uterus using a type of small vacuum cleaner. All the tissues are collected in a clean sealed jar and can then be sent off to the laboratory for analysis, if needed. The advantages of this vacuum method of cleaning out the uterus are that it is very efficient, and it is much less likely that any pieces of tissue will be left behind. It also reduces the risk of the tissues becoming infected by organisms in the vagina and cervix. As we discussed in Chapter 4, this can effect the chances of genetic analysis on the tissues being successful.

Sometimes the diagnosis that the pregnancy has died will be made with the ultrasound scan but the baby and the placenta are still intact within the uterine cavity. In this situation it is usually advisable to have the pregnancy evacuated rather than wait for the pregnancy to miscarry spontaneously. If the pregnancy is more than 12 weeks, it may be necessary to use special drugs to 'prime' or prepare and gently soften the cervix in order to minimise any potential damage to the cervix when it is dilated or stretched up. This is important because the size of the baby may necessitate the use of special forceps to remove some of the tissues before a final cleaning of the cavity is performed with the suction method.

When it is known that the baby is larger than 16 weeks' size, the doctors will probably advise you that they need to induce you to go into labour and for you to deliver the baby vaginally. This may sound very frightening to some readers but I think it is important for me to explain exactly what will happen so that you are prepared if you have the misfortune to be in this situation. The process of labour can take quite a long time because at this early stage in pregnancy the uterus is less prepared to contract and expel the baby. In order to make the cervix soften and start to dilate, a pessary is put into the vagina. It will probably be necessary for you to have several pessaries inserted at intervals of approximately four to six hours. The pessaries contain prostaglandins. These prostaglandins are chemical substances which are normally produced by the cervix at the time of delivery to 'prime' the uterus to contract. Recently it has been possible to give this prostaglandin drug in tablet form which is often more acceptable to women. However, a small proportion of women may experience side-effects such as nausea, vomiting and other gastrointestinal problems with the oral form of the drug.

The pessaries can only be used one at a time because occasionally they have a strong effect on the uterus, making it contract violently. It is likely that you will think that nothing is happening for many hours after the first one or two pessaries are inserted. The cervix will be softening silently and when it starts to open gently you will probably experience some discomfort in the lower abdomen, similar to period pains. A bit later, the uterus will start to contract and eventually the baby will be delivered. This usually takes about 24 hours, but may be a longer or shorter period of time.

Many women are understandably very worried that they will experience a lot of pain. Let me reassure you immmediately that you will not suffer much physical discomfort because you will be offered plenty of analgesia (pain-killing drugs). The most commonly used painkillers are pethidine and omnopon, which are given as an injection into a muscle in your bottom or upper thigh. The pain relief lasts about four hours, after which further injections will be offered to you. Some units will be able to offer you an epidural anaesthetic. This is an injection in your back which numbs your body from the waist downwards.

The great advantage of an epidural is that it can be 'topped up' at regular intervals to keep you pain-free without the need for further injections. Having said this, I must tell you that when a mother in this sad situation asks me for advice about the most suitable method of pain relief, I almost always suggest that she has pethidine injections. This is because the pethidine will make you feel a bit sleepy and gives you the feeling of floating on air. You will not be fully aware of events all of the time. An epidural anaesthetic will make you pain-free but you will be wide awake and conscious of everything that is happening to you physically and emotionally. Of course, you and only you must decide whether you want to be acutely aware or slightly numbed emotionally. However, I think most women will find some relief in the escape that pethidine can provide at a time like this.

There is one more physical hurdle to cross after this distressing labour and that is the delivery of the placenta. In very late miscarriages, after 20 weeks, the placenta may deliver spontaneously after the baby, or with the help of the midwife pulling gently on the umbilical cord. Before 20 weeks the placenta is usually, but not always, retained in the uterus. It needs to be removed to avoid further bleeding and later infection. If you have had an epidural for the labour this can be 'topped up' to allow the removal to take place. Otherwise you will need to undergo a light general anaesthetic.

Possible problems you may encounter in hospital

If you do have to go into hospital and have an ERPC the staff will try to arrange your operation as quickly as possible. But sadly, even the best laid plans can go wrong and you may experience long delays which are extremely distressing. If you have had to fill up your bladder by drinking water for an abdominal ultrasound scan, the anaesthetist will insist that at least four hours passes before he or she gives you a general anaesthetic. The operating theatre may be busy and, just as you think your turn has come, an emergency may claim your operating slot, forcing your ERPC to be delayed still further.

After the operation, the doctors may be so busy that no one is available to come and ensure that you are well enough to go home for some time. You may feel that no one cares about your problems and feelings and although this really is not the case, I understand how you may well feel this way. You are tired and distressed and the staff are overworked. The doctors may be unable to answer your questions fully and appear to have no time for the explanations you are looking for. You may end up with the impression that you are 'just another routine miscarriage' and from this point onwards everything goes from bad to worse. I am not suggesting that you should be trying to understand everyone else's problems at this difficult time, but I think it is helpful for you to know that the hospital staff do care and they do want to sort out your problems as quickly as possible.

If the only bed available is in the postnatal ward, the sound of crying babies can be the last straw. Although we try hard to prevent this situation, it is sometimes unavoidable. Indeed, this is one of the reasons why we aim to discharge you from the hospital as quickly as possible but this in itself may make you feel that no one wants to spend time with you. If you have suffered a late miscarriage, you may find that you are starting to produce milk and this is always very distressing after losing a baby. Tablets are available (called bromocryptine) to suppress milk production if this is very troublesome.

Your GP will be sent a summary of your admission and treatment as soon as you are discharged from the hospital. Sometimes the communications are slow – particularly at weekends – which is why we usually fax the report to the surgery these days.

New developments – drugs to clean out the womb

It is now possible to use drugs to empty the pregnant uterus for women whose miscarriage has occurred before eight weeks. The drugs used are a combination of an antiprogesterone and prostaglandins. The antiprogesterone blocks the action of progesterone hormone, which maintains the early pregnancy in the uterus, and the prostaglandins can then act upon the cervix and uterine muscle to expel the pregnancy from the uterus. This method is not yet available at all hospitals but it is likely that it will become increasingly popular over the next few years, since it avoids the need for an anaesthetic and an operation. It also reduces the amount of pain relief that is needed by most women. You may want to ask your doctor if this method is suitable for you, so I have included a few details about it here.

If you decide to have this medical evacuation of the uterus, you will be asked to attend the hospital where you will be given a tablet of mifipristone (often referred to as RU486) which is the anti-progesterone drug. You will be asked to wait on the ward for about 30 minutes, until the tablet has been absorbed and then you can go home. Some women feel a bit sick after taking the tablet but this usually settles quickly. You may have some period-like pain or bleeding the day after and if you feel uncomfortable you can take a paracetamol tablet.

Approximately 24 hours later you will return to the hospital and at this visit you will be examined vaginally and a pessary of prostaglandin will be inserted into the vagina. You will experience some pain and bleeding and will be offered painkillers if you need them. Most women will miscarry within four hours of having the pessary and can go home an hour or so later. Light vaginal bleeding may continue for up to 12 days after your admission but usually stops before the date of your clinic follow-up visit two weeks later. Treatment with prostaglandin drugs is not recommended for women with heart disease, asthma, or kidney and liver disease, but your doctor will be able to advise you about whether this method is suitable for you.

Saying goodbye to your baby

Having gone through all the physical events of your miscarriage, you may then have to face some emotional traumas. Most couples find that the miscarriage, surgical evacuation of the uterus, or the labour, feel like a bad dream and that it is only after these have ended that the full realisation of what has happened hits them emotionally. Whatever the age of the pregnancy, you may want to seek advice about how you can say goodbye to your baby. If the miscarriage occurred early in pregnancy, then there will be no specific practical issues that require you to make a decision. You will be grieving and ways of coping with this very natural response are discussed in the next chapter.

If you have had a late miscarriage, a late termination for medical reasons or a stillbirth, you will be asked if you want to see your baby. I urge you to do so and more than that, hold and cuddle your baby, give him or her a name, and spend as much time with the baby as you feel you want to. You may initially be afraid to see the baby because you feel he or she may be deformed or look odd in some way. What you imagine is usually far worse than the reality.

I shall never forget listening to the thoughts of a woman who had delivered a baby 60 years earlier with severe spina bifida. She recalled how all those years ago it was not recognised how important it is for the mother to be offered the chance of seeing and holding her baby. The baby was whisked away and for 60 years she had experienced nightmares, thinking that the baby she had delivered was some sort of monster. When she eventually told her new young GP about these fears he showed her a picture from a textbook of a baby with spina bifida. It was only then that her nightmares stopped and she was able to think about this lost baby without fear.

Many women tell me how important it is to have had some time with their baby and they find it enormously helpful in dealing with their grief, later on. This is because spending time with the baby provides you with an opportunity to say hello and goodbye to him or her. Most importantly, it will remove the fear of the unknown. I am absolutely confident in saying to you that every woman's baby is beautiful and special. Please do not miss the opportunity of realising this fact.

If you feel that you do not want to see the baby, he or she will be taken out of the room as soon as you deliver. However, most hospitals will take a photograph of the baby which will be given to you or kept for you in the medical notes in case you would like to see it or have it at a later date. These records are kept for many years. If you find that you want to come back to the hospital a long time after the pregnancy loss, these photographs will have been kept in your notes.

There is little doubt that you will be feeling very distressed after your late miscarriage. Try to talk to the staff involved in your care and ask them questions if there are any problems troubling you. I have never worked with a doctor, midwife or nurse who does not feel saddened and distressed by the plight of a woman who loses her baby in late pregnancy. They may have seen the problem many times before but this will not stop them from feeling great concern and sympathy for you. Talk to them, cry with them and be angry with them. They will understand and they will also have useful advice to offer you.

The doctors may suggest that your baby undergoes a post-mortem examination (autopsy) to try and identify a medical condition that may have led to the death of your baby. I know that this can be a cause of great anxiety and distress for parents who have just lost a baby. I would like to explain to you what happens at the post-mortem in the hope that it will comfort you, allay your fears and encourage you to find out all you can about why your baby died.

The post-mortem will be carried out by a pathologist who may have specialist training in disorders of children and babies (paediatric or perinatal pathologist). At the post-mortem the baby's body and internal organs will be examined. This examination needs to carried out as soon as possible after the baby's death and usually within 72 hours. The post-mortem will be carried out with great care and can take up to three hours. The pathologist will make sure that openings are made in places that are not visible when your baby is fully dressed. Your baby's face, arms and legs will not be affected by the post-mortem.

During the examination small samples of tissue and body fluids may be taken for special tests. The results of these tests may not be available for many weeks but this will not affect the funeral arrangements. The pathologist will write a detailed report and send it to the doctors looking after you. Most hospitals arrange to see parents about six weeks later when the test results are all available to discuss with them.

At the end of the post-mortem, the baby's body will be carefully repaired so that you can see and hold your baby again if you wish. The hospital will have suitable clothing to dress your baby, but you may want to dress the baby in your own baby clothes. If you do not want to see the baby again after the post-mortem, the body will be stored in the mortuary.

Unless a coroner has legally authorised a post-mortem to be performed on your baby, the post-mortem cannot be carried out without your consent. Some couples become very concerned that the post-mortem will be against their religious beliefs. Many of these worries can be easily sorted out by discussing them with your doctor or religious leader. If you decide that you do not want your baby to have a full post-mortem, talk to your doctor about other tests which may provide some limited information about the cause of death.

There is a legal requirement for any baby born after 24 weeks to be buried or cremated. If your baby has died at an earlier date, before 24 weeks, you can make arrangements for a funeral, but you will not require a death certificate. Some hospitals will organise a funeral on your behalf or help you to arrange it yourselves. If you have had a very early miscarriage, it is likely that your baby will be disposed of by the hospital.

The funeral may be a way of helping you with your loss. Many couples find that it provides them with a dignified way of saying goodbye to their baby. If you do not want the formality of a full funeral service, you may want to arrange for the hospital chaplain or a religious leader of your own faith to give a short service or prayer for your baby, either during or after your stay in hospital.

Some hospitals organise regular memorial or remembrance services for parents who have lost babies. At my own hospital we hold a special service twice a year to which both parents and the staff involved in their care are invited. It is always extremely well attended, which suggests to me that these more formal acts of remembrance can be very helpful after your baby has died. Some cemeteries have special areas for premature or stillborn babies. The hospital chaplain, patient affairs officer or one of the midwives looking after you should be able to give you the information you need to find out what is available in your area.

There are many different ways of remembering your baby. For many parents, this will be extremely important and can play a significant role in their grieving process in the short and the long term. Giving the baby a name is particularly comforting and will help you to remember him or her as a 'real' person. You will probably find that other people find it easier to talk to you about your baby by name, instead of 'the baby', which can sound so anonymous.

Many parents find that compiling a book of memories helps them enormously in the years to come. It may include a photograph of an ultrasound scan, antenatal test results, a photograph of the baby, a lock of hair, a hospital name bracelet, a copy of the memorial or funeral service, a few pressed flowers, perhaps some letters of sympathy. Some parents may prefer to remember their baby by planting a rose bush or tree, or marking a bench with a plaque placed in the park. Of course, you may not find any of these things helpful and there is certainly no reason to feel that you are expected to create memories of your baby. You may feel that your private memories are the most comforting and the most precious and if this is the case, then this is the right course for you to follow.

SEVENTEEN

IS IT NORMAL TO FEEL THIS WAY AFTER A MISCARRIAGE?

Yes, it is entirely normal. I promise you that whatever feelings you experience after a miscarriage, they are entirely normal. They may be different from the feelings that a friend of yours tells you she experienced, but you need to remind yourself that we all deal with grief, anger, despair, depression, guilt and self-blame in different ways.

The loss of a baby is a devastating experience. It doesn't matter how the pregnancy ended; all pregnancy losses, including miscarriage, ectopic pregnancy, stillbirth, neonatal death, or being forced to end the pregnancy because your baby is abnormal or your health is at serious risk, are equally heartbreaking.

It will be difficult for you, your partner and your family to come to terms with what has happened and you are likely to experience grief, anger and emptiness, not just immediately, but for a long period of time. No matter what kind of pregnancy loss you have experienced, you will probably be unprepared for the pain and anguish you feel. Instead of looking forward to the arrival of your baby, you are now left with a terrible sense of emptiness, frustration and even failure. All the love you were hoping to give this new person in your life has no outlet any more and this can give rise to very intense emotions. It is entirely normal for bereaved parents to feel isolated, angry with themselves, each other, the staff at the hospital, and jealous of other people who have healthy babies.

Grieving for your baby

It is quite normal for the shock of the pregnancy loss to numb all your feelings initially. With time, the process of grieving will start. Grief can be frightening and overwhelming especially if you think that it is abnormal to feel this way. Try not to fight it. Grieving is a natural way of expressing your feelings of loss and it needs to run its natural course.

The process of grief has different stages that may last for days, weeks or many months. It cannot be hurried up and if you try to skip one of the steps you will probably find that you have to revisit this stage at a later date. Undoubtedly, your feelings will change over time. The first feelings of shock, disbelief and denial are usually followed by severe emotional distress, including anxiety and depression. As the grieving process continues, you may experience feelings of anger, guilt and jealousy. Sometimes the yearning you may feel for your lost baby will be overwhelming. With time, these feelings will give way to a deep sadness. The acute grief will be replaced by feelings of mourning and regret for what has not happened. Eventually, you will feel resigned to what has happened, although this resignation will probably never take away the emotional pain entirely.

Even if you find it difficult, you should try to express your feelings and not bottle them up. By expressing them, you will find that it becomes much easier to understand these feelings and this will help you to deal with them. Easy for her to say, you may be thinking as you read this, but not so easy to do. I know that some people find it extremely difficult to express or share their grief. This is often because they are afraid of losing control if they let go of their emotions in any way. It does not matter if you lose control for a while. In fact, it is an essential part of the process you have to go through in order to recover from your loss.

If you are someone who is used to keeping your feelings to yourself, you may try to pretend – to yourself as well as everyone else around you – that you have recovered from the miscarriage. It may seem easier to try and brush aside or suppress your feelings of grief, in the hope that they will go away more quickly. They will have to come to the surface at some time. Let me say again that grieving takes time and there are no short cuts. Each one of us will need a different length of time to recover. I think it is also important to remember that the process of grieving does not always go in a straight line. Sometimes feelings you thought you had dealt with will return. You may think you have started to get over it and then suddenly you will be overwhelmed again.

Many women I meet in the miscarriage clinic tell me how distressed they feel by people who tell them that 'time is a great healer'. When you are grieving, you do not really want to hear that the acute feelings of pain and loss will fade with time. In some ways you do not want them to fade, at least for a while, because these feelings are the only part of your pregnancy that is still with you. You do not want to turn your back on your baby until you feel ready to do so. You should not feel guilty or fear that you are 'indulging' yourself. It is a perfectly healthy and normal response and an important part of coming to terms with your loss.

I have never been convinced that time heals completely, but I do believe that as time passes, the way in which we perceive grief changes. It becomes more manageable and less likely to catch us unawares. This does not mean that you will forget the pain and disappointment, but with time, it will become a part of your life that does not overwhelm you. You will be able to think about it and even revisit your emotions when you want to do so without feeling that you are helpless and out of control.

Similarly, you should not feel guilty if you feel strong and philosophical about your loss after the initial grieving period. You may find that you are ready to get on with your life quite quickly and I suggest that you do not allow other people's expectations of how long it should take you to recover to influence you. There are no right or wrong ways to deal with these important life events.

Depression

Depression is quite a common sequel to the acute phase of grief. You may feel tired or lethargic, with no energy and no desire to get on with anything. Changes in appetite and sleeping patterns, headaches and other aches or pains may develop, all of which can be symptoms of depression. Many women experience feelings of worthlessness and lose confidence in themselves. They often feel unable to cope with the daily routine of life or work. Other symptoms may be lack of concentration, irrational fears or behaviour, feelings of panic, or uncontrollable crying.

This type of 'reactive' depression usually passes of its own accord but it can last for weeks or months. If the symptoms continue, it is important that you are honest with yourself and recognise that you need some help. This is not a failure on your part, it is the only sensible way to help pull yourself out of the depression. Go and tell your doctor. He or she may be able to put you in touch with a bereavement counsellor, and occasionally it may be helpful to take some medication, either for depression or to help you sleep. Support groups have a very useful part to play in this situation. At the end of this book is a list of useful addresses and contact numbers.

Guilt

Guilt and self-blame are very common emotions after a miscarriage. 'What did I do wrong?' is a question that I hear regularly. This feeling is very understandable, particularly when there is no clear reason why the miscarriage occurred, but it is misplaced. You need to remember that it is highly unlikely that you did anything to cause the problem, so try not to punish yourself. You are not a failure. Nor are you a victim. You have had a miscarriage, which is a bitter disappointment, but it is not recompense for something that happened in your past. You will have a baby in the future and the quicker you start liking yourself again, the quicker a new pregnancy will end in success.

Your partner's grief

I think men have a particularly difficult role to play when their partner has a miscarriage. Remember that your partner will probably have had to watch you bleeding, in pain and, in many cases, undergo a general anaesthetic and an operation. It is very tough to see someone you love suffering and feel that you are powerless to help. It is also very frightening and this fear often leads to outbursts of anger. Distressed partners often ask me what will happen if something should go wrong in the operation, or if the bleeding cannot be stopped.

I meet many men who feel very frustrated and angry when their partner has to wait for an ultrasound, or for the doctor to see and assess the situation. If there is a further wait for an ERPC operation, the anger often bubbles over and explodes. This is an entirely understandable reaction which stems from the fact that he is trying to protect you. Many couples tell me that they later feel embarrassed if a scene developed during their hospital admission. Don't worry about it, no one will hold it against you. The hospital staff really do understand that your partner is concerned for your safety.

Your partner may find it difficult to express his feelings but he will be grieving too. He may well feel that he should hide his grief in an attempt to try and protect you from any more distress and help you through the physical traumas you have experienced. If this is the case, you will need to encourage him to talk to you about his feelings and not to keep them entirely to himself. Shared tears can be very therapeutic. When I see couples soon after a miscarriage, I often suggest to the man that he needs to do some crying too. I point out to them that he is also feeling the pain, and that they both need to accept that he cannot be the strong and supportive partner all the time.

For many couples, the experience of pregnancy loss brings them closer together. Sadly, for some couples the miscarriage raises feelings of resentment, guilt, self-blame and bewilderment, which can be very difficult to sort out. If you find yourselves in this situation, seek help – from friends, counsellors, a religious adviser – but don't allow the feelings to fester and get out of control. Throwing yourselves into work in the hope that it will all get better if you ignore your feelings seldom solves the problems and usually makes them much worse.

Telling your children

If you have other children, the pregnancy loss will almost certainly affect them too. However young they are, they will know that something is wrong. It is understandable that you may feel that you want to protect your children from something painful and difficult for them to understand. The reality is that the truth is usually less frightening for them than the things they may imagine are happening if you don't try to explain.

It is important that you tell them about the baby, and how you feel. You will need to listen carefully to what they say and ask them gentle questions to find out what they are thinking. Above all, answer their questions honestly, however painful it may be for you. There is no need to avoid using words like 'died' or 'death' as long as you try not to show them that you are frightened or anxious. They need to understand why you are feeling sad and in particular they need to be reassured that you love them and want to cuddle and kiss them even though you are distressed.

Many children may find it difficult to talk about their feelings immediately and you will need to be prepared for fears and difficult questions to emerge at a later date. Most importantly, you need to reassure them that they are not the cause of what has happened and try to stop them blaming themselves. They may feel lost and abandoned if you have needed to spend some time in hospital and they may be worrying about your safety in the future. Signs of emotional disturbances such as tantrums, sleeplessness, bedwetting and nightmares are all common. They will pass if you provide the children with love, support and constant reassurance that everything is going to be all right. Above all, encourage them to share their feelings with you.

Dealing with other people and their reactions

One of the most difficult things about having a miscarriage is dealing with other people and their reactions to your grief and distress. We human beings are not very good at coping with someone else's pain. We often take the easy way out and avoid talking about it. I am quite sure that this is not because we do not care but because we are frightened of saying the wrong thing, hurting feelings or reminding the sufferer of his or her pain. Embarrassment at the raw emotions that may be uncovered by a simple question is another reason. Few reactions in life could be so inappropriate. Most women who suffer a miscarriage positively want other people to talk to them about what has happened. Indeed, many women I meet tell me how distressing it can be when other people avoid the subject. Many feel resentful that someone they counted as a friend will not take the risk of asking them about the miscarriage. Worse, they may start to feel that their grief is unacceptable and should be hidden from public view.

One of the most important things I have learnt about miscarriage sufferers is the enormous comfort that you can offer by expressing your feelings of sadness for them. Of course, it does not take away the pain but a few spoken words or a brief note (however inarticulate) can make all the difference to someone who is grieving.

Losing a twin

Losing a twin or a triplet can be the start of a series of complex emotions. You may feel that you have a split personality for a while. One half of you will be mourning the death of the lost baby, while the other half will still be excited and relieved about the surviving baby or babies.

You may try to suppress your grief for the lost baby and put all your energies into thinking about the survivor(s). On the other hand, you may find it very difficult to cope with the remaining baby and be guilty that you feel this way. I think it is important for you to remember that just because you are still pregnant and can look forward to a baby being born, this does not mean that you feel the pain of your loss any less acutely. Once again, you need to allow yourself time and space to grieve properly. Remember, too, that you may need to find a way of explaining to the surviving baby what happened to his or her lost sibling.

Coping with anniversaries

When you have suffered a miscarriage, certain dates may suddenly take on great importance. As one patient explained to me, 'I could never remember dates without my diary before I lost my baby, and now I can tell you when I first missed my period, when I first started to bleed, when I miscarried and when my baby should have been born, right down to the last hour.' These anniversaries can be very painful and difficult to deal with.

I think the best way of tackling them is to give in to them and allow yourself to feel sad, robbed, disappointed, angry or whatever feeling they bring you. Just because the rest of the world does not recognise the anniversary is no reason for you to feel that you have to forget it or push it behind you. With the passage of time, the anniversary date will become much less painful. You won't forget it, but you will find that it becomes a wistful rather than a painful memory.

One of my miscarriage patients (who has subsequently had three healthy bouncing babies) tells me that she always takes a day off when her miscarried baby should have been born. She needs to spend a few quiet hours remembering the baby who 'did not make it'. When she first told me this, I was struck by how much comfort this had provided her with and asked her if she would share her idea with some other patients. She did and the letters I have received as a result of this 'self-help' suggest that it may be a very useful practice. Anniversaries for sadness can be as important as anniversaries for joy. The most important thing is that you recognise what you want to remember and remember it in your own way and in your own time.

Deciding whether to try again

This is a very individual decision. For some couples, there is no question – they want to embark on a new pregnancy without delay. There are no rules about when is the right time. If you feel emotionally prepared to embark upon another pregnancy, then it is likely that you are physically ready too. For others, it may take longer, particularly when the miscarriage was late. There is no doubt that losing a baby during the second and third trimesters of pregnancy is a particularly difficult blow to deal with. The emotional adjustments involved and the recovery time needed are often longer. Nonetheless, it will be you and only you who knows when and if you are ready to contemplate another pregnancy.

Most of the couples I meet decide that they do want to try for another pregnancy. The desire to have a child, whatever the obstacles met previously, is a strong and driving force. But there may come a time when you and your partner decide that you cannot expose yourselves any longer to the stress and trauma of repeated disappointments. I am often asked whether I think it is sensible to try again. I suspect that there will never be a correct answer to this question because it depends upon the couple, their history and their circumstances. The most useful advice I can offer is that you will know when you want to stop trying. Before this date, you will not want to give up because you believe that there may be a chance of reaching your goal.

The most important point here, I believe, is that whilst you still feel these emotions, you cannot and will not stop trying. The decision to put this quest behind you is rarely a sudden one. It comes after much soul searching and heartache. There may come a time when you feel that you need to stop trying for a baby and put your energies into other parts of your life. I certainly meet couples who feel relieved after coming to this decision because their lives have become dominated by trying to have a baby and they feel that this drive has started to become destructive. At the end of the day, only you can make the decision to stop trying. As long as you feel confident that you have pursued all the possible options available to you and that you will not be consumed by regrets that you did not try 'once more', then I think that this is the right decision for you and you need to take it.

Summary

Grieving for a lost baby is a process. It goes in stages and it has no set pattern and no time limits. For some women, it will be relatively quick, for others it will be longer. You do not need to feel that you should be over it because other people expect this of you. Nor should you feel that a short period of mourning means that you are odd or unusual. Give yourself as much time as you need to come to terms with what has happened.

EIGHTEEN

FINDING OUT MORE ABOUT THE PROBLEM OF MISCARRIAGE

Some hospitals are able to provide a counselling service for women who have suffered a miscarriage. If you think it may be useful, then find out whether this service is available to you and then use it for as long as you need to. If your hospital cannot provide help in this way, then go and see if your GP is able to help directly at the local surgery or can put you in touch with local organisations and self-help groups. A list of useful names and addresses of national organisations is included at the end of this book. A few telephone calls may provide you with some useful contacts that you never realised were available near you.

The Miscarriage Association is a very useful organisation to contact. Its members are voluntary and have suffered miscarriages themselves. They can provide you with details of members who live in your area, many of whom run support groups. These support groups can be enormously valuable and you are likely to find that becoming involved in such a group will mean that you meet many other couples with similar problems to your own. You will also be able to offer help to others in the future and this is another very positive way of coming to terms with your loss.

The Miscarriage Association also publishes a regular newsletter with articles from members, nurses, doctors and counsellors, all of whom have experience to offer you. In addition to locally organised activities, the association also runs an annual conference which you may want to attend. The annual conference usually invites doctors who are particularly interested in miscarriage to come and speak to the members.

If you have suffered repeated miscarriages, your doctor may suggest that you are referred to a specialist miscarriage clinic. These clinics can provide more extensive investigations into your problem and usually arrange to help you during the first few anxious months of the next pregnancy. Since there are not many specialist clinics across the country, it may be necessary for you to travel considerable distances for clinic appointments.

I know that most of the couples we see at the St Mary's recurrent miscarriage clinic do not mind the travelling and often tell me that they are prepared to go to any lengths to try and sort out their problem. If you are referred to the clinic at St Mary's by your GP or your local hospital consultant, you will be asked to fill in a detailed questionnaire about your general health and your pregnancies before you attend the clinic. The information in this questionnaire makes it possible for us to contact your local doctors for any missing pieces of information before we see you. It also means that when you first come to the clinic, the time can be spent talking about your specific problems, instead of trying to piece together the dates, scan results, complications and other details about your previous pregnancies.

While you are waiting for a clinic appointment, we will also try to arrange for you to have some investigations (usually blood tests) performed. This can save a lot of time and means that we have some of the results to discuss with you at the first visit. We can then arrange for further investigations that are suited to your individual case. For example, about one third of recurrent miscarriage sufferers also experience problems in getting pregnant. As I mentioned in Chapter 13, if these delays in conceiving are not clearly identified, then the chances of being able to sort out the problems are reduced. In other cases, complications in a previous pregnancy, which may have resulted in a live baby born prematurely, may provide clues about your particular problem.

Perhaps the most important function of specialist clinics is that they will also give you an opportunity to become involved in the most recent research into miscarriage (see Chapter 21). Joining a research programme is probably the most useful thing you can do to help yourself. Research programmes are crucial to the future development of successful treatments for miscarriage. As I frequently say to couples I see in the clinic, the treatment we can offer you today was an idea last year and the tests we want to perform today may result in a new treatment being available next year.

PART FOUR
THE NEXT STEP

NINETEEN

GETTING READY FOR THE NEXT PREGNANCY

General health issues – pre-conceptual care

Every woman trying to conceive should be as healthy as possible. It is sensible to consider several general health issues which can affect the chance of getting pregnant, the risk of miscarriage and the health of the baby. Certain risk factors can be avoided or minimised by simple precautions taken before pregnancy and during the pregnancy. Some hospitals and doctors' surgeries have introduced special clinics for women before becoming pregnant. These 'pre-conception' clinics are very helpful, offering general medical advice about diet, drugs, exercise, what to do and what to avoid doing when you are trying to become pregnant. Most importantly, they attempt to answer many of your queries and concerns about pregnancy.

It is important that a woman who is trying to become pregnant has a healthy, well-balanced diet and is of normal weight. If you are either under- or overweight, this can affect your chances of becoming pregnant. If you are underweight when you conceive, you are at risk of having a baby who is smaller than is ideal for his or her health. If you are overweight, avoid crash dieting and follow a well-balanced low-fat, low-sugar, high-fibre diet of approximately 1500 calories a day.

The Department of Health advises all women trying to conceive to take 0.4 milligrams (400 micrograms) a day of folic acid before pregnancy and to continue this for the first 12 weeks of pregnancy, in order to reduce the risk of having a baby with spina bifida or other neural tube defect (the name for disorders in which the brain and/or the spinal cord do not develop properly). It is likely that folic acid may also reduce the risk of other types of congenital abnormality and birth defects. Furthermore, it is useful to remember that there is some evidence to suggest that the levels of folate in our blood are increased more efficiently by the daily intake of 0.4mg in tablet form, rather than by eating an extra 0.4mg of folate in the diet each day. This dose of folic acid is available over the counter at chemists and is best taken on its own rather than in a multivitamin preparation, since these may put you at risk of taking too much vitamin A (see Chapter 20). If you must take a multivitamin tablet, do check that it contains 0.4–1.0mg of folic acid and not more than 5000 IU of vitamin A.

If a woman has had a previous pregnancy affected by spina bifida or another type of neural tube defect, it is recommended that she takes a higher dose of folic acid (a 5 milligram tablet) every day whilst trying to conceive, and for the first 12 weeks of pregnancy. This dose is available on prescription only, from your doctor. If you are epileptic, it is important that you discuss this with your doctor before starting to take folic acid, as it could alter the dose of anti-epileptic medication that you require. Women with epilepsy need to take the higher folic acid dose of 5 milligrammes each day because epileptics have a higher risk of having a baby with spina bifida (see further on in this chapter).

Alcohol can have a damaging effect on male fertility by a direct toxic effect which lowers sperm numbers. In heavy doses, alcohol can affect female fertility as well. It is sensible to restrict alcohol intake to 21 units per week for men and 14 units per week for women. However, I know of no data that suggests that becoming a teetotaller is helpful. So, if you enjoy a glass of wine with dinner – cheers!

Smoking cigarettes may make both men and women less fertile. It has been reported that the chance of conceiving is reduced by one third in women who smoke. Since smoking increases the risk of miscarriage as well, it is more than just a good idea to give up smoking before becoming pregnant. Passive smoking is also a risk – so if you live with someone who smokes as well, make an effort to give up together. There are several organisations which you can contact to help you, such as Quit and ASH (see useful addresses).

Rubella (German measles) infection during the first four months of pregnancy can cause severe handicaps to the baby. Most adult women in the UK and all children born after 1988 will have been vaccinated against rubella as a small child and we have now abandoned routine vaccination of teenage girls at school. The vaccination does not always provide long-term immunity, so make sure that you have a blood test to check your immunity before you try to become pregnant. And if this test shows that you are not immune to infection, get vaccinated straight away. Since the vaccination could potentially cause damage in very early pregnancy, it is sensible to have it done early in your menstrual cycle, just after your last period and before you could have possibly become pregnant, and to take contraceptive precautions until a repeat blood test four weeks later shows that the vaccination has been effective. In the past, women were advised to wait for three months after rubella vaccination before becoming pregnant, but we now know that only one month is necessary.

During the last few years I have met several patients who have become pregnant almost immediately after having a rubella vaccination. Their distress and fears that their tiny embryo may have been damaged prompted me to contact several virologists with special experience in rubella. Happily, I can tell you that there is a UK registry for all women who have conceived at the same time or soon after their rubella vaccination and that no abnormalities have ever been detected in the babies who have been born.

If you are rhesus negative and need to have an injection of anti-D after your delivery because your baby is rhesus positive, your doctor will probably suggest that your rubella vaccination is left to a later date. This is because the anti-D (which is another type of gamma globulin injection) can interfere with your ability to develop the correct antibody response in your blood to the rubella vaccination. This failure to 'sero-convert' is important because the only way to ensure that you and your baby are protected from rubella in the future is to measure a strong level of anti-rubella antibodies in your blood. This is why you will be asked to have a blood test a few weeks after your vaccination date to ensure that you have sero-converted. Rubella antibodies will be present in your blood if you have had the infection in the past or if you have been vaccinated.

Ensuring that women who wish to become pregnant are immune to rubella is something I feel very strongly about, both as a doctor and a mother. I will never forget the infertility patient I looked after many years ago who developed German measles in early pregnancy and had not been immunised. Despite this important personal lesson, I am ashamed to confess that when asked by my obstetrician during my own pregnancy if I was immune to rubella, I had to admit that I did not know! Fortunately I was, but my message to you, the reader, is please do not rely on being lucky. Go and get vaccinated today.

Exercise is obviously a good idea for general health and also in preparation for pregnancy. However, if you are an unfit 'couch potato', do not start a gruelling exercise programme on day one of your new fitness campaign. Regular, gentle exercise such as walking briskly for 30 minutes per day, cycling and swimming are all good ways to introduce regular exercise to your daily routine. If you are already used to more strenuous exercise like aerobics and working out in the gymnasium, you are probably quite fit already and should continue exercising to remain fit.

Serious medical disorders

If you have any long-standing medical condition, it is important to see your doctor when planning to become pregnant. It is also important to continue taking any medication that you have been prescribed for your medical problem until the doctor either changes it or stops it. If you are diabetic it is essential that your blood sugar levels are well controlled whilst you are trying to conceive. Poor diabetic control will reduce your chances of becoming pregnant and increase your risk of miscarriage.

If you suffer from epilepsy, it is particularly important that you are under close medical supervision when you are trying to become pregnant and during the pregnancy. Some anti-epileptic drugs can cause abnormalities in the baby, such as heart and limb defects, mental retardation, cleft lip and cleft palate, and are best changed to a different type of drug when trying to conceive. Pregnancy can change the way anti-epileptic drugs are metabolised in the body and you may need a higher dose. As noted earlier in this chapter, anti-epileptic drugs may reduce the mother's folic acid levels and it is very important that women with epilepsy take high dose folic acid supplements before becoming pregnant and during the first 12 weeks of pregnancy to minimise the risk of spina bifida.

High blood pressure (hypertension) is another medical problem which needs to be under good control when you are planning to become pregnant. The risk of developing pre-eclampsia (toxaemia) and severe problems with your blood pressure are greater if your blood pressure is high at the start of your pregnancy. Some of the anti-hypertensive drugs are not suitable for use in pregnancy, so please ensure that you have talked to your doctor about your plans to become pregnant well in advance, or as soon as the pregnancy test is positive. Asthma sufferers are another group who need to be carefully looked after before and during pregnancy. The aim is to reduce the amount of medication used without increasing the risk of an asthma attack.

Women with thyroid disease also need careful supervision during pregnancy. If you are taking drugs for your thyroid, the dosage required may alter during pregnancy. However, as we noted in Chapter 11, thyroid disease does not increase the risk of future miscarriage, although an under- or over-active thyroid may prevent you from falling pregnant.

Although acne cannot be classified as a serious medical disorder, I think it is important to remind the reader that some of the anti-acne drugs can cause serious abnormalities in the unborn baby. The vitamin A drugs which encourage the affected skin to peel off more quickly than usual are particularly dangerous and, as mentioned earlier in this book, the tetracycline antibiotics are contraindicated in pregnant women because the drug leaves deposits in the growing baby's teeth and bones and discolours them.

During the last five years, I have met an increasing number of women with renal disease requesting advice about pregnancy and miscarriage (see Chapter 9). Undoubtedly, one of the reasons for this is because the medical treatment of renal disease has improved so dramatically that some women who could never have risked a pregnancy before are now able to consider it as a distinct possibility.

However, if you do suffer from renal disease, it is important that you consult with your renal doctors before attempting to become pregnant.

Is there a place for alternative medicine?

I am often asked for my views about alternative medicine by women who are trying to become pregnant after having suffered a miscarriage. My reply is always the same – until conventional medicine can sort out every problem faced by women wanting to achieve a successful pregnancy, I will remain open-minded about any alternative treatment. In fact, I positively encourage some women to look at alternative options such as acupuncture and homeopathy. My reason for this is simple. I do not understand how they work, or even if they do work, but I do recognise that trying to do something for oneself is a good way to tackle the impotence and frustration that so many miscarriage sufferers experience. Most of the women I talk to in the miscarriage clinic are distressed by the feeling that they are not in control of what is happening to them both physically and emotionally. So if a visit to the Chinese herbalist or the Foresight organisation helps you to feel that you are back in the driving seat, then I recommend it. One word of warning, however. Try not to become obsessional about the alternative medicine. Cranky diets, worrying yourself silly that your hair analysis has suggested that you are deficient in zinc or magnesium, or taking so many vitamin tablets that you rattle when you jump up and down is not helpful. In fact, it is counter-productive, causing further stress and anxiety.

Period problems

If your menstrual periods are irregular or infrequent, you may experience a delay in becoming pregnant. In young, healthy women the commonest cause of irregular periods is polycystic ovaries (discussed in detail in Chapter 11). However, it is important to remember that for many women who have just experienced a miscarriage, normal, regular periods do not return for a couple of months. There is nothing abnormal about this and the best remedy is not to worry about it. In many cases it reflects the emotional distress of the recent miscarriage. However, if you know that you have polycystic ovaries, it is sensible to talk to your doctor about undergoing some tests to see if you are ovulating. If you are not ovulating regularly, it may be appropriate to have treatment to help you produce and release an egg every month. This treatment needs to be carefully monitored to prevent complications.

Heavy periods are unpleasant for a woman but they are not usually a cause of infertility. Nor do heavy periods increase the risk of miscarriage, unless they are due to the presence of a fibroid or polyp in the womb which may interfere with successful implantation of the early embryo. An ultrasound scan can help to determine what is going on. Periods that are too frequent usually reflect a problem with ovulation. Although an egg may be released, the next part of the menstrual cycle – the luteal phase – is too short and does not allow sufficient oppurtunity for a fertilised egg to implant properly. Light bleeding (spotting) in the middle of the menstrual cycle may be normal for some women, but it may also reflect hormonal imbalances or a physical problem such as a polyp in the womb or a raw area on the neck of the womb (cervix).

If you are experiencing period problems and you are preparing to become pregnant again, arrange to see your doctor. The likelihood is that nothing is seriously wrong, but establishing this fact will give you much more confidence. And if your doctor suspects that you do have a problem, a prompt referral to a gynaecologist is likely to sort the problem out quickly.

How long should I wait before trying again?

I am frequently asked by women who have recently miscarried if there is a recommended period of time to wait until trying to become pregnant again. The answer is no – there are no black and white rules. Most women will not conceive again until they have had a normal period, but this is not always so. Certainly, waiting for a normal period to come is a good way to reassure yourself that your hormones are back to normal and it will make the doctor's job much more simple if the dates of the next pregnancy can be calculated easily.

However, there are no data to suggest that falling pregnant again soon after a miscarriage increases the risk of a further miscarriage. I suspect the old advice offered to women that they should wait for three months is based on the idea that after that time the woman is more likely to be emotionally ready for another pregnancy. My personal advice is simple and individual. The right time to embark on another pregnancy is when you feel ready for it. For some women this will be straight away. For others, particularly those who have suffered a late miscarriage, a longer period of time will be needed to make all the emotional adjustments for a new pregnancy. There are only very rarely medical reasons for delaying a future pregnancy. One example is when a woman has suffered a blood clot, or thrombosis, during her previous pregnancy. In this situation, it is usually necessary to give the woman anticoagulant drugs for a couple of months following the pregnancy, during which time it is not sensible to become pregnant again. Indeed, most thrombosis experts will probably advise that any future pregnancies are postponed for at least 12 months.

What contraception should I use?

I meet many women in the miscarriage clinic who find themselves pregnant unexpectedly. This can be a cause of enormous distress, particularly if the woman is in the middle of investigations into the cause of the previous pregnancy losses. Invariably, the interruption to the investigations brings fears that a possible cause may have been missed. Worse, that there is no time to start treatment which may have helped prevent a future miscarriage.

It is sensible to use an effective type of contraception until you are ready, both physically and emotionally, to embark on your next pregnancy. I know that there are many old wives' tales told about the dangers of the combined oral contraceptive pill in this situation.

They are all untrue. There is no truth in the story that miscarriage is more common in women who conceive shortly after stopping the combined pill. If anything, the reverse is true. Several large prospective studies have shown that the risk of miscarriage may even be slightly lower in previous pill users.

Nor does the combined pill cause delays in becoming pregnant. In fact, there is some evidence suggesting that women with polycystic ovaries who have had ovulation problems, benefit from using the combined pill for several months before the next pregnancy. For some of these women, the pill appears to successfully correct the hormonal problems (most probably high LH levels) preventing regular ovulation, so that when they stop the pill they ovulate spontaneously for a short while and often conceive during the first or second month of trying. Hence, the widely quoted drug manufacturers' advice that women should avoid becoming pregnant for three months after stopping the combined pill (to allow time to clear the chemicals from her body) is both incorrect and unhelpful.

The situation with progestogen-only pills is not so clear cut. There is no evidence to suggest that they increase the risk of miscarriage. However, they do not offer the benefits of controlling ovulation and they do cause irregular bleeding in some women, which may cause alarm and confusion. However, for women who are not allowed to take the oestrogens in combined pills, they are very useful. All types of barrier methods can be used although these are not as effective in preventing pregnancy as hormonal contraception. The use of spermicide creams does not increase the risk of miscarriage, as has been suggested in the past.

The least suitable form of contraception for the miscarriage sufferer, in my opinion, is the intrauterine contraceptive device or 'coil'. I am always worried that they may cause infection in the uterus and pelvis, resulting in later infertility. Although the uncomplicated coil does not increase the risk of future miscarriage, if pregnancy occurs whilst the coil is in the uterus (IUCD failure), as many as 50% of the pregnancies will miscarry. In this situation, the best course of action is to have the coil removed as quickly as possible. The longer it remains in the uterus with the pregnancy, the more likely it is to cause bleeding, infection and miscarriage.

In summary, the best way to ensure that your next pregnancy occurs when you are physically and emotionally prepared for it, is to ensure that you use suitable contraception in the meantime. A combined oral contraceptive pill is probably the best method available for the majority of women, because it offers a low risk of failure, a low risk of future miscarriage and may even improve the chance of falling pregnant for some women when it is discontinued.

Your emotional health

Preparing yourself emotionally for the next pregnancy is often the most difficult task. What is more, every woman will have different needs. For some women, the only way to cope with the misery and disappointment of a miscarriage is to become pregnant again as soon as possible. The fear of 'losing valuable time' is one that is often expressed to me. This is very understandable, but can sometimes lead to further anxieties and distress if pregnancy does not occur straight away. I often suggest to couples who are experiencing some delay in falling pregnant again that they try to go on a holiday and promise each other that they will stop talking and thinking about another pregnancy for a while. This is difficult to do, I know, but if the number of delighted post-holiday telephone calls we receive at the early pregnancy clinic is anything to go by, then it is certainly worthwhile trying!

For other women, the fear of losing another pregnancy prevents them from wanting to try to become pregnant again for a while. Although they desperately want a baby, the horror of reliving their worst nightmare is a very real one. In this situation, the only cure is time. Time for the fears to lessen and the drive to be pregnant to return. Hopefully, you will be able to talk about some of your fears with friends or close members of the family. However, I think there are some occasions when your partner, friends and family are too close to the problem to be able to offer you the help you need. Arranging to see a counsellor may be the answer in this situation. Certainly, some time spent talking to an individual who is able to remain more detached and objective can be of enormous value.

Depending upon you and your lifestyle, this person may be your local doctor, health visitor, priest or a member of one of the voluntary bereavement organisations such as Cruise (see useful addresses). I regularly have cause to feel very grateful to the two miscarriage counsellors who are attached to our clinic. They play an essential role in the healing process for some women, and their contribution is entirely different to that offered by the doctors, nurses or research fellows working with us. If you have difficulties in finding someone like this, try contacting the Miscarriage Association (see useful addresses). They have a country-wide network of self-help groups and the vast majority of members have experienced miscarriages themselves and understand your need for support.

As I mentioned in an earlier chapter, one of the most important things to do when preparing for the next pregnancy is to collect as much information about your miscarriage as possible. Knowledge and understanding of your own problem is the best weapon you have for fighting the next battle. Even when there appear to be no answers to your questions, trying to help yourself is a positive course of action and will provide a measure of emotional comfort.

TWENTY

COPING WITH THE NEXT PREGNANCY

Diet

Every pregnant woman needs to give some thought and attention to what she is eating and drinking. Much has been written about the dos and don'ts of diet during pregnancy. Some of the advice handed on down through the generations is useful. Some is wrong or simply unpalatable. For example, braised liver was considered a 'must' by my grandmother's generation. Liver is an excellent source of iron and folic acid, but we now know that the vitamin A content of liver can cause birth defects in the baby, such as facial, heart and brain abnormalities. Since the vitamin A content of fresh liver is variable, I think it is best to avoid it altogether when you are pregnant. If you hate spinach, there is little point in feeling guilty that you cannot stomach a kilogram of soggy greens every day. Furthermore, in our affluent society, I rarely meet vegetarians in my antenatal clinic who develop anaemia because of their vegetarian diet, although strict vegans are more likely to develop anaemia and other dietary deficiencies during pregnancy.

A well-balanced diet of regular meals including a mixture of protein, carbohydrate and fat is the optimum during pregnancy. This has been the received wisdom for many years and I do not argue with one bit of it. However, I think it is important to add that first and foremost your diet needs to be enjoyable and to suit your appetite and lifestyle. In the first three months of pregnancy, nausea often dictates what you can or cannot eat. In my own pregnancy, I remember vividly that during the first few months the only things that I really enjoyed were asparagus sandwiches, Marmite sandwiches and grapefruit juice! The smell of cooking meat made me actually retch and the taste of coffee, which I usually drink continuously throughout the day, was extremely unpleasant. These fads soon passed and by 16 weeks I was able to eat regular well-balanced meals.

Fish is a particularly good source of protein, and offers the advantage of containing special oils which are particularly good for the growth of the baby's brain. Any type of fish is beneficial but the best fatty acid content is found in oily fish such as tuna, mackerel, sardines and salmon. If you are a meat eater, choose lean meat and cut off the visible fat. Nuts, lentils, beans and peas can all be eaten as an alternative or an addition to meat or fish.

Dairy products provide good sources of proteins, fat and calcium and also offer great variety to your diet. Try to include one pint of fresh milk in your diet each day. Remember that skimmed milk is just as rich in calcium, but has a lower fat content. Many women find that a small pot of yoghurt is helpful in combating early nausea. Yoghurt is also very good towards the end of pregnancy if heartburn is troublesome. One word of warning about dairy products, however: avoid products made from unpasteurised milk which is found in some soft cheeses, such as Brie, camembert and some blue-veined varieties. The unpasteurised milk can harbour many different bacterial organisms, which can cause serious problems such as late miscarriage and intrauterine death during pregnancy. There is no need to stop eating all cheese, just look at the details on the packet. If the cheese is made with pasteurised milk it will state this fact. For the same reasons, avoid eating raw or soft cooked eggs and foods made from uncooked eggs (e.g. mousses and mayonnaise). Make sure that any meat or poultry you eat is well cooked and avoid pâtés, terrines, liver and liver sausage. Ensure that all fruits and vegetables are carefully washed.

Bread and cereals are important sources of energy, fibre, vitamins and minerals. Wholemeal bread, wholewheat pasta, rice and whole-grain breakfast cereals all offer a high fibre content which helps to prevent constipation and keeps the gut healthy. Make sure that you include at least two pieces of fruit per day in your diet and particularly citrus fruits such as oranges and grapefruits. It is also sensible to eat foods with a high folic acid content. Green leafy vegetables (which should not be overcooked) such as spinach, brussels sprouts, broccoli, cabbage and lettuce are all good sources, as are green beans, okra, parsnips, bean sprouts and pulses (for example, peas, cooked blackeye beans and chick peas). Fortified breakfast cereals, fortified bread and yeast extracts (such as Marmite) are all good ways to supplement your diet.

Make sure that you do not put on too much weight. The average weight gain during pregnancy is about 10 kilos (22 pounds). Many women find that they start having little snacks when they are pregnant. During the early months, frequent small meals may be the only way to cope with nausea. However, when the snacks contain lots of sugar and are later added to regular meals, there is no way that you will escape unnecessary weight gain. The problem will be made worse if you pretend to yourself that all of the weight you are putting on is the baby and that another few chocolate bars do not matter now because you can shed the weight easily after the baby is born. You will need to be as fit as possible for the birth of your baby and the demanding months afterwards, so try to avoid gaining more than the average. The old adage about 'eating for two' should be treated with a pinch of salt. You are not eating for two, you are eating sensibly for you and your tiny baby. Your baby will take everything that it needs from your diet and you do not need to eat vast quantities of food to ensure that your baby has enough. If you need further reassurance of this fact, remember that the birth weight of babies born in Third World countries is not significantly less than that of babies born in this country.

Vitamins

There is now clear evidence that folic acid and folates have a major role to play in the prevention and recurrence of neural tube defects (e.g. spina bifida). As a result, the Department of Health recommends that all women increase their intake of folic acid and folates by an additional 400 micrograms (0.4 milligrams) a day before pregnancy and during the first twelve weeks of pregnancy. There are three ways to increase your folate intake: eating more folate-rich foods; eating foods fortified with folate (see Diet, above) and taking supplements of folate in tablet form. A normal healthy diet already provides you with an average folate intake of about 200 micrograms per day. The recommended supplement of 400 microgram tablets is easily purchased over the counter at your chemist and will bring your total daily intake up to about 600 micrograms. It will cost you approximately 30 pence per week.

Many women I see in the miscarriage clinic like to take multi-vitamin preparations during pregnancy. However, it is important to remember that not all multivitamin tablets contain folic acid, nor in sufficient quantities. Furthermore, if you try to achieve the recommended dose of folic acid by taking several multivitamin pills, there is a risk that you will be taking an excess of the other vitamins, particularly vitamin A. For this reason, it is best to take the 400mcg folic acid tablets on their own. If you have not been taking folic acid before pregnancy and suspect that you might be pregnant, start taking supplements straight away and continue until the twelfth week of pregnancy.

Iron tablets seem to be much beloved by patients and doctors alike. However, iron supplements are not needed routinely in pregnancy unless you are carrying twins or are already anaemic. Anaemia is definitely not a cause of miscarriage. I find that about a third of women taking iron tablets can take them without any complication, another third develop severe constipation, and the last third suffer from tummy upsets and diarrhoea as a result of the tablets. I think these are needlessly unpleasant complications to endure throughout your pregnancy if you are not actually anaemic. Your blood count will probably fall towards the end of pregnancy due to a dilution effect resulting from the increased amount of fluid in your blood. If, at this later stage of pregnancy, you are advised to take iron supplements and develop gastro-intestinal symptoms, ask your doctor to prescribe another brand. There are many different preparations on the market and it is usually possible to find one that suits you better. Remember that there are many foods such as dried fruits (particularly apricots and raisins) and chocolate that are very good sources of extra iron and also very palatable! But do make sure that you keep a watchful eye on your calorie intake.

Constipation

Lots of pregnant women suffer from constipation. Undoubtedly, this is partly due to the high levels of progesterone hormone that are produced during pregnancy and which cause the smooth muscle of the gut to be much less active than usual. As mentioned earlier, some women taking iron tablets find that the iron makes the constipation significantly worse. If you find that you are becoming constipated, start eating extra fibre in your diet. Wholemeal bread, fresh fruits and vegetables, dried fruits (such as raisins and apricots) are all good sources of fibre. If this fails, daily tablespoons of real bran (the sawdust lookalike purchased in health food shops, not the breakfast cereal called bran flakes) usually does the trick, but is virtually inedible unless you mix it into some yoghurt, soup or gravy. If this does not resolve the problem, then it is sensible to use a bulk laxative such as Lactulose, Fybogel or Isogel. Remember that you will not cure your constipation unless you drink plenty of fluids to help the fibre along. Try and drink lots of water, fruit juice or unsweetened drinks rather than coffee, tea or soft fizzy drinks. Fortunately, I am able to reassure you firmly that however badly you may suffer from constipation, it will not cause you to miscarry.

On no account should you use Senna or any purgative laxative during pregnancy. Senna and its relatives causes irritation of the bowel which can, in some situations, irritate the uterus and even lead to the onset of premature labour. Moreover, the continued abuse of these purgative laxatives results in the destruction of the nerve-endings in the bowel and, as a result, in later years your bowel will become more constipated and more resistant to the use of bulk laxatives and dietary fibre.

Tobacco and alcohol

Smoking in pregnancy can lead to a reduction of the baby's supply of oxygen and nutrients and can produce smaller babies who are at increased risk of infection and may have developmental problems.

Please try hard to stop smoking before becoming pregnant, and if this has not been successful, throw out your cigarettes the moment the pregnancy test is positive. I meet so many women who say, 'But I only smoke five cigarettes per day, doctor'. Any number of cigarettes per day is too many when you are pregnant. Think about the fact that five cigarettes a day during a 40-week pregnancy means that your baby will have been exposed to 1380 cigarettes before birth! If you are still not convinced, then please go back to Chapter 9 and read about all the adverse effects that cigarette smoking has on fertility and the growth and development of the fetus and placenta in pregnancy.

I have often reflected upon the fact that nature has some very clever ways of helping to ensure that women continue to produce healthy babies. What other explanation can there be for most women to hate the taste of alcohol in early pregnancy? Indeed, before the days of home pregnancy tests, becoming intolerant of alcohol was often considered one of the first symptoms of pregnancy. There are good reasons for this revulsion for alcohol, which fortunately (I think!) starts to fade later in pregnancy.

During the first three months of the baby's development, large quantities of alcohol can cause severe abnormalities. The fetal alcohol abuse syndrome has been well described in the children of mothers who are alcoholic and details are included in Chapter 9 of this book. Some reports have also suggested that moderate regular drinking is also associated with miscarriage, milder fetal abnormalities and growth-retardation in the baby. However, there are no data that suggest that the occasional drink is harmful, particularly in later pregnancy. One or two glasses of wine during the week may be a very good way of increasing relaxation. I am reminded that in years gone by, an intravenous drip of alcohol was the only known method to quieten the uterus which was threatening to labour prematurely. I am not suggesting that you should hook yourself up to a bottle of scotch, but would suggest to you that after the first three months of pregnancy are completed, there is no need to deny yourself the odd drink if you fancy it.

Bed rest

The question that I am asked more than any other is: 'Doctor, should I bed rest during the first few weeks of my pregnancy?' I find this a very difficult question to answer medically, since I do not know of any data that suggests that resting in bed reduces the miscarriage rate in early pregnancy. If you have an episode of bleeding, then lying flat in bed may appear to stop the bleeding but this usually recurs when you get out of bed again, and particularly when going to the toilet. This is because the blood which has leaked from behind the placenta passes through the neck of the womb into the vagina in the upright position. Nonetheless, for many hundreds of years, doctors and midwives have advised women to rest in bed if they experience bleeding in early pregnancy. One of the reasonings has always been that the more rest the pregnant woman has, the better the blood flow to the uterus, the placenta and therefore the baby, will be. This is certainly true in later pregnancy; indeed, plenty of rest during the last two months is the reason why maternity leave is a statutory right. However, in early pregnancy, there is no evidence that bed rest can affect the outcome of pregnancy.

Hence I think my response to the issue of bed rest in early pregnancy is that it depends on the woman. Her character and her past experience in pregnancy will be important factors to take into account. For the woman who has suffered repeated miscarriages in the past, resting in bed may provide her with the reassurance that she did everything she could to help the pregnancy continue, should anything go wrong in the future. For other women, resting in bed will lead to so much anxiety and distress that it is better for them to follow their usual day to day lifestyle including going to work. I suggest you ask yourself which of these two groups you fall into. If you are going to feel consumed with guilt and self-blame when some bleeding occurs whilst you are doing the shopping or are attending your yoga class, then stay in bed. On the other hand, if you need the distraction of domestic tasks or your job to help you cope with the fears and anxieties you have about this next pregnancy, then go to work. I really do not think it is necessary to wrap yourself in cotton wool in the first few weeks of a pregnancy. The reality is that a pregnancy that is going to miscarry is going to miscarry, and a pregnancy that is going to stick will stick.

Similarly, the value of a period of time spent in hospital which coincides with the time at which the previous miscarriages have occurred, is of no proven benefit. Some women will want to be hospitalised. Others will consider going into hospital to be the realisation of their worst nightmares. I am often asked to arrange admission to my hospital for patients with a history of miscarriage, particularly for those who have suffered late losses. I always manage to find a bed, however short they are reported to be, because I believe that a positive response to this request to be 'looked after' is extremely important emotionally. And since I cannot pretend that I understand all the reasons why some women miscarry repeatedly at the same time in pregnancy, perhaps it is helpful. I shall continue to advise this open-door policy unless someone persuades me that it is harmful.

One more point is worth mentioning on this subject. I meet many women who feel very pressurised by family and friends to retire to their bed if they have suffered a miscarriage in the past. I am sure the advice is meant well, but it can cause needless distress. Make up your own mind, with the help of your partner if possible, about what is the right thing for you to do. After all, it is your feelings that matter and only you know how best to cope with them.

Sex

It is usually quite safe to enjoy making love throughout pregnancy as long as you do not experience any pain or discomfort. I know that many doctors advise avoiding sex during the first 12 weeks of pregnancy, particularly if the woman has had a miscarriage in the past. There is no scientific basis for this viewpoint. I think the reason why this advice is offered is to protect the couple from feelings of guilt and self-blame if the woman should happen to have some bleeding after making love.

This is another situation in which it is important for the individual woman/couple to make their own decisions. I know of no data that could persuade me that sex is dangerous in early pregnancy, but if you are anxious about miscarriage and bleeding, I suggest you avoid sex until you feel more confident. Remember that it takes a big insult to disturb a healthy pregnancy!

Exercise and sport

Over the last few years I have received many more questions about the safety of exercise in pregnancy. So I feel that it is important to spend a bit of time at this point discussing the issues in more detail. Gentle regular exercise is a good thing in pregnancy. Current evidence points to the fact that exercise is safe and beneficial for the majority of pregnant women. Even if you have had several miscarriages in the past, there is no reason to stop the exercise that you are used to. And if you have not been taking regular exercise, start walking every day, or swim a couple of times per week. Daily exercise will help you to keep fit during pregnancy and is actually very relaxing.

If you are a keen sportswoman, you are probably quite fit anyway. Many female athletes now continue training programmes throughout their pregnancies and even go on to improve their sporting performances after childbirth. The reason for this is not entirely clear but it has been suggested that the increased blood volume and effort required to exercise at a greater body weight has long term physiological benefits. An alternative explanation could be that there are important psychological benefits for a competitive sportswoman after enduring pregnancy, labour and motherhood!

Historically, women and their doctors have worried about the effect of exercise and sport on the unborn child, but this is really a bit misguided. The baby within the uterus is enclosed by the bony pelvic cage until 12 weeks of pregnancy. After this time the fetus is protected by thick, spongy layers of the uterine wall and at least a litre of amniotic fluid. As a result, damage to the baby because of maternal trauma or activity is very rare. On the other hand, because of the mother's increasingly lax ligaments, her shifting centre of gravity and changes in the curvature of her spine, she is at increased risk of trauma to herself towards the end of pregnancy. It is probably best to avoid contact sports such as field and court games during the last three months of pregnancy.

I think that much of the advice that strenuous exercise may put the baby at risk stems from animal studies which have suggested that the blood flow to the uterus is reduced. But there are just as many other studies that have demonstrated that even strenuous exercise is of no risk to the baby, certainly in the first half of pregnancy. It appears that some of the uterine blood flow is directed to the placenta during exercise and that the uterine circulation is able to increase the amount of oxygen it extracts from the mother's blood as a compensatory mechanism.

It is obviously very difficult to monitor the baby's response during exercise. Nonetheless, cardiotocography (fetal heart rate tracings) studies have been performed and usually show a short period of tachycardia (speeding up of the heart rate) after exercise, or alternatively that the baby's temperature increases slightly. Overall, the experts have concluded that maternal exercise up to 70% of maximal capacity does not interfere in any way with normal fetal growth and development. The only women whose babies appear to suffer are those who undertake daily endurance training near to the time of delivery and have poor weight gain – these babies are sometimes small for dates. Hence professional athletes need to be reminded to pay particular attention to good nutrition and should probably be advised to scale down their training schedules towards the end of pregnancy.

I recently had the pleasure of a medical sports expert as a patient. She provided me with a list of points to offer the pregnant athlete which I include here for you.

- Avoid exercising to exhaustion – you should be able to carry on talking normally during prolonged exercise
- Avoid exercising in the heat – especially in early pregnancy – and make sure you do not become dehydrated and that you drink sufficient fluids
- Begin and finish your exercise gradually – the message is warm up and warm down

- Always stop exercising if you experience any pain
- Exercise regularly to maintain fitness, rather than in fits and starts
- Aim to reduce your exercise programme in later pregnancy

Scuba diving is one sport that should not be undertaken during pregnancy because of the potential risk of bubbles (gas emboli) developing in the placental and fetal blood vessels as a result of the pressure changes in deep water. Parachute jumping should also be avoided and water-skiing enthusiasts are usually advised to wear a wet suit during pregnancy to avoid forceful vaginal douching.

Another very commonly asked question is 'Is it safe to take saunas while I am pregnant?' It is true that there was a single report in the 1970s which suggested that regular saunas may increase the risk of fetal malformations but this has never been confirmed. Reassuringly, there are more recent studies which have shown that maternal hyperthermia (overheating) during exercise does not result in fetal abnormalities. In summary, I don't believe that sport is harmful in early pregnancy. I suggest that you adopt a middle-of-the-road approach and if you enjoy sport, continue to play, but avoid very strenuous activity which tires you out. You will find it difficult not to blame yourself if you start miscarrying in the middle of a squash tournament.

Travel

Long distance travel is one activity that I do think should be avoided if you have a history of miscarriage. Not because a transatlantic flight or a long car journey can cause a miscarriage, but because being a long way away from home and the doctor and hospital that you are familiar with, is bound to cause you even more distress, if you start to miscarry again. Imagine what it feels like to stand in the casualty department of a hospital in a foreign country, when you cannot speak a word of the language and you are trying to explain to the doctor (they are tired and overworked overseas as well) that you want to have an ultrasound scan before anyone examines you or ships you off for a quick 'clear out'.

You may have had the misfortune to have experienced going into a hospital before with a miscarriage, but did you have to fight to make yourself understood or have to worry about whether you have the correct insurance documents with you before anyone medical will pay you attention? No, I am not a reactionary British doctor who considers that the UK is the only country in the world capable of delivering good health care. Nor am I recounting a bitter personal experience. What I want to share with you is the misery that so many women have described to me, in graphic detail, when they have miscarried a long way from home. Fortunately, the chances of this happening to you are small, but it is possible to avoid the risk completely by not exposing yourself to it.

I think I need to make a few comments here about the safety of air travel in particular. I am struck by how many more questions I have been asked on this subject in the clinic recently. In theory, there are two potential areas of concern. The first is that spending a lot of time thousands of feet above the ground may lower the mother's oxygen levels because the pressure in most passenger cabins is lower than atmospheric pressure on the ground. The second is cosmic radiation – which simply means the radiation you receive from the sun – which of course is greater if you are nearer the sun, as is the case in an aeroplane.

I have scoured the literature in an attempt to answer the above questions, but there is really very little data to be found. One study from Finland recently reported that there may be a small increase in the risk of miscarriage among female flight attendants. Certainly most airlines offer their crews the option of switching to ground duties during pregnancy, but when I contacted the medical advisers to several airlines recently, they explained to me that this employment concession is not based on any firm evidence that flying regularly during pregnancy has any detrimental effect on pregnancy outcome.

Early pregnancy fears – what can I do to allay them?

If you have suffered previous miscarriages, it is entirely natural that you will have fears and anxieties in the next pregnancy. I think the best way of dealing with these worries is to try to ensure, before you become pregnant, that you know how to contact medical help promptly as soon as you get pregnant again. If you are able to obtain an appointment with your doctor, local hospital or early pregnancy clinic (if this is available in your area) quickly, many of your worries will probably be resolved very simply. Feeling that you are unable to access help and advice is certain to induce panic and distress if you are a miscarriage sufferer who has just become pregnant again. Fortunately, the value of early pregnancy clinics is becoming much better understood. More and more hospitals are introducing ultra-sound services that are immediately accessible to women and their general practitioners. I hope that it will not be long before early pregnancy referral clinics are routine services offered by our health services. For anyone reading this book who has doubts about the importance and cost-effectiveness of such clinics – please read Chapter 21, which describes the proven benefits that such expertise and care can offer to women in early pregnancy.

If I was to recount all of the worries told to me in the early pregnancy clinic at St Mary's Hospital, this chapter would never be completed. However, I think it is useful to mention a few of the most frequently expressed concerns here.

By sheer weight of numbers, I have to conclude that the fear of bleeding is the commonest fear experienced by miscarriage sufferers. Try to remember that the majority of women who develop bleeding in early pregnancy will go on to have a normal pregnancy. If it is possible to have an ultrasound scan, this may provide some reassurance that the pregnancy is progressing and that there is no obvious cause for the bleeding. Some women are frightened of having a scan because it may confirm their worst fears – that the pregnancy is over. Although I understand the emotions involved here, I always strongly encourage women to establish what is happening as early as possible. It is only by making a diagnosis and obtaining as much information as possible, that you can move forwards. Burying your head in the sand will not help in the long term and may even prevent you and your doctor from obtaining useful information for the future.

Fears that the baby may be abnormal are also very common. This is always a difficult anxiety to allay because even the most sophisticated tests can only offer a degree of reassurance – it is never possible to promise a woman a 'normal' baby (see Chapter 7).

Another very common concern is that the woman has taken certain medical drugs before she realised that she was pregnant. In practice, these are usually antibiotics and fortunately only a few antibiotics cause abnormalities in early pregnancy. For example, tetracyclines (usually prescribed for acne or for infections caused by chlamydia) cause discoloration and deformity in the teeth and bones of the baby and chloramphenicol (rarely used nowadays) is responsible for the blue baby syndrome. Penicillin taken for a throat infection, a whitlow on your finger or an episode of cystitis has never been known to cause harm to the baby directly.

The nausea that invariably accompanies the early weeks of pregnancy can be very distressing and at least 50% of pregnant women also experience repeated episodes of vomiting. Despite the popular name of 'morning sickness' many women experience nausea throughout the day and for some women the symptoms continue way beyond 20 weeks of gestation. Some women may benefit from small doses of an anti-emetic (anti-sickness drug). However, the lessons learnt from the thalidomide disaster (thalidomide was prescribed for pregnancy nausea) have rightly resulted in doctors and patients being both wary and vigilant of all medications taken during pregnancy. I therefore think it is important that I do not sound too reassuring in this book about the use of drugs in early pregnancy and, instead, encourage all women who are planning to become pregnant and who are in early pregnancy, that they should take no drugs at all unless they are absolutely necessary.

I promise you that if your nausea is so severe that you become dehydrated, all doctors will recognise this problem (which is called hyperemesis gravidarum) and arrange for you to be admitted to hospital and treated with an intravenous drip to give you the fluids necessary to rehydrate you. I think it is important to remember that in the days when intravenous drips were not readily available, some pregnant women became very ill indeed as a result of the dehydration associated with hyperemesis. Fortunately, this is no longer the case. Although the intravenous drip obviously does not stop the woman feeling miserable because of her symptoms, it does prevent her getting into danger because of dehydration.

A wide variety of treatments have been tried to alleviate hyperemesis. Pyridoxine (vitamin B6) three times a day is probably the least likely to cause any side-effects. There is also a suggestion that powdered ginger may be helpful, although direct evidence is lacking and it can be difficult to eat sufficient quantities of dry powder. Acupuncture has also been reported as a successful alternative treatment. Steroids have been shown to be helpful but this treatment is usually reserved for very severe and unresponsive cases, in order to avoid the risks of steroid therapy in pregnancy.

It is interesting to note that there have been quite a few studies demonstrating that hospital admission, IV fluids and a small dose of an anxiolytic drug such as diazepam or lorazepam can be very effective. Most obstetricians will agree that many women suffering from hyperemesis gravidarum in early pregnancy may have some emotional or domestic problem as the underlying cause. No, I do not think that such patients are hypochondriacs, but yes, I do think that the debilitating nausea and vomiting is a physical way of expressing a cry for help. Recognising this fact may allow her family and her doctor to identify the root cause and offer constructive help and support for the problem.

Viral infections are very common during pregnancy, so it is not surprising that many women worry about the effects these illnesses may have upon their unborn child. Viral infections that cause specific abnormalities in the baby are discussed in Chapters 4 and 10. A bout of 'flu or a nasty headcold is much more common and considerably more difficult to give specific advice about. My impression is that these common respiratory viruses may cause miscarriage if they are severe enough, because they result in a major upset to the system, but they do not cause abnormalities in the baby. Similarly, an episode of food poisoning may be the cause of a sporadic miscarriage, but if the pregnancy continues, no fetal abnormalities are later recognised.

Should I ask my doctor for hormone treatment?

If only I had a shilling for each time that I have been asked this question . . . My answer is always the same. Giving injections of progesterone or HCG (human chorionic gonadotrophin) during early pregnancy with the aim of reducing the miscarriage rate is worthless. There are several well-conducted treatment trials that have shown that these hormone treatments are not helpful. The only function they have is to postpone the inevitability of a miscarriage by a short interval.

The reason for this is simple. If the pregnancy hormones are low, this reflects the fact that the placenta has failed and cannot produce sufficient hormones to allow the pregnancy to continue. Injecting a small dose (compared to the amounts of hormone that the placenta should be producing, the dose is tiny) via a hypodermic syringe cannot make the placenta come alive again, although it may increase the levels of hormone circulating in the blood slightly. As a result, the bleeding and/or miscarriage that was scheduled to start today may be delayed for a short time. However, since the placenta is not functioning, it will not be long before the process of miscarriage continues.

So why, despite this knowledge, are some women still offered progesterone and HCG supplements in early pregnancy? I think the reason for continued differences of opinion on this subject can be explained by the emotional distress which accompanies so many miscarriages. These emotions are powerful and, if allowed, can override factual knowledge. The miscarriage patient wants to try anything that may help her hang on to her baby. She may have a friend or relative who has received hormone treatment in early pregnancy which appears to have resulted in a successful pregnancy. Not surprisingly, she exerts pressure on her doctor to do something. The doctor feels helpless because he or she has no magic solution to offer. It goes against the grain to do nothing and it is particularly difficult to be seen to 'deny' treatment that may just 'do the trick'. As a result, I think many prescriptions for hormone treaments in early pregnancy are written out because they make everyone concerned feel better that some action has been taken.

I have to confess here that there have been rare occasions when, faced with a distraught miscarriage patient, I have succumbed to the same pressures and prescribed hormones. I felt guilty afterwards, because this was the easy way out for me. I still feel guilty, because by allowing anecdotal reports to override my knowledge of the facts, I have contributed to the confusion and stood in the way of progress.

Further confusion has arisen from the infertility world. Many of the assisted fertility treatments now include the use of drugs which shut down the ovary and are followed by further drugs which stimulate the ovary to produce multiple eggs. Because all natural ovarian hormone production has been turned off, it has become standard practice to give progesterone or HCG supplements after the eggs have been collected. This improves the chances of pregnancy by making the womb lining more favourable to the implanting embryo. The treatment is usually continued until about eight weeks into a successful pregnancy. Many infertility clinics have reported that the use of progesterone/HCG in this way improves the ongoing pregnancy rate. However, the reasoning behind this treatment is entirely different. It cannot be extrapolated to a patient who becomes pregnant spontaneously and then miscarries.

For the miscarriage patient, starting hormone injections after the pregnancy has already implanted is akin to shutting the stable door after the horse has bolted. If the placenta cannot produce sufficient progesterone or HCG to support the pregnancy during the first few weeks because it has implanted poorly, no amount of hormone treatment given as injections or pessaries can improve the quality of implantation, and the pregnancy will founder.

In the future it may be possible to use hormones to improve the quality of implantation. If this proves successful, I am sure that the treatment will need to be started long before the pregnancy test becomes positive.

Antenatal diagnostic tests

I meet many couples who are worried about the risks of miscarriage which are associated with invasive antenatal diagnostic tests such as amniocentesis and chorion villus sampling (see Chapter 7 for details). If you have suffered repeated miscarriages, you will feel particularly wary about undergoing any procedure that may put your pregnancy at risk. However, there may be very specific reasons why your doctor discusses these tests with you.

Your age may be an important factor – the risk of Down's syndrome increases steeply after the age of 35 years. Alternatively, it may be that one of your previous pregnancies is known to have miscarried because of a chromosomal abnormality, which does increase your risk of a future chromosome abnormality in the baby. If you or your partner carry a genetic abnormality such as a balanced translocation (see Chapter 7) there is a risk that the baby may inherit the unbalanced chromosome. In this latter situation, all doctors are agreed that, whatever the woman's pregnancy history, an amniocentesis should be performed to ensure that the baby is normal.

Of course the decision to have one of these tests is a very personal one. So, too, is the action that you may choose to take if you find out that your baby has an abnormality. There is no right or wrong way to deal with this difficult situation and it is important that any advice you seek from your doctors is individual to you and your pregnancy. There are only a few general points of guidance that I believe can be offered. The first is that you are not more likely to miscarry after an amniocentesis because you have suffered miscarriages in the past. The second is that amniocentesis is usually performed between 14 and 16 weeks. If your miscarriages have been after this date it is probably best to avoid an invasive test unless the results of detailed ultrasound scans and blood tests suggest that there is a specific problem. I have always found it impossible to reassure a woman who miscarries after an amniocentesis that the test was not the cause of the miscarriage – so if you have suffered late miscarriages, this is one potential source of self blame which can be avoided.

TWENTY-ONE

THE IMPORTANCE OF JOINING A RESEARCH PROGRAMME

Recurrent miscarriage is an enormously distressing problem for both the sufferer and her doctor. It is common for both parties to experience feelings of helplessness and despair. One of the hardest issues to deal with, in my opinion, is that the emotions of everyone involved are so raw that it can be very difficult to look at the problem objectively. If you have just had another miscarriage, it is understandable that you will want to try anything that may help you to have a baby. You want the results of the test that has just been discovered to be abnormal. You want this test to lead to a new treatment option. At that moment you do not care if the treatment has not been subjected to the rigours of a controlled trial. You do not care that it has no logical basis. All you want to do is try it and hope that it will work for you.

Your doctor may well be having similar feelings. It is really quite difficult to look after recurrent miscarriage patients and resist falling into the trap of trying out some new treatment idea before it has been properly evaluated and tested. After the umpteenth miscarriage, your doctor has to look you in the eye and tell you that the only advice to be offered is to try again because he or she does not know why your miscarriage happened. This doctor will probably feel that he or she has let you down, because they have failed to give you an answer or solve your problem. After all, medicine in the twenty-first century is meant to have conquered most common medical disorders and, on many occasions in this book, we have noted just how common the problem of miscarriage is.

All of these emotional feelings encourage the use of treatments for miscarriage before they have been properly tried and tested. Once they have been introduced, it is almost impossible to then subject them to the rigours of a randomised controlled trial. Which patient wants to be in the 'no treatment' group of a trial when their underlying problem is recurrent miscarriage? Which doctor wants to be in the position of deciding who receives what treatment? It is not difficult to see why it has proven so difficult to conduct research in this field. As a result, fact and fiction become muddled and are difficult to separate.

Why are we still so ignorant about the causes and treatment of miscarriage? This is a conversation that I embark on very frequently in the clinic, and many patients have told me that they found it helpful in understanding the complexity of the problem. Some of the answers are contained in the paragraphs above. I do not pretend that I have any more answers hidden up my sleeve, but I do think that it would be useful for the reader to appreciate that, in no other field of medicine, do we have to try and treat the abnormal before understanding the normal.

This may sound a strange comment, but remember that we are still incredibly ignorant about how a tiny embryo manages to implant successfully in the womb lining. If we knew the answer to this, we would soon be able to achieve 100% pregnancy rates for women who were undergoing IVF treatment. Getting pregnant is the first hurdle, staying pregnant is the next. How does this barely visible embryo manage to cope with all the obstacles that it faces during the first few months of its life? If you have had early pregnancy scans you will, I am sure, have marvelled at the transformation that you have witnessed with your own eyes as the tiny blob on the screen turns into a comma and then into a recognisable fetus. If we understood all the mechanisms involved in this development, we would probably be able to prevent a large number of miscarriages, providing that the embryo was chromosomally normal.

The reality is that we know very little about these early stages of pregnancy and we have to glean our knowledge from the pregnancies that miscarry, since we cannot experiment on the pregnancies that are developing properly. Of course, we can watch the pregnancy develop on the scan and we can measure the baby's growth, blood flow and movements, but we are unable to find out what is causing all these changes at a molecular level unless we can examine the tissues of the fetus, placenta or the endometrial lining. We have to content ourselves with working backwards, looking at those pregnancies that went wrong and trying to deduce what should have happened. When you appreciate these difficulties, I think it is easier to understand why both you and I are often faced with the problem of 'not knowing why' the miscarriage occurred.

I do not want to give the reader the view that the outlook for the future is bleak. On the contrary, there are many research groups working in this field and using animal models, human blood samples and tissue biopsies (often obtained from pregnancies that have miscarried or been terminated). They are trying to unravel some of the mysteries using molecular biology techniques. Although progress is not fast, it is constant and I believe that we can look forward to great advances in our knowledge during the next few years. As the theories emerge, they will need to be carefully translated into practical treatment options. This is where the readers of this book will have their best opportunity to make a contribution and benefit from their efforts. We are all working towards the same goal – a live, 'take-home' baby.

The best advice that I can give to couples who have miscarried repeatedly is to visit a clinic that is actively involved in research. You will find that the doctors running these clinics are interested in and knowledgeable about your problems. Ask them questions and make sure that all the treatment trials they are involved in have control groups. Remember that the only way to determine whether treatment A is superior to treatment B is to examine them carefully in a controlled trial. Try to resist the temptation to go and find a doctor elsewhere who will give you the new treatment without comparing it to anything else.

During the course of the treatment trials that I have described to you in this book, there were several occasions when patients from our clinic dropped out of the trial before their treatment had started. They thought that they should ensure that they received the new 'wonder treatment' rather than risk being in a control group. I understand their motives, but I believe that they were misguided.

Certainly, most of them returned to see us at a later date. Your future pregnancies are much too important to be looked after in isolation. What you need is evidence and the benefit of pooled knowledge with which you can give yourself the best opportunities for a successful outcome to your pregnancy. I should also mention here that control groups do not necessarily mean 'no treatment'. More usually they mean that the new treatment is being measured against the best available treatment known at the time that the trial was being performed.

When you join a controlled trial, you are not a guinea pig – you are doing the most useful thing that you possibly can to sort out your own problem. This is the time when you can get back into the driving seat. Now you can stop feeling lost and out of control and start to help yourself. It is impossible for me to emphasise this point strongly enough. I am absolutely convinced that the treatment trials that we have performed recently at the St Mary's clinic owe a part of their success to the fact that the couples participating have understood what the trial is trying to achieve and why. There is no doubt that being informed has a remarkable capacity to make people feel confident and optimistic. These important emotions are very valuable when you want to embark upon a new pregnancy.

There is one more important issue to mention about the importance of miscarriage research. It needs dedicated effort and money to push it forward. If you have benefited from being involved in a research project, remember that many patients before you contributed to the research without any promise of a happy outcome. Their efforts have helped you and your efforts will help the next group of miscarriers in their quest for a child. Encourage everyone you know with a miscarriage problem to seek help in centres that are actively involved in research. The only way to change the distress of repeated miscarriages into success stories is to ensure that every woman with this problem contributes her experience to the pool of knowledge.

And when you have succeeded and have a beautiful baby, please remember those women who are still waiting to experience this joy. There are many ways that you can help to raise money and campaign for research funding for miscarriage. Please explore them!

TWENTY-TWO

THE VALUE OF TENDER LOVING CARE IN EARLY PREGNANCY

A question that I am asked repeatedly is 'What happens to those miscarriage patients who undergo all the available tests and have completely normal results?' I have saved this account for the end because it is so important. Much of the work carried out in the miscarriage clinic at St Mary's is aimed at identifying the reasons why a woman miscarries repeatedly. Since we are a research unit, we are regularly assessing the benefits and the failings of new investigative tests and treatments.

Most of our miscarriage patients and their doctors hope that one of these tests will be abnormal and that, as a result, they will identify a definite cause for their miscarriages. Of course, they hope there is also a suitable treatment that is capable of curing the abnormality that has been identified. However, there are always some patients in whom all the test results are persistently normal. As a result, there is no known medical treatment available for them. Sadly, these patients are frequently offered a variety of treatments (hormones, antibiotics, aspirin, immunotherapy – the list is a long one) in the hope that 'doing something' will help to resolve the miscarriage problem.

The reader will have noticed on several occasions in this book how important I believe it is to resist giving patients treatment for miscarriage when no cause can be identified. This is because I firmly believe that one of the most important reasons why our understanding of recurrent miscarriage is so incomplete is due to the use of 'empirical' treatments. Of course, every woman and her doctor wants to maximise the chances of her next pregnancy being successful. The trouble is that when a particular treatment is given empirically (given anyway) although no cause has been identified, the results of this treatment become impossible to assess. The waters are muddied and, most importantly, the true benefits of an individual treatment will remain a mystery.

Over the last ten years, we have identified several thousands of couples with recurrent miscarriage in whom we can find no obvious abnormalities. We refer to this group as having unexplained pregnancy losses, although we recognise that a substantial proportion of these unexplained miscarriages are probably cases of bad luck or sporadic pregnancy loss. I was particularly interested to know the outcome of future pregnancies in these women, since this is obviously valuable information for me to pass on to my miscarriage patients. Helped by my research fellows, the early pregnancy clinic was expanded to include these women. Alongside all the miscarriers who were undergoing trial treatments, we encouraged the 'unexplained' group to visit the early pregnancy clinic every week and undergo the ultrasound scans and receive tender loving care from the research fellows, clinic nurses and scanners.

We found that the unexplained group who received this supportive care were extremely successful in their next pregnancy. Nearly 80% of them had a live baby. From a scientific point of view, I would argue that this is not surprising, since these women have no evidence of any specific causes of miscarriage. However, convincing a distressed miscarriage sufferer of these facts can be very difficult, which is why I am so delighted that we have been able to demonstrate how very successful these women can be in their next pregnancy.

Even more remarkable is that this study of the future outcome of women with unexplained recurrent miscarriages also demonstrated that the tender loving care plays an important part in achieving a successful outcome. Among the unexplained miscarriage group was a subgroup of women who, for a variety of reasons, decided not to return to our early pregnancy clinic. Some of them felt disillusioned by the fact that we had been unable to identify an underlying cause for their miscarriages. Some of them felt that the geographical distances were too great to travel on a weekly basis. I should mention here that many of our patients travelled 400 miles to visit us each week, and I feel sure that this sort of dedicated attitude must have played a part in their success.

Among the women who did not attend the early pregnancy clinic, the live birth rate was much lower – only 50%. I cannot give you a scientific explanation for this, but I do recognise that tender loving care in early pregnancy improves the outcome for women who have experienced repeated, unexplained miscarriages. Perhaps the supportive care has a beneficial effect on the woman's hormones, or on the way in which her immune system responds to the pregnancy in those first few crucial weeks. Certainly, there are other workers in this field who confirm my opinion, which is why I feel it very important that as many units as possible set up early pregnancy clinics for their miscarriage patients.

Before closing this chapter, I should mention that some sceptical doctors have asked me why I bother to look for new tests and new treatments for women with recurrent miscarriages, when I can achieve a 70–80% live birth rate just through the policy of a little tender loving care. I hope that the readers of this book are now so well informed that they can answer the question themselves! If I was to treat women with phospholipid syndrome with supportive care alone, and no aspirin or heparin, the miscarriage rate would rise to 90% and the live birthrate would drop to 10%. If, on the other hand, I decided to give all women aspirin and heparin, even those with no identifiable causes for their miscarriages, it would not be long before some of them developed side-effects from the treatment.

Even more worrying is the likelihood that if I had given everyone with unexplained miscarriage the aspirin and heparin treatment, the success rate for this treatment for the phospholipid syndrome would have been much lower and the true benefit of this therapy would never have been established. Until we reach the point where we understand the underlying cause for every miscarriage we cannot afford to second guess and offer women empirical treatments. If we let ourselves fall into this trap we will never be able to identify new research tests and new successful treatment options.

I believe that the first role of a miscarriage clinic is to identify causes of recurrent miscarriage that we can treat and continue to look for further tests that will identify new causes that are amenable to treatment in the future. The second role is to offer early pregnancy care and support. If, after careful investigation, we can find no cause for your pregnancy losses, it is now possible to reassure you that your chances of a successful pregnancy are about 75% if you are looked after carefully in the early weeks. I know of no other type of treatment for miscarriage that can better these excellent results! At the end of the day, your chances of a healthy take-home baby are very high – so please do not give up.

A FINAL WORD

In the introduction I explained that my aim in writing this book was to try and take the mystery and the fear out of the subject of miscarriage. I have attempted to describe the known causes and treatments of miscarriage in ways which my patients tell me they have found helpful. I hope that I have achieved what I set out to do, although I am conscious of the fact that at the present time, there are still questions for which I cannot offer you an answer.

The answers will come if we continue to research them carefully. We must also resist the temptation to give miscarriage sufferers treatments until they have been shown to be of benefit in properly controlled trials, as the use of empirical treatment for women with unexplained miscarriages only serves to make this important subject more difficult to understand and conquer.

Happily, I can reassure you that the vast majority of women with a history of recurrent miscarriage eventually succeed in their aim of having a healthy child.

Good luck in your new pregnancy!

GLOSSARY

ACA: anticardiolipin antibodies – one of the family of anti-phospholipid antibodies. The IgG and IgM variants are associated with miscarriage and placental insufficiency in later pregnancy.

ADHESIONS, OR SYNECHIAE: fibrous bands joining one tissue surface to another. When present inside the uterus, the walls of the uterus stick together, distorting the shape of the cavity.

ALLOGRAFT: a tissue or organ taken from one human and transplanted into another human being. Kidney transplants are allografts.

ALLOIMMMUNE: immune reactions which occur between the tissues of different human beings.

AMNIOCENTESIS: a procedure in which a fine needle is inserted into the amniotic sac via the mother's abdominal wall to obtain a sample of amniotic fluid for genetic or chemical analysis of the baby.

AMNIOTIC SAC/FLUID: two layers of membranes (the amnion and chorion) form the amniotic sac. The sac lies in the uterine cavity filled with amniotic fluid, which bathes the fetus.

ANEUPLOIDY: too many or too few chromosomes present in the cell. Normal cells contain 46 chromosomes arranged in 23 pairs.

ANTICOAGULANT: a substance that makes our blood less likely to form clots. Certain drugs can do this and normal blood contains natural anticoagulants.

ANTI-D: an injection of immunoglobulin (antibodies) capable of destroying rhesus positive (D) red blood cells. This is given to rhesus negative mothers after delivery of a rhesus positive baby to prevent them developing rhesus disease in a future pregnancy.

ANTIPHOSPHOLIPID SYNDROME: a condition in which antiphospholipid antibodies in the bloodstream lead to recurrent miscarriages and/or thrombosis.

APA: antiphospholipid antibodies – a family of autoantibodies, the most common of which are the lupus anticoagulant and anticardiolipin antobodies.

APCA: antipaternal cytotoxic antibody – an antibody which develops when the mother's immune system has recognised that the fetus contains cells from the father.

APCR: activated protein C resistance – an inherited type of blood clotting disorder which is found in some women with late miscarriages.

AUTOIMMUNE: immune reactions caused by antibodies which are directed against our own tissues (anti-self). The reactions usually cause damage to our body tissues.

BICORNUATE UTERUS: a congenital abnormality in which the two uterine horns do not fuse together but are joined by a single cervix.

BIOCHEMICAL PREGNANCY: a positive pregnancy test followed soon after by a menstrual period.

BROMOCRYPTINE: a drug used to reduce high prolactin hormone levels.

BRUCELLA: bacterial organism causing brucellosis or undulant fever. An important cause of infertility and miscarriage in cattle. A rare cause of miscarriage among farm workers.

CERCLAGE: a stitch inserted into the cervix to close the cervical canal.

CERVIX: the muscular neck of the uterus (womb).

CHLAMYDIA: a sexually transmitted infective organism halfway between a bacterium and a virus. Common cause of damage to the fallopian tubes leading to infertility, and conjunctivitis in newborn babies. It does not cause miscarriage in humans.

CHORION VILLUS SAMPLING: a procedure in which a sample of placenta is obtained for genetic or chemical analysis of the baby, using a special needle introduced through the mother's abdominal wall.

CHROMOSOME: rod-shaped bodies in the nucleus of cells which carry the genes that transmit inherited characteristics.

CONGENITAL: a structural or functional defect or malformation present at birth.

CORDOCENTESIS: a procedure used to sample the baby's blood in utero. A special needle is inserted into the umbilical cord under ultrasound control.

CORPUS LUTEUM: 'yellow body' – formed in the ovary from an ovarian follicle which has released an egg. The corpus luteum produces progesterone hormone until the placenta takes over production.

CT: computerised tomography – a special imaging technique for body tissues.

CYTOGENETICIST: a specialist in the genetic makeup of cells.

CYTOMEGALOVIRUS: a viral infection which may cause neurological problems in the baby.

D&C: dilatation and curettage – a minor operation in which tissue is removed from the lining of the uterus (a scrape).

DE NOVO: an event that occurs out of the blue.

DNA: the chemical building blocks that genes are made of.

DOPPLER SCAN: measures the flow of blood through vessels and can be used to identify blood flow problems in the placenta and baby.

DRVVT: the dilute Russel's viper venom time test is the most accurate way to identify the presence of the lupus anticoagulant in blood.

ECTOPIC PREGNANCY: a pregnancy that implants outside the uterus, usually in the fallopian tubes.

ENDOCRINE: hormones that are produced by a gland (e.g. pituitary, ovary) and carried in the bloodstream to act on another organ in the body (e.g. uterus).

ENDOMETRITIS: inflammation of the uterine lining, usually caused by infection.

ENDOMETRIUM: the uterine lining that is shed during each menstrual period and is the site for implantation of the embryo.

EPIDURAL: a local anaesthetic inserted into the back which numbs pain from the waist downwards.

ERPC: evacuation of retained products of conception – a surgical procedure to empty the uterus of pregnancy tissues that have not been expelled after the pregnancy has died.

FACTOR V: one of the factors involved in the complex pathways which control the ability of our blood to coagulate (clot) and to dissolve these clots.

FETAL POLE: the term used to describe the tiny fetus before it has developed a recognisable form.

FETOSCOPY: a specialised test using a fine telescope inserted into the amniotic sac to visualise the fetus or baby and through which tissue samples can be taken.

FIBROID: common non-malignant tumours that arise in the muscular wall of the uterus.

FOLIC ACID: one of the B vitamins. When it occurs naturally in foods it is known as folate.

FOLLICLE: the fluid-filled cysts in the ovary containing an egg surrounded by layers of cells.

FORMALIN: a chemical which preserves tissues for histological analysis under the microscope.

FSH: this follicle-stimulating hormone is secreted by the pituitary gland and stimulates the growth of the ovarian follicles.

GENE: a single unit of inheritance. Each chromosome is made up of thousands of genes which control the development and function of all the tissues of our body.

GNRH AGONISTS: drugs which stop the secretion of FSH and LH from the pituitary gland when they are given for more than a few days.

GONADOTROPHINS: the collective term for FSH and LH hormones produced in the pituitary gland. These hormones can be used to induce multiple ovulation.

HAEMATOLOGIST: a medical doctor who specialises in blood.

HAEMATOMA: a collection of blood (clot) inside the body tissues.

HALF-LIFE: the time taken for a drug or hormone level in the body to reduce by 50%.

HCG: human chorionic gonadotrophin. A hormone produced by the embryo which is measured in standard pregnancy tests.

HEPARIN: an anticoagulant most commonly used to prevent or treat thrombosis.

HIV: human immunodeficiency virus which causes the AIDS disease.

HYDATIDIFORM MOLE: a tumour of the placental tissues (trophoblast).

HYPEREMESIS GRAVIDARUM: extreme nausea and vomiting in pregnancy which can lead to severe dehydration.

HYPOTHALAMUS: a control centre in the brain which plays a crucial role in the functioning of the pituitary gland.

HYSTEROSALPINGOGRAM: HSG – an X-ray examination in which a special dye is injected through the cervix to visualise the cervical canal, the cavity of the uterus and the fallopian tubes.

HYSTEROSCOPE: a fibre-optic telescope which is passed through the cervical canal into the uterus to visualise the uterine cavity.

ICSI: intra-cytoplasmic sperm injection. A recently developed fertility technique in which a sperm is injected into an egg to improve fertilisation, using specialised microscopic instruments.

INCOMPETENCE (OF THE CERVIX): a cervix that starts to open during pregnancy due to weakness of the muscular wall.

IVF: *in vitro* fertilisation – infertility treatment involving the collection of eggs and sperm which are then fertilised in the laboratory. The resulting embryos are then replaced into the mother's uterus.

KARYOTYPE: a person's individual chromosome pattern. In women it is normally 46XX and in men 46XY.

LA: lupus anticoagulant – one of the antiphospholipid antibodies (APA) which have been strongly implicated as a cause of recurrent miscarriage.

LAPAROSCOPY: an operation during which a lighted telescope is introduced into the abdominal cavity to visualise the uterus, ovaries and fallopian tubes.

LH: luteinising hormone – secreted by the pituitary gland. The normal mid-cycle surge of LH triggers the process of ovulation. High levels of LH at other times in the cycle are associated with miscarriage and infertility.

LISTERIA: bacteria present in animals and contaminated soil. If the mother becomes infected during pregnancy, listeria can cause late miscarriage.

MEIOSIS: a special type of reduction cell division which only occurs in eggs and sperm. The numbers of chromosomes are halved to 23 in preparation for fertilisation.

MONOSOMIES: the defect arising when one chromosome is lost. The most common example is Monosomy (45) X or Turner's syndrome.

MOSAICISM: two different cell lines in the same tissue or organ, made up of different chromosome numbers.

MRI: magnetic resonance imaging – a specialised three-dimensional scanning technique.

MULTIPAROUS: a woman who has delivered babies in the past.

MYOMECTOMY: surgical procedure to remove a fibroid (myoma) from the uterus.

OESTROGEN: one of the female hormones produced by the ovary and placenta.

OMNOPON: a painkilling drug which also acts as a sedative.

PARTUM, INTRA/POST/ANTE: labour and delivery of the baby – hence intra (during), post (after) and ante (before) delivery.

PARVOVIRUS: a viral infection which only rarely causes miscarriage or intrauterine death. The baby may accumulate fluid in the abdomen, chest and brain 'hydrops'.

PETHIDINE: a painkilling drug frequently used for women in labour.

PITUITARY GLAND: a small structure lying under the brain and behind the eyesockets. It controls the production and secretion of hormones from several other glands.

POLYCYSTIC OVARIES: ovaries in which the follicles are arranged around the outside of the gland in a 'pearl necklace pattern'. These ovaries tend to be larger than normal and may be associated with infertility and miscarriage.

POLYPLOIDIES: the defect caused by the embryo receiving extra sets of 23 chromosomes; triploidy = 69XXY, tetraploidy = 92XXYY.

PRE-ECLAMPSIA: a pregnancy disorder characterised by high blood pressure, swelling of the hands and feet and protein in the urine.

PRIMIGRAVIDA: a woman who is pregnant for the first time (gravid = heavy).

PRIMIPAROUS: a woman who has never delivered a baby before.

PROGESTERONE: one of the female hormones produced in increasing quantities by the ovary after ovulation and by the placenta during pregnancy.

PROSTAGLANDINS: naturally occurring chemicals present in many tissues of the body. Some types cause the uterine muscles to contract, leading to labour.

REACTIVE DEPRESSION: depression which develops in response to major life events or crises.

RESECTION: the paring away of a tissue (as opposed to complete removal) usually using telescopic instruments.

RHESUS ANTIBODIES: antibodies produced by a rhesus negative mother in response to the presence of rhesus positive red blood cells entering her bloodstream from the baby.

RU486 OR MIFIPRISTONE: an anti-progesterone (progesterone antagonist) which can be used to terminate early pregnancies without the need for surgery.

SLE: systemic lupus erythematosis – the commonest autoimmune disease in women during the reproductive age. A woman who has lupus anticoagulant in her blood does not necessarily have or develop fullblown SLE.

SPINA BIFIDA: a congenital abnormality in which the baby's delicate spinal cord is not covered by the bony spine. This one type of neural tube defect.

SUB-CLINICAL: a very early pregnancy that is recognisable by biochemical tests but with no evidence of a pregnancy sac on the ultrasound scan.

SUBFERTILE: a delay or difficulty in becoming pregnant.

THROMBOSIS: a blood clot which blocks the flow of blood in a blood vessel.

TORCH: the name of the infection screen that used to be advised for recurrent miscarriers. (T=toxoplasma, O=other, R=rubella, C=chlamydia and H=herpes).

TOXAEMIA: another term for pre-eclampsia (see above).

TOXOPLASMA: a parasitic infection which can cause miscarriage and congenital abnormalities. It is most often found in communities with lots of cats or where meat is undercooked.

TRANSLOCATIONS: when a piece of one chromosome becomes attached to the broken end of another.

TRIMESTER: pregnancy is divided into 3 trimesters of approximately three months.

TRISOMIES: the presence of three copies of one chromosome instead of the normal two. The best known example is trisomy 21 – Down's syndrome.

ULTRA-SOUND SCAN: high frequency sound waves that are used to produce a grey-scale image of tissues in the body. Obstetric ultrasound has become extremely sophisticated and can now visualise tiny abnormalities in the baby.

UNICORNUATE UTERUS: a single uterine horn usually accompanied by a redundant second horn which has failed to develop.

UTERINE SEPTUM: a dividing wall or curtain of tissue extending downwards from the top of the uterus.

UTERUS: the womb – consisting of a hollow muscular body and neck (the cervix). A canal through the cervix connects the body of the uterus to the vagina.

VIABILITY: the age at which a newborn baby is capable of survival outside the mother's womb.

Useful addresses

For those readers who would like further information and the opportunity to meet other women with similar problems, the following addresses should be useful.

THE RECURRENT MISCARRIAGE CLINIC
St Mary's Hospital
Winston Churchill Wing
Praed Street
LONDON W2 1NY
Tel: 0207 258 0285
Fax: 0207 886 6479
(Specialist clinic for the investigation and treatment of miscarriage)

THE MISCARRIAGE ASSOCIATION
C/o Clayton Hospital
Northgate
Wakefield
WEST YORKSHIRE WF1 3JS
Tel: 01924 200799
Fax: 01924 298834
(Support and information on pregnancy loss)

THE CHILD BEREAVEMENT TRUST
Aston House
High Street
West Wycombe
BUCKS HP14 3AG
Tel: 01494 446648
(Support and counselling for grieving families)

FORESIGHT
(Association for the Promotion of Preconceptual Care)
28 The Paddock
Godalming
SURREY GU7 1XD
Tel: 01483 427839
(Pre-pregnancy advice for infertility and miscarriage)

ARC (Antenatal Results and Choices)
73-75 Charlotte Street
LONDON W1P 1LB
Tel: 0207 631 0280 and 0207 631 0285 (helpline)
(Self-help charity offering support by parents who have had a similar experience)

SANDS (Stillbirth and Neonatal Death Society)
28 Portland Place
LONDON W1N 4DE
Tel: 0207 436 7940
(Supplies one-to-one advice and leaflets for bereaved families)

ASBAH (Association for Spina Bifida and Hydrocephalus)
ASBAH House
42 Park Road
PETERBOROUGH PE1 2UQ
Tel: 01733 555988

TAMBA
PO Box 30
Little Sutton
South Wirral L66 1TH
Tel: 0151 3480020
(Bereavement group attached to Twins and Multiple Births Association)

CRUSE
126 Sheen Road
Richmond
SURREY TW9 1UR
Tel: 0208 940 4818
(Bereavement counselling)

ASH (Action on Smoking and Health)
102 Clifton Street
LONDON EC2A 4HW
Tel: 0207 739 5902

QUIT
Victory House
170 Tottenham Court Road
LONDON W1P 0HA
Tel: 0207 388 5775
Helpline: 0207 487 3000
(Practical help to stop smoking)

NATIONAL CHILDBIRTH TRUST
Alexandra House
Oldham Terrace
Acton
LONDON W3 6NH
Tel: 0208 992 8637
(Useful booklets on miscarriage, clinical trials and medical research)

ISSUE
114 Litchfield Street
WALSALL W51 1FZ
Tel: 01922 722888
(Formerly the national association for the childless)

COTS (Association for Surrogacy)
Gruids
Lairg
Sutherland
SCOTLAND IV27 4EF
Tel: 01549 402401

LONDON SCHOOL OF HYGIENE AND TROPICAL MEDICINE
Keppel Street
LONDON WC1E 7HT
Tel: 0207 636 8636
(Useful advice on vaccinations and tropical diseases during pregnancy)

ENDOMETRIOSIS ASSOCIATION
Suite 50
Westminster Palace Gardens
Artillery Row
LONDON SW1P 1RL
e-mail: AngelaBarnard@compuserve.com
(Self-help group and newsletter for endometriosis sufferers)

MIND (National Association for Mental Health)
Granta House
15–19 Broadway
LONDON E15 4BQ
Tel: 0208 519 2122 and 0845 7660163 (information line 9.15am–4.45pm Mon–Fri)

SENSE (National Deaf-Blind and Rubella Association)
11–13 Clifton Terrace
Finsbury Park
LONDON N4 3SR
Tel: 0207 272 7774

REACH (The Association for Children with Hand or Arm Deficiency)
12 Wilson Way
Earls Barton
NORTHAMPTONSHIRE NN6 0NZ
Tel: 01604 811041
(Information and support to parents of children with hand or arm problems)

MENCAP (Royal Society for Mentally Handicapped Children and Adults)
MENCAP National Centre
123 Golden Lane
LONDON EC1Y 0RT
Tel: 0207 454 0454

DOWN'S SYNDROME ASSOCIATION (National Office)
155 Mitcham Road
LONDON SW17 9PG
Tel: 0208 682 4001

CYSTIC FIBROSIS TRUST
11 London Road
BROMLEY BR1 1BY
Tel: 0208 464 7211

CLEFT LIP AND PALATE ASSOCIATION (CLAPA)
235–237 Finchley Road
LONDON NW3 6LS
Tel: 0207 431 0033
(Support to families of babies with cleft lip and palate)

ASSOCIATION OF PARENTS OF VACCINE DAMAGED CHILDREN
78 Campden Road
Shipston-on-Stour
WARWICKSHIRE CV36 4DH
Tel: 01608 661595
(Advises parents on claiming vaccine damage payment)

COT DEATH RESEARCH AND SUPPORT
(Foundation for the Study of Infant Deaths)
Artillery House
11–19 Artillery Row
LONDON SW1P 1RT
Tel: 0207 222 8001 (administration) and 0207 233 2090 (24-hour helpline)

CHILD (National Infertility Support Network)
Charter House
43 St Leonard's Road
Bexhill-on-Sea
EAST SUSSEX TN40 1JA
Tel: 01424 732361
Fax: 01424 731858

HFEA
(Human Fertilisation and Embryology Authority)
Paxton House
30 Artillery Lane
LONDON E1 7LS
Tel: 0207 377 5077
Fax: 0207 377 1871

Index

SAVE THE BABY

There are a number of ways that you can help us to raise money for **'Save the Baby'**. Please tick any of the boxes you can, fill in your details and send this form to the address below:

☐ **I would like to make a donation**
(Please see below for details)

☐ **I might have a fund raising idea**

☐ **I would like to be on your mailing list for information on future fund raising events**

Name: _

Address: _

_ _

_ _

_ _

Tel: _

Please make cheques payable to: **Save the Baby** and send your donation with this form to: **Save the Baby. Department of Obstetrics & Gynaecology, Imperial College School of Medicine at St Mary's Hospital, Norfolk Place, London W2 1PG**
Tel: 0207 886 1461 or: 0208 940 6654   Fax: 0207 886 6054

Registered Charity No. 285594